RUN MITCH, RUN

RUN MITCH, RUN

The Hard Decisions One Man Faced for the 2012 Presidential Election

DON V. COGMAN

Afterword by
MITCH DANIELS

RUN MITCH, RUN
THE HARD DECISIONS ONE MAN FACED FOR
THE 2012 PRESIDENTIAL ELECTION

iUniverse books may be ordered through booksellers or by contacting:

iUniverse
1663 Liberty Drive
Bloomington, IN 47403
www.iuniverse.com
1-800-Authors (1-800-288-4677)

ISBN: 978-1-4917-5106-0 (hc)
ISBN: 978-1-4917-5105-3 (e)
ISBN: 978-1-4917-5577-8 (sc)

Printed in the United States of America.

iUniverse rev. date: 12/08/2014

For Susie, Bryan, Marc, Clay, and Caroline,
the loves of my life forever

and

In Memoriam

W. Dennis Thomas
Friend and Colleague of Forty Years
12/8/1943 – 9/23/2014

Democracy is not a numbers game. A good leader does not count opinion, but weighs it. We urgently need leaders who dare to tell us what we need to hear, not what we want to hear.

—Richard C. Halverson
Chaplain, US Senate
July 1984

Contents

Part III – 2011

Part IV – 2012

Author's Notes and
————— Acknowledgments

If you've been as fortunate in your professional life as I have, to work with exceptional people and experience significant events, you come to a point where friends and colleagues of many years attain positions of leadership in both business and government.

It always amazed me to stop occasionally and look around:

There's Haley Barbour, a friend and field man for the Republican National Committee (RNC) when I was working as an aide in the US Senate. He's now the governor of Mississippi.

There's Roy Blunt, a friend and former lower-level state official in Missouri when I was running a corporate Washington office. He's now a United States senator.

There's Dennis Thomas, a fellow senate administrative assistant on Capitol Hill. He's now deputy chief of staff to the president of the United States.

And on and on.

One day, my amazement reached a new peak as I browsed the *Wall Street Journal*. A longtime friend and colleague from my Washington days was mentioned on September 26, 2009, as perhaps the most successful Republican governor in the entire nation. The columnist, Kimberley Strassel, asked, "What if he ran for president?"[1]

So began the odyssey of Mitch Daniels and his pursuit, or non-pursuit, of the presidency of the United States. This passionate, arduous journey

---

[1]   Kimberley Strassel, columnist, "We are the Initiators," *Wall Street Journal*, September 26, 2009.

that would take nine of us around the nation and through profound emotional highs and lows started on that day, September 29, 2009. It ended on May 21, 2011. Another two years passed until I decided someone needed to tell the story. I had kept my files and voluminous notes locked away in a storage box just in case. I was finally motivated by a call from Rick Powell, a friend and colleague who worked for me right out of college for nearly ten years in both Washington and New York and who participated in those meetings with Mitch as one of the "group of eight."

I told Rick I had been contemplating writing the story myself but had never committed myself to the project. I had written one book several years ago—a memoir for my kids and grandkids—so I knew the time and effort it took for such an undertaking. As I told Rick, "The hardest part is just starting."

Rick told me I needed to do it, saying, "It's history." I recalled a statement from someone years ago who said that if you are fortunate enough to participate in history, you have an obligation to tell the story to others who follow. I gathered my notes, organized my thoughts, tried to balance the inside story with sensitivity to others, and just … started.

This was indeed history, a story that deserved to be told—the story of what it takes to run for president and the choices one faces and the hard decisions one makes.

* * *

When writing a book, an author often wonders why anyone would want to read it.

I wrote this book for three reasons:

First, it is a brief glimpse into the nuts and bolts, the mechanics of the necessary steps to making a decision on whether or not to run for president of the United States. For those individuals, be they historians or practitioners who are intrigued by this process, this is a book that may be of interest.

Secondly, it is a story of Mitch Daniels' set of beliefs—his principles and values—his attempt to answer the questions of what kind of country we are and, even more importantly, what kind of country we want to be for generations to come. It is about policy and issues and an approach to government that is quite different from what we are experiencing today. It is about competence and what is required to actually get the job done.

Thirdly, it is an inside look at the emotional journey of living in an age where "good" people are increasingly reluctant to get into the game of national politics because it has become so marred with lack of civility and a negativity that borders on the obscene. The savagery of the process is a primary reason why the ultimate decision is so hard.

Ultimately, I wrote this book because I thought it was an interesting story—a narrative in need of reflection and historical context for future generations.

The key players from beginning to end were "the group." That is how we always referred to ourselves. We were Tom Bell, Al Hubbard, Charlie Black, Bob Perkins, Rick Powell, Mark Lubbers, Eric Holcomb, and myself. Each of my seven partners in this endeavor gave of their time and talent to see if this could be done. They did it for love of country and respect and admiration for Mitch Daniels. This is their story as much as mine, and I salute them as comrades in arms with appreciation for their friendship and their many contributions.

And, of course, Mitch Daniels himself. US Senate staffer, White House aide, cabinet member, business executive, two-term governor, exceptional writer, Mitch is a person of phenomenal intelligence combined with acute political instincts and extraordinary leadership abilities. Mitch was a person many thought could be president of the United States, but in the end, he said no. In his words, "I love my country, but I love my family more."

Above all this is Mitch's story. I write it with pride in his accomplishments and gratitude for thirty-five years of friendship.

Introduction

Every four years, we hold a presidential election in this country. But, for months and years prior to that day, men and women and their families have hard decisions to make. This is the story of one individual, Mitch Daniels, but it could apply to others who will wrestle with this same problem in years to come. The process of making hard decisions never changes.

Running for president in its rawest form is a great deal like selling a product. In the case of the presidency, the product being sold could be a vision or a governing philosophy or, in its most basic form, a person. Therefore, the objective is to differentiate yourself, just like you try to differentiate a product, as you take your message to the public.

So the question was, why Mitch Daniels? What made people believe that 2012 was his time, that he had something unique to offer, and that he was "different" from all the rest, particularly when the presidency was never a part of his career game plan?

Mitch had the normal impressive résumé that most candidates for the presidency have by the time they declare an interest. He came from a middle-class Indiana family and graduated from Princeton and then Georgetown Law School. He was experienced in local government, serving as chief aide to then mayor Richard Lugar of Indianapolis; experienced in state government, serving two terms as governor; and experienced in Washington, having served as chief of staff to Senator Richard Lugar, assistant to the president for Political Affairs for President Ronald Reagan, and a cabinet member with President George W. Bush as director of the Office of Management and Budget (OMB).

He also had an impressive private sector career, both in the profit and nonprofit worlds. Mitch was the president and CEO of the Hudson Institute, a well-respected think tank headquartered in Indianapolis. Next he went to Eli Lilly & Co., serving in various capacities, including president of North American operations, and ultimately taking charge of strategic planning for the entire global company.

Mitch became a grandfather a few years ago with all of his four daughters now married and living nearby in Indiana. He was known to be smart (very smart); competitive; and personally, famously frugal. He had a dry sense of humor and a winning smile that would occasionally help him when dealing with adversarial opponents who might invite confrontation. But most of the time he was the picture of humility, always willing to stop and talk with any citizen. He was famous for staying in the homes of ordinary Hoosiers when traveling the state in his RV.

At times, Mitch could be impatient and exhibit a stubborn streak. But most of all he was the definition of competence. He had that rare combination of great political skill and instinct combined with an intellectual intelligence that enabled him to expertly deal with most major policy issues.

The most relevant evaluation of Mitch Daniels is to analyze what was arguably his most difficult job and one in which he was actually in charge, being governor of the state of Indiana.

Mitch himself, however, has said the experience that contributed most to his ability to be a good governor was his stint in private business. That manifested itself in the way he tried to operate government as any business would, by having a central objective that all aspects of the enterprise serve. He said, "For us in Indiana, that objective was raising the net disposable income of all Hoosiers."

After sixteen years of Democrats in the statehouse, Mitch turned a $700 million deficit into a $1 billion surplus. When asked how he did it, he famously said, "Prepare to be dazzled. We spent less money than we took in."

As governor, Mitch used a previously unused power called "allotment" that gave him the ability to not spend money appropriated by the legislature. He cut $800 million from state government in fiscal 2009, another $190 million in renegotiating state contracts, and another $250 million in unnecessary spending and eliminated five thousand government positions.

However, he also provided additional funds for things he believed important—800 new child protection caseworkers, 250 more state troopers, and increased spending for education. Health and welfare expenditures and efficiency increased in categories ranging from child immunizations to developmental disability to welfare benefits management. Veteran's benefits, child services, prescription drug benefits—all increased.

In 2005, Mitch's Kids, a partnership between state government and the Boys and Girls Clubs in Indiana, was created. Tens of thousands of students have participated in the program to improve reading and math skills. In 2006, 10,000 Indiana children were in a full-day kindergarten program; in 2012, over 66,000 were participating, and the program was fully funded throughout the entire state. Indiana led the nation in its dedication to K–12 education with 55.4 percent of its general fund being spent on this most critical area. Meanwhile, the graduation rate of Indiana students at the end of his term was up 10 percent.

Midway through his first term, Mitch signed legislation that established the Healthy Indiana Plan, a program that gave state employees the option of switching to health plans with health savings accounts. It covered 130,000 uninsured, where participants contributed to their account based on income, with the state of Indiana and private insurance also participating. It was designed to make certain everyone, with a few exceptions, had skin in the game and didn't expose taxpayers to the catastrophe in other states that had an entitlement program.

His reputation was that of a governor who restored fiscal integrity to the state. He paid back over $750 million to local government and schools that had payment delays initiated by previous administrations. He enacted the biggest tax cut in state history with property taxes cut and capped permanently.

Customer service was improved and state government streamlined. He created the Office of Management and Budget at the state level for financial oversight and management. He changed the culture of state employment through pay for performance (the only state to provide it for every state employee), and Indiana now has the fewest state employees per capita in the country.

One significant action impacting nearly every citizen was reorganizing the Bureau of Motor Vehicles. It is now a model for the country, where the average visit time of seven minutes and thirty-six seconds is a remarkable accomplishment, due to new incentives for government workers that reward efficiency and speed.

Economic development was the key to enabling Indiana to experience an unprecedented, record-breaking job growth during his tenure as governor. Average wages were substantially increased, and corporate tax rates were decreased. Multibillions of dollars were attracted in foreign investment due to Indiana's business-friendly tax environment.

In addition, sweeping ethics reform and increased transparency had become a mainstay in state government by the time Mitch concluded his two terms. The Office of Inspector General was created in 2005 to fight fraud and abuse in state government. The state received multiple awards from national organizations for achievement in transparency and governance.

* * *

Those of us who had known Mitch Daniels for many years knew he was smart. We knew he had leadership qualities and was capable of managing large enterprises. He was experienced in both business and government. What we didn't know was, could he be a good candidate? How would he do at "retail politics"?

During both his campaigns for governor, Mitch traveled the state in an RV, labeled RV One. He visited counties and towns that had never even seen a real candidate for governor, let alone personally talked with one. At the end of the campaign, Mitch wrote a book entitled *Notes from the Road: 16 Months of Towns, Tales and Tenderloin*. Hundreds of examples of Mitch's expertise in retail politics were demonstrated, but one story gave us a clue. Mitch reported:

> Nothing could top our Unplanned Stop of the Week, which came after dinner in Kentland. County Assessor Janice Wilson mentioned to me at dinner that she was headed to band practice that evening. Now, Janice is a beautiful lady, but let me just say that she's a few decades out of high school, so I inquired what kind of band she was in.

Turns out they have a Newton/Jasper Community Band, made up almost entirely of senior citizens who just love to get together and play for events in the area. So I invited myself, and before the night was over, two great things had happened. First, I realized my lifelong ambition to conduct a band, and feel that sense of power that Mr. Laswell had over us back at Westlane Junior High.

Second, as I was thanking the band, a hand went up in the French horn section and a sweet little lady asked, "If you get elected governor, can we play at your inaugural?"

So, be on notice everybody. If this project of ours should go the distance, you are in for a treat, because you are going to hear the Newton/Jasper Community Band, and they can really play. Even with a rookie conductor.

And, they did, twice, in both 2005 and 2009. Now, that's retail politics.

* * *

Mitch always said that he wanted the people of Indiana to expect great things from their government—to expect it to do things that would benefit all citizens.

So, what makes Mitch Daniels "unique"? Columnist Ryan Streeter wrote, "Daniels is not like other political creatures. His sober sensibility is a part of his appeal. He was a frugal cost-cutter before it was cool. He has regular-guy appeal and efficacy as a public executive, riding his Harley and stopping in run-of-the-mill diners."[2]

Asked by Streeter why he was a Republican, Mitch explained that he always tried to stay away from labels. For him, it was an issue of unity and a very strong belief that individual liberty and dignity was far more important than any label. He also believed that government was there to protect the freedom of individuals, not overstep its role in dictating how they were supposed to live.

---

[2] Ryan Streeter, "8 Questions for Mitch Daniels," *American Outlook*, December 15, 2010.

Why Mitch Daniels? Why did a group of eight individuals devote nearly two years to working on the idea that perhaps this was his time? We did so not only because we believed in Mitch Daniels, the individual, but also because of our concern for the future of our country.

Mitch believed we needed a "survival agenda," that our country was going down the wrong path with policies that would burden the next generation with a debt so overwhelming it would change the very fabric of our nation. His focus was to have an honest "adult" conversation with the American people and be willing to talk truth about critical issues.

He believed strongly that you had to run to govern, not just to win an election. His stance on social issues was very much in sync with a majority of Republicans, but he believed it necessary for people to understand that we needed to focus on our fiscal crises first and foremost.

Why Mitch Daniels? Because, in fact, he *was* different. He was willing to meet *the* major crisis—government's continual propensity to spend money we didn't have, thereby mortgaging the future for generations to come—head-on.

Multiple and diverse reasons fuel an individual's difficult decision to run for president of the United States. Many who have no chance whatsoever of winning run. What made this story different was that Mitch Daniels had a realistic chance. At one point in this journey, Mitch was on the cover of the three most important publications impacting the race for the Republican nomination—*National Review*, the *Weekly Standard*, and the *American Spectator*.

The momentum was building for the "un-Obama, an ideal contrast to the incumbent," as stated in the chronicle of the 2012 campaign *Double Down* by Mark Halperin and John Heilemann.[3]

Hard decisions lay ahead. Could we convince him the country needed him at this unique time in history?

Equally important, could we convince his family?

---

[3] Mark Halperin and John Heilemann, *Double Down: Game Change 2012*, (New York: The Penguin Group, 2012), 131. Following the election, in one of the myriad of electoral analysis sessions, David Axelrod (Obama's chief strategist) was reported to have said that the Obama campaign had its biggest sigh of relief when Mitch made the decision not to run.

Prologue

The day was cold in Indianapolis, December 14, 2010. But "the group" had just finished a two-day strategy meeting in the residence of the governor of Indiana, and we were warm, even hot, with enthusiasm and optimism.

After nearly a year of indecision and uncertainty, Governor Mitch Daniels had answered the last question of the day put to him by Tom Bell. "So, where is your head? Are we going to do this or not?"

Mitch answered, "I'm 80 percent there."

We were all stunned and ecstatic. He said the family was still an issue, but he didn't see anyone else who could do it. He was convinced we had the right message and believed it just might be possible.

The group, the same eight people who'd first gathered in my living room in Scottsdale, Arizona, at the beginning of the year, had just finished a two-day meeting where we talked issues, scheduling, personnel, financing, and a host of other items on which to focus as we entered 2011. We had come a long way since that first phone call in 2009 when Mitch told me, "That is the dumbest idea you've ever come up with," and proceeded to completely dismiss the idea of considering a run for the presidency.

Most of the group was leaving for the airport, but I had already planned to stay the night to have dinner with Mitch and his wife, Cheri. The last decision we made at our meeting was to have me bring up the subject with Cheri at dinner. We were to have a serious conversation about our yearlong efforts and why we thought this was his time. I had known Cheri almost as long as I had known Mitch, so I was the elected person to have what we thought might be a pivotal conversation.

As the meeting was breaking up, Mitch asked me to join him downstairs in the study when everyone had departed. As I entered the room with the fire blazing in the fireplace, he closed the door and said he didn't want to say this in front of the group because everyone was so enthusiastic, but he thought the family was a major problem—perhaps a greater problem than he had even thought several months ago.

My warm feeling immediately turned cold. All of us had concluded our meeting with a feeling that this really might be happening. Now, something was telling me we had an obstacle that was real and perhaps unrelenting. I asked if it was Cheri or the girls or all of the above. He replied all of the above. I asked what he thought I could say that would change their minds, and he said he didn't know.

I then suggested it might be better if I met her before we had dinner and had a conversation just between us. I thought perhaps the talk might be more productive with just the two of us, and he agreed. So we set it up, and I returned to Al Hubbard's, where I was staying, and began to prepare.

Many highlights occurred in this journey with Mitch, but this one was perhaps the most critical of all. How do you convince a spouse and four children, grown children, that our country needed their husband and father? It was a decision that would potentially change their lives forever.

That was what consumed my thoughts as I walked into the residence three hours later to have a conversation with my old friend, Cheri Daniels.

PART 1
2009

The Beginning

I t started with an article in the *Wall Street Journal*, an interview for the Saturday edition on September 26, 2009, by Kimberley Strassel. When asked about running for president, Governor Mitch Daniels laughed and said, "You'll be the first to know, but don't hang around the phone," completely dismissing the idea and moving on to other subjects having to do with Indiana.

Strassel wrote, "The Indiana governor is answering a question he gets asked a lot these days. Will he run for president? He keeps saying no, but the collapse of such GOP notables as Sarah Palin and Mark Sanford has people looking north. Mr. Daniels is today something rare indeed: a popular Republican."[4]

A few other articles, mostly local, had raised the question columnist Chris Cillizza asked on May 12, 2009, with his column in the *Washington Post*, "Can Mitch Daniels Save the GOP?" He contended the Republican Party was continuing to search for fresh faces and new leaders, and Daniels' success in his 2008 reelection campaign as governor was built on two pillars—populism and competence.

It is interesting to note Cillizza's comment: "Daniels may be overshadowed somewhat by his fellow governors with higher national profiles, Bobby Jindal (La.), Mark Sanford (S.C.) and Tim Pawlenty (Minn.)."[5] Jindal never seriously considered a run after a lackluster convention speech among other things, Sanford resigned in a personal

---

4   Strassel, "We are the Initiators."
5   Chris Cillizza, columnist, "Can Mitch Daniels Save the GOP?" *Washington Post*, May 12, 2009.

scandal, and Pawlenty was the first in and first out as a presidential candidate who never got any traction.

Later in the year, a guest columnist in the *Washington Times* called Mitch "reform-minded," outlining his success as governor and pointing to his push for Republicans to appeal to young voters on a national level—not just to gain votes but because today's young people will be tomorrow's leaders (and the inheritors of the nation's debt). The column noted that Mitch had won the youth vote by wide margins in both his gubernatorial races and quoted him as saying, "Our deficit levels threaten the well-being of the next generation; we are stealing from our sons and daughters."[6]

A few weeks went by, and I decided to call Mitch just to get his reaction to the article. He was appreciative of the call—and of a few others he had received—but basically took none of the chatter seriously. He again dismissed the notion of even considering a run for the presidency.

I then traded e-mails with a number of friends, asking whether or not they had seen the article and generally soliciting opinions on the state of the Union and Republican prospects for the future. One in particular mentioned well-known columnist George Will, who in her opinion would be very interested in a Daniels candidacy, saying, "He would respect Mitch's intelligence because George's #1 goal from now on is to only support smart candidates!"

Several more weeks passed, and I decided to send Mitch an e-mail on September 26, saying the *Wall Street Journal* article had interested multiple people and, "Could we not have a small, quiet meeting somewhere with a few people just to discuss it?" His response that same day was, "Okay, if only for the fun of seeing you guys." I told him I'd work on it.

On October 1, I sent him an e-mail indicating that Tom Bell was interested in getting together. Tom was an old friend, now a leading businessman in Atlanta with years of political experience. Tom made the suggestion we include Al Hubbard, local Indianapolis businessman, former national economic advisor in the White House to President George W. Bush, and a longtime friend of Mitch.

The idea was to get together for golf, dinner, and discussion. I offered my home in Scottsdale, Arizona, and also suggested the Greenbrier, in

---

[6] Frank Donatelli, guest columnist, "The Reform-minded Conservative," *Washington Times*, October 26, 2009.

White Sulphur Springs, West Virginia, where Mitch had a home, or New York City, where all of us had other things we could do and where Mitch could visit one of his daughters. We also considered coming to Indianapolis to make it easy on him, and he indicated we could stay at the governor's residence (he didn't reside there).

His response was that he would look at the calendar and think about it. He indicated he didn't want to put us through a useless exercise, because "I'm pretty dug in on this subject, but appreciate the thought and interest on everyone's part."

Ultimately, we decided we shouldn't do it in Indianapolis for security and confidentiality reasons. As I told Mitch in an October e-mail, "I'm a bit concerned about doing it in Indy primarily because if Cheri finds out why we are coming she will have the highway patrol troopers meet us at the airport with handcuffs." I was only partially kidding. For the same reason, we decided against the Greenbrier.

A few weeks passed, and I called Tom Bell and said I hadn't heard from Mitch with specific dates. I asked whether I should keep bugging him to get something on the calendar. Tom said, "I think I know how to get him to commit to a meeting. Let's do it at Augusta." I said, "That should do it. I'll call him." In twenty-four hours, we had the time, date, and place. Augusta National Golf Club in Augusta, Georgia, is the home of the storied Masters Golf Tournament and one of the most revered golf destinations in the world. Any opportunity to play the course and reside in one of their cottages is an invitation rarely declined.

Shortly thereafter, Mitch called and said Hubbard couldn't currently play golf due to a back injury. He said, "We have you, Bell, and me, but we ought to have someone who actually knows something about running for president!"

"Not a bad idea," I said. "How about Charlie Black?"

Charlie was an old friend from Washington days, and I knew he was a fan of Mitch. Charlie had indicated he was through working for any future presidential campaigns and, therefore, was not committed to anyone.

Mitch asked if I thought Charlie would come to Augusta. Already knowing the answer to that question, I got Charlie on the phone and told him of our idea to talk seriously to Mitch about considering a run for the presidency. I asked him if would be interested in helping us strategize on at least considering the possibility. He said yes. I then asked if he'd be willing to come to Augusta for our first, secret meeting, and before I could even tell him when, he said yes again!

Augusta is a special place for many reasons. Tom told Mitch when we got together, it was the place where Dwight D. Eisenhower was first approached to run for president. So, as far as we were concerned, it had multiple meanings.

Prior to coming to Augusta, I had sent Mitch and the group a memo outlining a general agenda for discussion purposes. I asked Mitch to put in writing why he thought this was the "dumbest idea you've come up with yet," and he did so prior to our meeting.

His memo said, "Here's a partial list. I'm sure I'll have thought of more by the time we get together. I'm counting on you guys to be smart enough to already be negative on the idea, or at least not smart enough to talk me into anything ridiculous!" He then listed the nine "reasons why not" that were bothering him the most:

1. Just ran for four-year term, stated repeatedly I would not run for anything else
2. Don't have the fundraising potential
3. Former pharmaceutical executive
4. Former Bush Administration official
5. College drug arrest
6. Not a matinee idol or close to it
7. Limited foreign policy expertise
8. Policy positions that wouldn't fly in primaries and/or afterwards (list available on request)
9. Recession and fiscal challenges mean I'd be leaving while state still in tough position

Then, he said: "How's that for openers?"

Two days later, I sent a memo to Mitch, Tom, and Charlie prior to our meeting that responded to these items, in addition to laying out a structure for our time together.

My memo said:

> For the past week I have been reading *The Clinton Tapes* by Taylor Branch, and it has made me wonder why I would ever encourage a friend to be president of the United States, let alone run for it. Then I pick up the newspaper, listen to the radio or turn on the television and see what is happening to our country, and I have my answer.
>
> Mitch sent me the top nine reasons why this was a bad idea, and most, but not all, were on my list also. However, what I tried to do was list the positive aspects of a candidacy, the potential negative aspects, and then a separate list of questions that I either don't know the answer to or I feel need to be addressed. In that context here are some ideas to consider prior to our trip to Augusta that we can then thoroughly dissect when we are together.
>
> In my view, #1 and # 9 on Mitch's list are the most relevant, depending upon some answers to elements of some of the other points[7]:
>
> My list of positives is:
>
> 1. Gubernatorial record of achievement
> 2. Ability to attract independents and Democrats
> 3. Fiscal discipline reputation; anti-pork and anti-financial gimmickry
> 4. Ability to connect with the average citizen; RV travels as gubernatorial candidate and Harley riding reputation
> 5. Reformist credibility on education, healthcare, budget
> 6. Non-ideological on social issues in terms of focus, although solid on positions
> 7. National contacts; ability to raise money

---

[7]   These two "negatives" actually declined in importance as time went on.

8. Sense of humor
9. Washington experience but still an outsider
10. Quality of opposition, particularly in the primary
11. Substance over style
12. Low-key charisma
13. High intelligence that is immediately evident once you hear him speak
14. A results driven approach to governing
15. A reputation for innovative ideas to solve problems
16. A record of bringing real change that produced real results for real problems
17. A belief in a Republican Party of ideas and a big tent
18. A belief in limited government that works and the principles of freedom
19. Cheri and the kids

My list of negatives (put together before I ever received those from Mitch):

1. Member of Bush Administration and potential backlash
2. Pharmaceutical experience/issues/red flags
3. Not perceived as ideological enough for some primary voters
4. Cynical reaction from voters to whom he pledged no more campaigns for office
5. Lack of "fire in the belly"
6. Previous proposal for surtax on high-income voters (that he later admitted was a mistake)
7. Not finishing term as Governor in a full-time manner
8. New large house in Indianapolis
9. Cheri and the kids

Questions I believe we need to address when we get together:

- Can Indiana state experience and successes translate nationally?
- Are there any serious pharmaceutical issues associated with Eli Lilly and/or you during your tenure there?
- Did your healthcare reform issues, prescription drug plan and health savings accounts, work?
- Can you finish the gubernatorial term, or would you have to resign at some point? What are the ramifications?
- Who would you consider friendly in the media?
- What other governors would support you or at least wait on you to make a decision?
- How do you keep key people from committing while making up your mind?
- Do you have a pollster, ad firm, FEC lawyer?
- How did you do among young voters in both 2004 and 2008?
- What speaking venues could/would/should you do?
- What is a reasonable timetable for decision-making?
- What are reasonable activities to undertake that will assist in the decision making process?
- Cheri/kids; how serious an issue is this?

As Mitch said, this is just a beginning list in all three categories, but hopefully enough to get everyone thinking. My initial view is that finishing the gubernatorial term is perhaps the most serious issue—along with the family issue—but many of the above are real and need careful thought and discussion.

So, think on these things and others and perhaps we'll come up with some brilliant solutions.

Finally, to balance out my reading regimen, I went back and revisited the *Reagan Diaries*, also a fascinating read. As one might expect, it was so much more hopeful and positive and "Morning in America" inspiring. It even gave me confidence to encourage a friend to think about running for president.

* * *

Tom, Charlie and I arrived in Augusta the afternoon of October 21, 2009, and settled in one of the cottages on the property. We had a couple of hours before sunset, so we decided to play the par 3 course until Mitch arrived later. Halfway through the round, he pulled up in a golf cart and finished the round with us. When we returned to the cottage to prepare for dinner, we gathered in the living room for a drink.

Tom then said, "Let's get this out of the way right now so we can enjoy dinner and golf and perhaps not worry about it anymore." Looking directly at Mitch, he said, "I have two questions that will determine if we continue this conversation at all. One, do you think you could do the job of president? Not do you want to do it, or do you think you could win, or would you want to go through a campaign, but do you think you could *be* president? Secondly, do you *want* to be president? Not do you want to go through a campaign or do you think you could win, but would you *want* to be president?"

Mitch basically said he thought he could do the job. He had been in the Oval Office many times, both with Ronald Reagan and George W. Bush. He knew many of the challenges of the job and understood the complexities of being president. All in all, he believed he had the basic capability.

The second question was a bit more difficult for him. Yes, there were things he thought he could contribute to the country, and he had many concerns about the direction in which we were headed. So, from that standpoint, part of him would like the opportunity to make a difference that being in that job would afford him. But the personal sacrifice and toll on his family were a major concern, and he wasn't certain this was a hurdle that could be handled.

Mitch then expanded on the subject by saying he just didn't think it was possible for someone like him to do this. He had never even considered the possibility. He felt like his political career was over after this term as governor. He reiterated he was pretty certain Cheri and the girls would not be enthusiastic, particularly about going through a national campaign. He was also concerned about going back on his statement to the Indiana press that his reelection bid for governor was his last campaign. He felt very negative about not finishing his second term, to which he had just been reelected.

Later at dinner, Tom told the story of Ike and his cronies having dinner in that same dining room in the early 1950s. As Tom told it, Ike was having dinner with several titans of industry, and they told him he needed to run for president and listed all the reasons why. They talked about it during dinner, and Ike said he would sleep on it and discuss it further in the morning. The next day at breakfast, he sat with the same group, and reportedly said, "I've been thinking about this all night and I just have one question, am I a Republican or a Democrat?" His colleagues assured him he was a Republican, and he supposedly said, "Okay, let's do it."

We had multiple conversations over the next thirty-six hours, through dinner, thirty-six holes of golf, and a final dinner before departing the following morning. We had our picture taken in front of the famous Eisenhower tree on the seventeenth hole,[8] and someone commented this was another "sign." Mitch questioned Charlie about timing and mechanics, and we continued to discuss alternative candidates.

From the beginning Mitch would say, "There has to be someone else with a better chance we can get behind." Our response was, "Okay, who is it?" So, we went down a rather lengthy list over the two days we were together. The only person in whom we had any confidence was Jeb Bush. However, all of us were of the opinion he wouldn't do it, and, in fact, we believed it was still too soon for another Bush to make the race.

* * *

---

[8]   Since destroyed by a storm, sadly

It wasn't until we were walking up the eighteenth fairway on our thirty-sixth hole played that day that I said to Mitch, "So, what do you think? Can we at least explore this possibility a bit more?"

Our entire objective for this trip was to see if we could expand this idea in a more organized fashion and to gauge Mitch's true feelings and interest in the job. We were convinced, based on his answers to Tom's initial questions, that he thought he could do the job and he believed he had something to contribute if given the opportunity. We clearly understood his reluctance and the multiple hurdles that stood in the way, but what we wanted was a green light to continue to investigate the opportunities. On the eighteenth fairway of Augusta, we got that green light.

After we returned home, Mitch wrote this note to all of us:

> It was unforgettable. Huge thanks to TB and everyone for coming. My daughters, who knew nothing of the Augusta trip, are petrified at what they are reading and hearing about a national effort. But there is lots of time for us all to marinate on this idea, maybe enough time to realize how dumb it is!!!!!!!!! Thanks everyone, Tom especially as host, for a wonderful experience.

Clearly, there was still a long way to go.

Next Steps

Following Augusta, I was given the responsibility to summarize our initial conversations and develop a starting point for the next steps in the process. We also agreed to have a monthly phone call among the four of us just to keep in touch.

On October 28, 2009, I sent Mitch, Tom, and Charlie a memo outlining what I thought we needed to do next. It read:

> As per our conversation following Mitch's departure, this is not a "plan" but merely in the simplest of terms, a list of things to do in the next six months. Depending on multiple factors, a "plan" certainly would be necessary in the future, but that is down the road.
>
> Having talked with a number of people this week and trying to sift through the various elements of our discussions last week, this is a compilation of thoughts for consideration as we explore this interesting idea. Don't be alarmed with the multiple tasks, none of this has to be done tomorrow, but I do believe this is a representation of the type of activities on which we should embark as we explore.
>
> 1. Events/Travel/Speeches
>
> Either in conjunction with things you are already doing, or specifically seeking out speaking platforms in the next

several months relevant to current topics of concern, consideration should be given to New York, Washington, Chicago, Dallas, Los Angeles, and Phoenix (for a special reason).

In each venue the focus should be on meeting with selected individuals who are friends wanting to help with this effort, potential fundraisers who we either want committed or at least moved to a neutral stance, target media who are friendly, and a speaking platform that expands the network.

New York is ripe with major business leaders and formidable, experienced fundraisers in addition to close friends eager to help.

In terms of Washington, I had an interesting conversation with George Will yesterday, and I understand you are trying to find a mutually acceptable date for dinner in his home. As you know, he invites other guests, primarily from the conservative press in addition to other Washington luminaries. It is off the record and well worth the time. He also mentioned the Ronald Reagan Lecture at the annual C-PAC event is something to consider.

I put Chicago on the list not because I have any great ideas, but because I know you have had several encouragements from people there and it is a close destination. We would try to put together the same type of itinerary—finance people, press, and a speaking platform. We need to discuss specific people and leadership.

Dallas is primarily to take advantage of the phone call you received to both touch base with President George W. Bush and try to lock up some key finance people. A speaking platform of some kind (Economic Club) would need to be developed. This visit needs to be after the Texas March primary so all of that "clutter" is behind us.

Los Angeles is primarily about money and locking up some key people. There are numerous former Bush Administration ambassadors there, in addition to other Bush stalwarts.

Phoenix (actually Scottsdale) is listed because the National Federation of Independent Business (NFIB) Board of Trustees and the NFIB Education Foundation Board is meeting here January 1–February 2, 2010, for their winter retreat. It would be a good platform to speak to a cross section of twenty small business leaders in addition to some other local heavy hitters financially that we could put together for a small dinner. We might consider using this time as our next face-to-face get together. It wouldn't be Augusta, but it would be warmer than where you come from!

I'm sure there are other places that would also be beneficial, but these are ones that come to mind to consider in the next six months. All, of course, need prior planning and lead time to make them successful. We should make this a point of discussion when we next get together on the phone.

2. Media Strategy

We need to give some serious thought to timely op-eds, radio, television and print interviews, editorial boards such as the *Financial Times* and other "new media" outlets. They need to be strategically scheduled as to not be too overt, but getting your expertise and opinion out there on issues that are important and where you have something to say. This obviously needs the attention of a specific person knowledgeable in this area, another point of discussion when we talk.

As a part of this effort, an entire social media strategy should also be considered, both in terms of issues, fund raising potential and general communication with key influencers. Unless you have someone already schooled in how to aggressively utilize this new phenomenon, politically, I would think about having Jeff Hunt and Paul Walker have an initial conversation with you on how this might work. Jeff and Paul used to work for us at Burson-Marsteller[9], and are doing some unique things in this area.

3. Lists

Updating, expansion and general accounting of various people lists needs to be completed. This would include the obvious elements—fund raising lists, "friends and family," friendly media, etc. Some thought needs to be given to housing such lists and the care and feeding of them.

4. Perceived Negatives

This came out of one of my phone calls, and I think it bears discussion. The idea is to take into account any and all major perceived negatives that one might come up with if a candidate for president, and take steps now to develop strategies to deal with them.

For instance, if *Hispanics* are not a major constituency with which you have dealt in your current position as governor, are there things to be done to build up your credentials in this area that would be useful and helpful in the future?

The fastest growing segment of new business creators in the country are *women*. How would you be perceived generally in the area of focusing on women's rights, opportunities, and concerns? Are there things you could do now to enhance your reputation in this area?

Something to consider and discuss.

5. Ongoing Communication

The idea of a phone call every month or so is still a good one and necessary to keep this effort going. I believe we

---

[9]   A global public relations and communications firm

left it to Mitch to initiate, and we probably need to try to do one between now and Thanksgiving. We can use this memo as the first discussion guide in addition to whatever else we need to review.

We also discussed expanding the group at some point to an additional four people (need to discuss when and how to do that)-Mark Lubbers, Al Hubbard, Bob Perkins, and Haley Barbour. After a phone call today, we need to rethink Haley. I am told by a couple of good sources that Haley wants to see where his RGA role might lead him before absolutely taking himself out; unlikely but still possible. As Charlie suggested, it would be good for you to continue to talk to him personally, but I would suggest not yet bringing him into the circle. Additionally, at some point we need to meet Eric Holcomb, who is the one staff member of Mitch being brought into the circle right now.

I am certain there are multiple other issues, some of which are probably best said personally rather than in print, but this will at least get us started. As was said last week, we have time to do things in an orderly manner, but it will take some discipline to at least make progress on various things as we proceed. Give us as much notice as possible for the next phone call.

* * *

One of the other things we asked Mitch about in Augusta was whether or not he would like to hear from people he knows and respects in terms of their opinion of this "dumb idea." He said, "Sure, happy to hear from others, as long as they know this is the longest of long shots that we'd even be interested." That gave us another green light to urge people to contact him directly with their opinions, pro or con.

Some of the immediate contacts shortly thereafter included:

- **Dennis Thomas**—A longtime friend of mine and Mitch's, former Senate AA, and White House deputy chief of staff to Reagan,

Dennis recently retired from International Paper. Dennis sent Mitch a lengthy e-mail, a portion of which said:

> Let me preface what I am going to say by acknowledging at the outset that I am shamelessly asking you to consider something other than retirement and contentment in your future.
>
> It is both my experience and reading of history that convinces me great leaders are a product of an intersection of individuals and issues. Simply and directly put—I hope you will reconsider your "no way" thoughts re running for President. The overriding reason is found in the "why" you should run. My favorite all time American philosopher and thinker, Lou Holtz, puts it pretty well. He says we should stop arguing about politics and simply "do what is right for America." Sounds corny, but my sense is he has it about right.
>
> A year ago we wanted "feel good"—today we want "do good." For sure candidate Obama touched a nerve—he offered up hope and optimism when there was precious little coming from the other side. Like Jimmy Carter, Obama offered the public relief from the previous eight years. That was then and this is now. Today a majority of folks believe we are way off track and need someone to in fact, "do good"—do what is right with deficit spending/big government, etc. And, like Ronald Reagan—they are looking for the real deal.
>
> An awful lot to think about my friend, but I do hope you will seriously think about it. My thoughts are selfish, because I care about where the country is going.

- **Dina Powell**—Dina worked with Mitch during the Bush Administration and now with Goldman Sachs in New York. Dina immediately committed to Mitch and offered help in multiple areas, both in meeting with Goldman executives and in working her many Bush contacts due to her time as head of White House personnel.

- **Cleta Mitchell**—One of the leading FEC lawyers in the country, specifically working with Republican candidates, Cleta had presidential campaign experience (the Forbes campaign) and was very influential in the conservative movement. She was the one initiating the George Will contact and offered to do work with us pro bono until Mitch made a decision.

- **Eddie Mahe**—One of the veterans in national Republican politics, he was initially committed to Haley but was very excited about the fact that Mitch would even consider the race. He believed that, in the end, Haley would not run, so offered any assistance possible.

- **Joe Allbaugh**—Veteran Bush operative and campaign manager for the first Bush campaign, Joe was very interested in becoming involved.

- **Jim Cannon**—A well-respected Washington veteran, former key Gerald Ford staffer in the White House, author, journalist, and longtime friend, Jim immediately pledged support. *(Now deceased.)*

- **Joe Wright**—A New York businessman and former OMB director and deputy Secretary of Commerce in the Reagan Administration, Joe indicated he was a "big fan" and would help him with the business community in New York, expressing the opinion he needed to start meeting with small groups both to seek their advice and to get them at least to wait on a decision.

- **Stan Anderson**—A veteran Washington lobbyist and attorney, currently working with the US Chamber of Commerce, Stan was being courted by several potential candidates but indicated support for Mitch if he were to go. His particular interest and experience in convention politics was a potential asset.

In terms of events, Mitch attended most of the National Governors' Conference meetings, which gave him the opportunity to speak with Haley and others regularly. In late 2009, he attended a governors' meeting in Dallas, where he was able to have a private conversation with George W. Bush. The former president was nothing but positive in urging him to consider the race. His basic message—there was still plenty of time to decide.

* * *

Mitch was invited to keynote CPAC, but in a personal phone call to David Keene, president of the sponsoring organization, declined, saying he didn't want his acceptance to speak to be misconstrued at this point. He indicated that Keene fully understood his position and agreed with it. George Will offered to introduce him when and if he made this keynote, which Mitch noted with gratitude.

Every time Mitch would go to Washington for an event or have any other contact with the media, speculation would continue to mount. Ralph Z. Hallow of the *Washington Times* wrote, "Mitch Daniels might be the best kept secret in the country as well as in his own Republican Party." Hallow went on to describe Mitch's record as governor on fiscal matters and the success he'd had in turning a billion-dollar debt into a surplus, without raising taxes. Additionally, he said, "Having been a manager in the worlds of business and politics for most of his 60 years on the planet, Mr. Daniels has the kind of experience any candidate thinking about running for the nation's highest office would die for. If you ask him if he will seek the 2012 GOP presidential nomination, his oft-stated answer is no."[10]

Probably the most significant conversation to finish off 2009 came in a telephone chat I had with Eddie Mahe on December 8, followed by an e-mail he sent to Mitch. Eddie's basic message, which was often

---

[10]   Ralph Z. Hallow, columnist, "Indiana's Daniels Offers Austerity as a Virtue," *Washington Times*, November 29, 2009.

repeated in the coming eighteen months was, "Do nothing that denies the option of running for president." That was Eddie's recommendation, and I repeated it many times during the coming year as we proceeded through the process. I think the formulation of that statement finally got Mitch's attention. He understood that was a way to at least keep people interested until a decision could be made.

The final action of the year was to make the decision to get together in person in early 2010 with a small but expanded group of people for purposes of strategy and further discussion. In response to my efforts to secure a commitment from him, Mitch finally sent me an e-mail two days before Christmas that said, "Okay, I guess we should do it. As long as everyone knows how far from a decision I am and may remain, I just don't want to mislead anyone."

We decided to do it in Scottsdale, in my home, and work several other things around it to keep the actual meeting secret. We expanded the group to include (in addition to me, Tom Bell, and Charlie Black) Al Hubbard, Bob Perkins, Mark Lubbers, Eric Holcomb, and Rick Powell for a total of nine including Mitch. Each person brought something unique to the meeting, in addition to a long-standing relationship with Mitch.

Every candidate for higher office has a group of individuals on whom he or she can rely for advice, counsel and support. In the case of Mitch Daniels he had a reservoir of talent, friends, colleagues, and former associates due to his many years of both public and private leadership positions.

The core group that came together from the very beginning lasted until the very end. Much will be said about these individuals throughout the story with greater detail on their contributions and involvement. Why these particular individuals? Two primary reasons guided their inclusion—trust and confidentiality.

Mitch trusted every single one of these individuals, and he knew they would keep quiet about the many aspects of the journey that required confidentiality. Without question, if the decision had been to run, the group would have been greatly expanded both in terms of talent and diversity. Until that time, Mitch wanted a very "personal" group that had his total trust and confidence.

The group consisted of the following:

Tom Bell

The first call I made after talking to Mitch was to Tom Bell. A friend for nearly forty-five years, Tom was the person who actually introduced me to Mitch in the late 1970s when we were all working for US senators as their chiefs of staff. Tom brought not only years of friendship with both Mitch and myself, he brought years of political experience and wisdom. Additionally, if there was ever a person destined to become a CEO, it was Tom Bell, and he did it several times in different industries. He was a master at creating a vision for an organization and was never afraid to state his opinion or make the tough decisions that are required of leadership. His record of achievement in business, civic leadership, and political campaigns was instrumental in determining the direction of our effort. Whenever there was a difficult conversation needed with Mitch, either Tom or I were designated to have it. In every case, Tom came through with a meaningful outcome.

Charlie Black

As detailed further in the story, one of Mitch's first comments as we proceeded on this journey was, "Don't you think we need someone involved who knows something about this!?" My immediate response was, "Yes, I'll call Charlie." Charlie Black and I came to Washington the same year, 1972, both with newly elected Republican US senators. We had been great friends ever since. We served on boards together; worked campaigns; and for the last ten years of my professional life, worked as colleagues in the same company. There hadn't been a presidential race since the early 1970s with which Charlie had not been involved in some capacity. His reputation as a strategist, an experienced presidential campaign veteran, and a cool head under pressure was invaluable every step of the way.

If there was a "wise man" in our group, it was Charlie Black.

Al Hubbard

A Harvard Business School classmate of George W. Bush, Al was the individual in the group with the most recent White House experience, having served as chief economic advisor to President George W. Bush in his second term. A highly successful businessman from Indiana, Al had known and worked with Mitch for decades, both in business and in politics, at the state and national level. His access to the finest policy minds in the country was a critical component in helping develop analysis of the myriad of issues needed to compete at the presidential level. Beyond his access, his own intellectual prowess and sound judgment on multiple issues was a key ingredient in our effort to articulate why Mitch Daniels was unique in this endeavor. Al's thoughtful, probing, insightful comments on nearly every public policy issue discussed were a continual contribution to our effort.

Bob Perkins

All one has to do to truly understand the value of Bob Perkins is to look at his résumé. He had held some of the most important marketing positions in corporate America, and his experience in understanding what sells and what doesn't was always an important component of our deliberations. Additionally, his background in political research and political fundraising was a bonus, including his appreciation for and knowledge of the importance of social media in any national campaign. Bob worked with Mitch in the late 1970s, both in the US senate and through the National Senatorial Campaign Committee when led by Senator Lugar with Mitch as the executive director. Any successful national campaign is in need of ideas—creative, innovative ideas. Bob Perkins was a person who had an idea a day. His constant influence in the necessity of creating new ideas was an important aspect of our effort.

Rick Powell

From the very beginning, we believed Mitch Daniels could appeal to the young voter, a key demographic that Republicans needed to recapture in order to win. Rick Powell was the "youngster" in our group, but one with years of political and communication experience and expertise at the national level. I hired Rick directly out of college, and he worked with me for a decade in Washington and New York. At the time of the campaign, he was head of global communications for Bloomberg LP. He brought great insight to the communication of key issues. Additionally, Rick provided a perspective on a range of difficult situations that required strategic thought and a clear path to communicating with various constituencies, in addition to his new media expertise. I have always said that Rick Powell was one of the two best people I ever hired in my professional life, and he proved me right again as he contributed to our overall objective.

Mark Lubbers

Probably the closest personal friend to Mitch and his family in our group was Mark Lubbers. Mark had worked for Mitch in Washington with Senator Richard Lugar and had been his number two at the Hudson Institute. With an MBA from Harvard, he had trafficked in and out of senior positions in business and politics. Mark had directed Senator Lugar's presidential campaign in 1995–96. The campaign was short-lived but gave him experience on the ground in the early key states of Iowa and New Hampshire. Mark was also behind the media innovation that helped define Mitch as a person when he ran for governor, the *Mitch TV* reality shows. They were composed of twelve thirty-minute episodes, completely unscripted and spontaneous, that surprisingly garnered high ratings and communicated Mitch as we knew him, a genuine, likable person with a good sense of humor. We also relied on Mark to be candid and direct with Mitch on difficult personal issues. He wasn't afraid to tell him when he thought he was off base, an invaluable asset in the world we were about to enter.

Eric Holcomb

Eric was the only staff member on the governor's staff who was involved in this effort. He had managed the most recent successful reelection campaign of Mitch for governor and was considered the "political" person in the governor's office. He was unknown to all of us except the Indiana folks, and the first time we met was our first meeting in Scottsdale. Eric was a Navy veteran who loved politics. In his position, there were many instances when he bore the brunt of Mitch's reactions to unpleasant situations. His coolness under fire and measured responses to crises was always a welcome addition to our group. Even more, he was a person who knew none of us personally and had every right to be resentful of this group of "outsiders" who wanted to come in and tread on his political territory. However, Eric never once exhibited anything other than support and complete professionalism. This effort could never have happened without the valuable input and participation of Eric Holcomb.

The eighth person was me. For over thirty-five years, Mitch and I had worked together through nearly every one of his numerous positions. From chairing Senator Lugar's Washington finance committee, where I first met Mitch, through his time in the Reagan White House to the Hudson Institute to Eli Lilly to OMB to the governor's campaign, Mitch and I were in it together. I can't think of one time when we didn't collaborate one way or the other. We served on boards together; played golf together; visited each other's homes; and for a time, had a contest on who would have the most children. We were friends and colleagues. I'd once commented that the only interest I would ever have in seriously working on a presidential campaign was if I knew the candidate personally and was willing to really invest in the effort because I believed in his quest. That happened with Mitch Daniels.

PART II

— 2010 —

2010 Begins

As we prepared for the first meeting of the inner circle (the "group") in Arizona in January, the goal was to develop an agenda to allow for a freewheeling but structured conversation to produce tangible results out of the meeting. As with our time in Augusta, the principal objective was to determine whether or not there was any real sense in continuing this effort and, if so, what to do next.

I sent a brief e-mail to the group asking them to think about the agenda and offer any suggestions for discussion. Several ideas came back, including the need for an issues strategy and a social media strategy, how to participate in the 2010 off-year elections, whether or not our group should be broadened (particularly in terms of young people, women, and Hispanics), the influence of the newly formed Tea Party, and an emphasis on potential negatives and how to deal with them.

I had a conversation with Cleta Mitchell regarding FEC regulations dealing with expenditures relevant to a presidential campaign, an issue raised by Tom Bell. He wanted to make certain all our expenditures to date were not covered by any prohibition, and Cleta assured me they were not. She indicated there was no problem in meeting with Mitch to plan, think, and strategize. Once a person says, "I'm running" and spends five thousand dollars or more to further that goal, he or she then has ten days to file and register a committee.

She did surprise me by saying, in terms of "exploratory" committees, the FEC doesn't even recognize them. The law includes an entire process that is known as "testing the waters." In this process you can:

- Open a bank account, confidentially, with no registration or filing
- Raise money from individuals—at that time $2,400 was the limit, but that increased to $2500 in 2011—without disclosing it
- Use money for polling, research, travel, and anything relevant to your "testing the water" in terms of a candidacy, except for public communication regarding your candidacy

If the determination is made to publicly announce a candidacy, the contributions are transferred to the campaign account, and you must disclose both contributions and expenditures. The contributions are counted toward the primary contribution limit.

The idea would be to start such a process after the November 2010 elections; we'd open a bank account and name a treasurer.

A couple of weeks before our Arizona meeting, I received an e-mail from Mitch that was to become a fairly regular occurrence. He was asking our opinion of whether or not he should do a specific media interview. This was a request from Jim McTague of *Barron's* to do a feature story, initially a cover story but later changed, with the theme that Mitch Daniels wasn't running for president, but if he was president, these are the steps he would take to save the US economy and other such considerations. Mitch believed Jim would come at this from a positive viewpoint, but stated there were obvious risks. The general consensus from all of us was he should do it.

In addition to sending the e-mail to our small group relevant to the agenda, I also sent it to Mitch, with more specific ideas I was proposing for the agenda. He responded that it looked fine but suggested we start out with a discussion of the potential negatives he had listed. He said, "If that can't be addressed, the rest is moot."

He also wanted to address the "who?" Who would be our political allies, even more important than the financial people, who he said, "Amazingly, are a smaller problem"? (He was coming around to the fact we could raise the money.) Also, he wanted to address the "why?" He was referring to themes and issues and what the issue platform would look like. He concluded by saying, "If this is going anywhere, I would want people to leave with assignments to scope out options on the hardest questions we would need to address."

A week before the meeting, I received another e-mail from Mitch that exemplified another aspect of this journey that would soon be familiar—an increasingly typical attitude among folks who believed Mitch should seek the presidency. Mitch had received an e-mail from a friend who'd been in conversation with Bill Bennett, former cabinet member and now a political commentator. Bennett, who had just seen some interview with Mitch, expressed the opinion that Mitch had to run and would win if he did so. Mitch's friend had attempted to explain that Mitch didn't want to run. "Who cares what he wants?" Bennett had responded. "If he is our man, it won't matter what he wants!"

On January 15, 2010, I sent out the agenda and timetable for our Arizona meeting to the group. I said:

> We are gathering simply for the purpose of continuing to explore options. We have the luxury of time, so patience on behalf of everyone is critical. Even if nothing comes of this, all of what we will be discussing has potential merit for whatever Mitch decides to do next.
>
> This agenda is just a guideline to initiate discussion, debate, and conversation. Just come prepared to add whatever you feel is relevant and important. One specific request, please bring your personal list of key people who might help in a major way, both in terms of influence and an ability to raise money and/or issue expertise.
>
> Obviously, confidentiality is paramount.

That last point was particularly important in terms of the necessity to keep this meeting, our personal views, and our strategic intent very confidential. Many ramifications were in play here, not the least of which was his current job as governor and the fact that his family, at this point, knew nothing about our plans other than what they read in the paper. Mitch was very sensitive to leaks, probably due to his White House experience, and it was important to him this group was one he could trust implicitly.

The final proposed agenda for the meeting included:

1. Update from Mitch, and anyone else that had current political intelligence.

2. Why *Not* Do This? Specifically requested by Mitch, a candid review of all the downsides.

3. Why Do This? Our differentiation, overall theme, platform? What are the two, three, or four issues we want to "own"?
   - Economic issues—jobs, fiscal discipline, budget deficits, regulations
   - Cap and trade; climate change
   - Health care
   - Campaign finance reform
   - Education reform
   - National security; infrastructure, immigration, intelligence
   - Foreign affairs; North Korea, Iran, Iraq, Afghanistan, China, Russia
   - Others; how to handle social issues

4. Outreach—Who are the most important potential political allies we need and how do we get them?
   - Groups that perhaps need attention: Hispanics, women, Tea Party members, bloggers, who else?
   - Geographical outreach in terms of places to go in 2010, primarily for quiet, influencer contacts including significant potential individual fundraisers in New York, Washington, Chicago, Los Angeles, and Dallas.

5. Media Strategy, thought pieces on current issues for op-ed; talk radio and business television appearances focused on a specific issue or topic.
   - What is our "message focus" for 2010?
   - Who is the point person on staff that focuses on this element?
   - Social Media, how do we become a significant player in this space?
   - Press outreach, who and when?

6. Perceived Negatives—A discussion of items with which we need to be prepared to deal. This could include:
   - Pharmaceutical career
   - Bush Administration experience at Office of Management and Budget (OMB)

- Gubernatorial issues that are controversial
- Personal life issues

7. 2010—What is the goal for 2010?
    - What should Mitch's role be in various campaigns for US House, US Senate, and governor?
    - Aiming Higher PAC, the PAC already established to raise money for state legislative races in Indiana; their goal was to win both houses of the state legislature. What to do with it in terms of this effort?

8. Next Steps
    - How do we keep careful track of contacts and people willing to help?
    - Potential additional professional help—FEC lawyer, pollster, etc.?
    - How and when do we broaden this group? Or should we?
    - How and how often do we communicate among us?
    - Should we develop a list of major influencers we want to contact and divide up the list?
    - What are the most difficult questions we need to address to move forward?
    - What can each person here be assigned to do to help?

As indicated previously, this agenda was formulated from the input of everyone, including Mitch. We veered from it somewhat as the meeting progressed but generally tried to follow it. It gave us a guideline to get back on track when the conversation wandered.

We built several other things around the meeting—dinner with the National Federation of Independent Business (NFIB) board, a breakfast with local people who had a tie to Indiana or some other reason for being interested in Mitch, and a luncheon with a local Young Presidents Organization (YPO) group from Oklahoma that was meeting in Arizona. All had an element of presidential candidacy discussion, which was brought up during the Q & A sessions.

The Arizona Meeting

Peaple started arriving in Scottsdale on Friday, January 29, 2010. Tom Bell, Bob Perkins, and Mitch were staying in my home, and Charlie Black hosted Mark Lubbers and Eric Holcomb in his Cave Creek home. Al Hubbard and Rick Powell stayed at the Westin Kierland, where the NFIB board meeting was being held. Because Mitch and the Indiana crew were arriving late, we started the actual meeting late Saturday morning, January 30. We met all day, through dinner, and concluded after lunch on Sunday, January 31.

As we gathered in my living room and everyone took a seat, I looked around the room and said to myself (and someone later said it out loud), *What are we doing here?* We're getting ready on January 30, 2010, in my living room in Scottsdale, Arizona, with friends, in some cases of forty years, to discuss running one of us for president of the United States. It was mind-boggling.

The meeting started with Mitch saying, "I'm not looking to do this. I'm concerned about the country; however, I don't see anyone else at this point. Christian faith teaches humility. We currently have an incredible arrogance of power going on in Washington. I don't see how a normal Republican effort can win."

Then, he wondered out loud, "Why and what should we be about if we were to undertake this? There is simply a list of prerequisites I would need, principally the ability to advocate some real solutions to real problems and a clear, defensible set of ideas with which I could go to the American people."

He stated he believed we were facing "survival issues" as a country. He articulated, "Over centuries, people have said this experiment of democracy would one day fade away, that it wouldn't last forever, because people would ultimately opt for the security of the state above all else. It is a choice between the private sector and the public sector—which is to be paramount? The choice is between individual freedom and the right to make individual choices and decisions and a system by which the government makes those decisions for you, whether it is health care or any number of other areas."

In the first five minutes of hearing Mitch just sit there and articulate his belief, I think all of us understood why we were there. His conviction and clarity and ability to fluidly express his beliefs reinforced our belief that we had an obligation to at least see if this couldn't be done. Here was a person who clearly got it—someone we all believed could make a difference to the world in which we lived.

Mitch personally articulated his "survival issues" in this way:

- **The Debt** (spending money that can't by any imagination possibly be there)—Will we have the discipline and the courage to make the hard decisions to deal with the deficit? Cleaning up earmarks won't solve the problem; that's a positive step, but it is a tiny step in the scheme of things. Our nation's debt has now become a matter of arithmetic. The numbers simply don't add up. How do we develop a program that actually fixes the problem long term? How do we sell the idea that everything—everything—has to be on the table in terms of potential solutions?

- **Radical Islamic Terrorism** (coupled with modern technology)— How do we protect the American people? How do we secure our borders? What would we do to make America more secure? How do Iraq and Afghanistan play into this overall equation? Why are we there and do we need to stay forever? What is our differentiation on this issue?

- **Foreign Oil Dependency**—This is both an economic issue and a national security issue. We are paying our enemies billions of dollars for our oil; that is a bad strategy. How do we do it? Raise the price of oil and gas to a new high with taxes and then rebate, in certain circumstances, to force people to look at alternative fuels? Put a floor on the price of oil? Is natural gas the way to go? Alternative fuels? Drilling in the United States in Alaska and offshore?

- **Jobs**—How do you create 20 million new jobs? What is a long-term plan, over twenty years, to do this? We should dismantle some of the regulatory structure, but how do you leave the proper oversight without destroying jobs? The average government worker now makes more than the average private sector worker, and the average federal government worker makes half again more. The majority of union members now consist of government workers. What does this mean for the future of the private sector and its ability to be the engine of growth?

- **Other**—I support infrastructure rebuilding, choice in education, health care reform, tax reform, and the notion that everyone should pay something. How do we get there? We must do something other than just cut taxes. Income taxes are only 14 percent of GNP.

- **Banks**—I know some regulatory reform is needed, but what kind? We need to do away with the notion of too big to fail. Do we need a single regulator? Is Congress going too far? Banks won't loan money, so jobs aren't being increased.

- **Social Issues**—We need to call a truce. A truce is not a surrender. I'm not trying to get people to change their opinions. I'm saying we need to agree to disagree and put these issues aside while we first tackle the "survival issues." My own personal positions on these issues are clear and "right" for most of the Republican constituencies. However, we need to concentrate on the first three issues mentioned above first. The country deserves our focus and attention on the issues that threaten our very survival.

Obviously, some red flags were raised that warranted more discussion and in-depth thought. Primarily, these included the notion of raising energy taxes, disengagement from Iraq and Afghanistan and how that would work and be articulated, tax reform, the social issue truce concept, and the development of a "world view" in terms of global issues.

* * *

Mitch went on to say the campaign would have to be conducted in a civil manner. He said, "We never disparaged our opponent in the governor's races." He understood the need to counterpunch but wanted to determine a way to have an honest, civil discussion of the issues.

Everyone agreed the campaign needed an overall theme that played to Mitch's strengths. Mitch said, "Are we going to pull together and save our institutions of democracy and freedom or not? Is that a theme? Reconstruction? What does it mean to be an American today? Independents would be very receptive to this approach."

A major subtheme was, "We're not running just to win; we're running to govern." Mitch said, "It would be foolish to go through all you have to go through in a national campaign just to win with no chance of then actually getting something done."

Mitch summed up his approach: "Here's what you have to do to fix our problems. If you have other ideas, bring them on. Let's work together to fix our problems even if it means making the tough decisions, even if it means taking the second or third best solution. Are we willing to do what is required to save the American experiment? We need to 'prove' our point of view with facts, creatively presented, and then develop mechanisms to test these ideas. We then need to get input and feedback from a variety of sources."

* * *

A major discussion ensued about who else could do this. Basically, the opinions were that no one else would ultimately run except Mitt Romney and Tim Pawlenty, neither of which could do it. Opinions were that certain voters still had concerns about Romney's Mormonism, not to mention his reputation of flip-flopping on certain issues due to his propensity to respond to polling data. Pawlenty, on the other hand, excited no one.[11] Palin, Gingrich, Barbour, Huckabee, Pence, Thune—in the end, none of these potentials would do it for various reasons.[12] It was suggested Mitch call Newt in particular on a regular basis for advice and counsel.[13]

---

[11]   This proved to be accurate.

[12]   Note that Rick Santorum and Ron Paul weren't even brought up in this conversation.

[13]   Looking back on the race, it's interesting to note that the negatives associated with Romney weren't really a factor in his demise. His inability to connect with the average voter, his unwillingness to walk away from his health care reform

Mitch said during the meeting and in subsequent conversations that his choice to run was Jeb Bush, and he indicated he had talked with Jeb several times urging him to do it. Most people believed it was just too soon for a Bush to make the run. Right or wrong, too much baggage still remained from the previous Bush Administration. Additionally, Jeb's family was not for it, at least not now, and he was in the process of trying to make money for the first time.

Mitch's second choice was probably Haley Barbour. Haley was a very close friend, and Mitch considered him to be one of the smartest political minds ever, which is why we (including Mitch) thought he ultimately wouldn't do it. He was smart enough to know a Southern, good old boy, Washington lobbyist, even though a very successful governor, could never make it against the first African American President.

* * *

Charlie Black noted that only three states matter in the beginning—Iowa, New Hampshire, and South Carolina—and Mitch should focus on New Hampshire. Then, he'd include maybe three more states; one need not organize in twenty-five states. Iowa and New Hampshire were tailor-made for the "RV approach"—the mix of staying in homes, Harley riding, and one-to-one campaigning that was so successful in the governors' races.

Charlie told Mitch he could wait until June 2011 to make a decision if necessary. Mitch said if the Republicans won the Indiana House in 2010, a major reform initiative would be attempted and completed by that time.

Charlie also indicated it would take $25 to 30 million for a serious effort through New Hampshire. Eric thought he and his colleagues could raise $6 to 10 million in Indiana alone in six months.

* * *

in Massachusetts (that basically took "Obamacare" off the table as an issue), his lack of a real organizational ground game (far inferior to Obama's), and his media buying strategy that proved flawed (and again, was outmaneuvered by Obama's)—all of these were much more relevant in the end.

Next, it was only natural that Mitch wanted to spend some time on the subject of "why *not* do this." He again reiterated what he considered to be negatives:

- Foreign policy inexperience (we reminded him Obama had none, less than him)
- Monetary policy—uncertain about what the right answers are (which is why you hire good staff)
- Global financial markets—lack of knowledge (our answer was the same as the other two points)
- No direct military experience (no one else had any either; less an issue today than before)
- Personal appearance (it is what it is; substance over style was our answer)
- Pharmaceutical executive (needed to be researched and defended)
- Bush Administration baggage (same answer as above)
- Some issue differences with traditional allies
- The need to resign as governor before his term ended
- Fear—public intrusion, scrutiny, ugliness—more scared of that than the job
- Family—petrified he will do it
- Fire in the belly—uncertain if he had the required obsession

* * *

We then asked the question of the group, "How do you run this approach up the flagpole?"

It was suggested we should ultimately put together a manifesto of ideas, real solutions to real problems. To enable us to monitor public opinion on all our "survival issues," it was important to put them out there to evaluate the reaction.

A good deal of time was spent on how to answer the question, "Are you running or not?" This proved to be a constant problem, particularly in the first six months of this effort. Suggestions were made to say, "If I would consider running, I would want to talk about ... I would want to propose ... I would want to have a 'grown-up' conversation about ..."

Another suggestion was to do an *Inconvenient Truth* type of documentary. What happens when Medicare goes bankrupt? What are the consequences when social security runs out of money?

* * *

Other issues were put on the table for discussion.

How do you deal with the immigration issue? Mitch was not for open borders but didn't mind having some type of immigration process that leads productive immigrants to citizenship. It would be important to stress border security first and then lay out plans for the rest of the process.

It was determined we needed our own "think tank" to put together facts and figures, real data, on these key issues. We needed to convene a group of individuals to come up with answers on a range of alternatives to our survival issues. It was necessary to pull together the massive material already out there to determine what else we needed and to come up with some solutions with serious experts to validate. Al Hubbard was designated the leader of this effort and indicated he would try to get Keith Hennessy, from the Bush White House, involved with him. As a part of this effort, we made a list of the top ten things we needed to stop or change.

On international affairs, Mitch indicated he would take this on himself, primarily right now to begin reading more. He asked everyone to send him articles on anything they thought would be useful to him on both domestic and international issues.

* * *

What to do next consumed the final hours of discussion. The primary next steps included:

- **Residence visits**—Since Mitch was still governor, it was difficult to travel outside the state on a regular basis, so the idea was suggested we get people to come to him. The goal was to organize a series of small dinners in the residence with six to ten people attending. We could include up to sixteen, but the smaller, the better. Our positioning was, "Many of us think Mitch should think about running for president. He is now listening at least, but the most important thing for him is to have a program to govern, one that actually has solutions to problems. He wants to listen to your ideas and get your reaction to some of his." We wanted to organize a dozen of these dinners in the next six months and start as soon as possible. I was designated to take the lead in organizing this effort, with Eric coordinating on his end.

- **Financial**—We needed to neutralize the major fundraising people. Al Hubbard was to get Travis Thomas (deputy finance director for the George W. Bush presidential campaign) to develop a list of George W. Bush principals. Al would then share these with me, and I would check them out with Dina Powell. We then needed to prepare a strategy to approach them.

- **The Aiming Higher PAC**—This was a local political action committee organized to assist Republican state legislative candidates in Indiana. Eric was leading this effort but indicated he could use our help and our personal contribution. As we talked to people and they wanted to know how they could help immediately, this was one mechanism. It was also a good avenue for people who didn't want to commit immediately or who had already committed to someone else but believed in what Mitch was doing. It was a way to support him "under the radar." The pitch was simply that, if we could take back the Indiana House (now 48–52), the governor would initiate one final major reform effort in the state, particularly education reform, parts of which could be a blueprint for national consideration. It would also help Mitch with his personal concern of potentially leaving unfinished business in the state to make a national race.

- **Social media strategy**—Bob Perkins was to coordinate the development of our strategy in this arena, along with help from Rick and myself. The objective was to bring together experts both within Indianapolis and outside to create something unique and differentiating in how we strategically use social media in all aspects of this effort.

- **Media**—We wanted to try to do one national interface of some kind every month. This needed the constant input of Charlie

Black and Mark Lubbers to creatively and strategically determine the best outlets.

- **Policy formation and recruitment of experts**—Al Hubbard was to put together a list of people and subjects and then recruit Keith Hennessey to help. Tom Bell would work on the idea of setting up a 501(c)(4) to raise money for travel expenses[14]. We needed to determine the best way to get these experts in front of Mitch. The objective was to pull together facts and figures and data on the survival issues and then recruit the people necessary to develop ideas and solutions to validate our findings.
- **Specific contacts of other key people**—A list of other people to contact was formulated.

* * *

Finally, we concluded the discussion with some miscellaneous comments:

- All agreed we should keep the group as is for the time being
- We decided to establish a password-protected "bulletin board" and put together a contact sheet for our group that would be sent to each of us
- We wanted a once-a-month conference call with Mitch—weekend or evenings
- We needed to send out the "to do" list

In many ways the outcome of the meeting was exactly what we wanted. We succeeded in getting Mitch to agree to continue to listen to what others had to say on the subject of running for president. He agreed that survival was at stake and wanted a coherent plan for attacking the big issues; he wanted to run to govern, not just to win. He agreed to think harder, listen to others, come up with some ideas on his own, and consider other ideas. Finally, he agreed to sit tight and wait to see if we could move forward.

---

[14] This was later deemed not necessary.

Tom Bell then asked, "Are you getting over this, 'I'm not worthy' bullshit?"

Mitch said, "Competing for it scares me more than doing it. The family and I are torn to shreds. I know there are other potential candidates out there, but I don't know who they are."

We all acknowledged this was a burden, but in the words of Tom Bell as only he could say it, "Mitch, this is bigger than just you; it is the country at stake."

And we adjourned.

* * *

Mitch and I had other discussions over the next twenty-four hours as we were doing these other events. The most memorable one was the night before he left as we had a final glass of wine in front of the outdoor fireplace when I raised the subject of Cheri.

He said if he would decide to do it, he would just let her stay out of it, if that was what she wanted. That's the way we did it in the governor's race," he said, "and it worked just fine."

I looked at him and said, "Mitch, you're running for president of the United States, not governor, and they'll never let you get away with that." I don't think he believed me then, but as time went on, that opinion would change.

* * *

All in all, it was a very successful meeting, and our principal objectives were achieved. Mitch agreed to listen and seriously consider the idea. We heard his vision and concept of a campaign if there was to be one. We were all convinced this was the person we wanted. Some red flags were raised that would need to be discussed. Some creative ideas like the residence dinners were developed, and a plan of action for the next six months was created.

It was a great comfort to all of us that the existence of this meeting never leaked. It wasn't until over a year and a half later, toward the end of the effort, that a reporter called me and asked about it, a conversation I declined to have.

The only press that immediately followed the meeting was a picture and story on local Indianapolis TV station, WISH-TV, of Governor Mitch Daniels sporting a "shiner." When asked about it by reporter Patrick Tolbert, Daniels jokingly said, "It was from a Ravens fan." He then clarified saying his injury was "accidental and entirely self-inflicted."

The truth is, on Monday morning when getting ready in our upstairs bathroom, he opened the inside door somehow right into his face! Blood, ice packs, and then a small bandage followed. It made for an interesting story as we proceeded to our schedule of meetings that day. He told me his lawyer would be in touch. "I've always wanted to own a home in Arizona!" he said.

The elephant in the room was never really addressed. Would Cheri and the family ever agree to do this, and would he do it without them? That would have to evolve, and in the end, it would be the deciding factor.

Post-Arizona Meeting

For everyone participating in the meeting in Scottsdale, the work now began. The immediate follow-up was to summarize the meeting and everyone's tasks, which was done in a memo from me. Additionally, some immediate new developments came to our attention, along with some feedback from the three additional meetings in which Mitch participated before leaving Arizona. These were communicated to our group.

The new developments included:

- Two different people had spoken with Haley Barbour, and both indicated he was very definitely considering a run. We needed to monitor and keep in touch with him.
- Romney was aggressively going after fundraisers. We needed to step up our efforts at neutralization.
- Recent homeland security issues had arisen due to congressional testimony that another attack was imminent in the next six months. Given that activity, it was suggested we consider increasing our effort to meet with the people we mentioned in this area, Fran Townsend, Michael Chertoff, and others, to develop our own ideas on what we would do both in prevention and in response.
- Regarding the budget deficit, since it was becoming an even hotter topic, which was good, some thought needed to be given to Mitch's response on Bush era deficits and his role. There were plenty of good answers; we just needed to get them down into clear, credible sound bites.
- The recent Supreme Court decision on corporate dollars opened up

some opportunities. The opportunity was far more than just getting companies to spend money on advertising, which most wouldn't do. We could also encourage them to more effectively utilize corporate resources to educate their employees and shareholders on various elements relating to campaigns. It had been suggested we test some ideas in this regard with some targeted state legislative races in Indiana in 2010.

Even though we each had specific assignments following the Arizona meeting, several items demanded attention by all of us. I asked that each person conduct his own one-on-one "focus groups," testing our survival issues, our run to govern not just to win philosophy, and our "social truce" approach. The idea was then to share that feedback with others when we reconnected.

Each person was encouraged to bring one or more groups to the residence for dinner. I emphasized that we needed to know the subject matter on the table (if in a specific area, such as economy, energy, banking, or something else) or the reason behind the group (small business or Wall Street, for example). Most importantly, we each needed the actual names of the people we would invite, including the host if we were unable to attend. I indicated I would be sending a "rules of engagement" outline shortly for everyone's consideration.

I also encouraged each person to expand his contact list. The lists should include people's names, why each person should be contacted, and who should make the first touch.

In addition, I again urged each person, if possible, to make a personal contribution to the Aiming Higher PAC and think of others who could do the same. I told Mitch getting people who had no relationship to the state of Indiana to give to an Indiana PAC was not an easy sell. The only way we would be successful is to position it as a way to support him and encourage him to seriously think about the presidential race.

* * *

The next round of communication with the group and Mitch centered on feedback from our individual one-on-one focus groups, beginning with the response to Mitch with the three groups he immediately met with in Scottsdale following our meeting. It gave him an opportunity to try out some of our themes and language, and the response was most interesting and helpful.

The first meeting was with a group of ten local business people, some with Indiana connections and some who were just interested individuals. A couple of serious heavy hitters were in this group, as well as many others. Some notables in attendance were:

- **Bob Hunt** of The Hunt Corporation, builder of the new Indianapolis Colts stadium along with other large construction projects
- **Ed Gaylord III**, third generation of the Gaylord family in Oklahoma (Gaylord Hotels, Newspapers, Gaylord Entertainment)
- **John Voris**, former Lilly executive now living in Scottsdale
- **Mike Meyers**, CEO of a major health care consulting firm with ties to Indiana

The "running to govern not just to win" approach resonated very well, in addition to the idea you could have an "adult conversation" about serious solutions for serious problems.

The second group was a YPO Forum made up of Oklahomans who were on retreat in Arizona, again including some heavy hitters:

- **Fred Hall**, who actually informed us he had bought three companies in Indiana in the last year
- **David Rainbolt**, a very successful banker from a historically well-known Democrat family
- **Art Swanson**, the host, an independent oilman living both in Oklahoma City and Scottsdale

David Rainbolt asked the question about social issues and Mitch gave the truce answer, which was universally praised.

Eventually, someone asked, "Why don't you run?"

Mitch answered, "If I could have an adult conversation and tell the truth and discuss real solutions to serious problems, if I could call a truce on social issues to concentrate on survival issues, if I couldn't find someone else … *maybe.*"

I almost jumped to my feet in a standing ovation!

Finally, the National Federation of Independent Business (NFIB) board of trustees retreat meeting was at the end of the day. All the key words and phrases we discussed—run to govern not just to win, the survival issues, and the notion of a social truce—were well presented and well received. We discussed the importance of determining the "what" in terms of the issues, not just the "who" in terms of the candidate.

Being on this board myself, over the next three days, I conducted what amounted to a focus group with many of these board members, asking them, "Is this realistic? Can a candidate willing to tell the truth to the American people and have an adult conversation about real solutions to our problems ever be successful?" The responses by and large were positive. Everyone thought people were ready for this, particularly if they could be educated about why it had to be this way and what it would take to actually solve the problems. They believed it was all in how you packaged it, but most felt the seriousness of the situation was starting to resonate.

Generally, among all the groups, in terms of the survival issues, several said we needed to combine the pain and suffering of making the hard decisions with hope in the future, a happy ending in other words. This was referred to by one as the Reagan "Morning in America" approach—we have serious problems, but as Americans if we work together, we can fix them.

Some believed it was important to "prove" our case with facts, figures, and indisputable data that the problems can't be fixed without everything being on the table, including perhaps tax increases. If we could prove it could be done without tax increases, as many of these people believed, then we needed to carefully explain the political realities of getting something through Congress and what form that might take.

Specifically on Mitch's opposition to signing the Grover Norquist "No New Taxes Ever" pledge, one interesting proposal was to expand that notion. It was suggested that Mitch not sign any litmus test, nor complete any interest group candidate questionnaire. The idea was to reject any no-holds-barred pledge for any organization for any reason or special purpose. The thought was to indicate that Mitch's record as governor, as manifested

in two terms of office, should be sufficient for any such purpose or issue.[15] His answer might be, "My only pledge is the oath of office I will take on the Bible pledging fealty to the United States Constitution upon the occasion of my swearing in on January 20, 2013."

The energy crowd believed you could solve the problem of energy dependency without abandoning the free market system or levying additional burdensome taxes. Obviously, this group had a stake in this argument. They did have a great deal of data that could be useful in working on this problem. For instance, the statistics on what natural gas could do in solving the dependency problem were quite interesting.

Generally speaking among these groups, the social truce idea was overwhelmingly received in a positive manner. Granted, the principal audiences had been business-oriented individuals who generally thought like us in terms of priorities, but the approach resonated very well with these people.

A suggestion by one person, not necessarily in the business category, was worth thinking about as we went forward. This was a very tricky area, but her idea was for Mitch to begin to build greater trust among the people who cared deeply about social issues by doing things in Indiana to reinforce his own beliefs. This might include calling in some of the social conservative leaders with whom he already had relationships (and perhaps new ones) and asking what could be done in Indiana to promote and protect life and the family. In addition, Mitch could remind people that he signed the first three pro-life bills in Indiana when he was first elected. This could illustrate the fact that he didn't hide from the issue; he'd actually taken a leadership role.

It was pointed out that most of those issues were best left to the states to decide anyway, except for federal judge selections, and if Mitch ran he could point to his record of leadership on those issues at the state level. She went on to point out the importance of not treating the underpinnings of the GOP coalition in a dismissive manner, instead building a framework that brought this core group inside the tent.

It was easier said than done, but this was a subject that deserved more discussion. The question was, were there steps we could take to make

---

[15] Charlie Black later pointed out organizations such as the National Rifle Association and the National Right to Life, while not requiring a pledge, do require a questionnaire to be completed before they will consider an endorsement.

the social truce approach doable and successful without disenfranchising people who believed social issues were of prime importance?

* * *

As time went on, all of us in the group had multiple conversations with other people around the country. The feedback we received was valuable as we evaluated the various ideas and issues with which we needed to deal. A sampling of comments included:

- A friend in Los Angeles—"He needs to talk to Cheri sooner rather than later."
- A participant in the YPO meeting—"Everyone was really impressed with him and hoping he will decide to run."
- From New York—"At a very important dinner last night, we encouraged three significant people to 'hold their powder'; we're ready to get going when you are."
- From the Business Roundtable—"Our members like Governors because they have experience running something; Mitch would be very popular among our members."
- A veteran Washington insider—"The nomination will be tough due to ideologues' purity tests" (referring to the social truce idea). And, "You have to want it to go through it."
- From New York—"Even if he doesn't do this in the end, he will make a great contribution by this approach and getting the discussion into the public realm. Obama is incapable of doing the job—campaign mode is all they know."
- Paul Zurawski—started a *Draft Mitch Daniels* website.[16]

* * *

The other phenomenon that now began was media attention, particularly the written press, to rumors about a possible Mitch Daniels candidacy. Part

---

[16] Interestingly, no one knew who Paul Zurawski was or how this happened.

of this was self-generated, almost by accident. However, once the door was slightly opened, the onslaught began.

George Will, in a February 7, 2010, *Washington Post* column started off by saying, "In 2013, when *President Mitch Daniels*, former Indiana Governor, is counting his blessings, at the top of his list will be the name of his *Vice-President: Paul Ryan*."[17]

This led to a rash of phone calls to the governor's office requesting comments and other interviews and generally kicked off renewed interest in the idea that Mitch might actually be a candidate. It also initiated what would be a continuing discussion of how to answer the question about running and not a few arguments and gnashing of teeth among the group.

On February 12, 2010, Nick Schneider, assistant editor of the *Greene County Daily World*, quoted Mitch as saying he was not a candidate for higher office in the future, and while he was flattered that some were urging him to be a candidate in 2012, it wasn't likely to happen. He said, "I don't think I have a political future. This is the only job I've ever run for and the only job that I have really thought about." He went on to say the possibility of a presidential run would "scare him to death."[18]

The groans of his group could be heard all across the country.

However, the real media storm started when he made the trip to Washington, DC, on February 22 for the National Governors Association meeting. A number of interviews had been set up months before, as is usual when he attended such meetings. The *Washington Post*, the *Christian Science Monitor*, *Politico*, the *Indianapolis Star*, *U.S. News & World Report*, *Roll Call*, the *Weekly Standard*, *National Review*—to name just a few—all had interviews and/or columns written and filed by the time the month ended.

The interviews started out pretty well. On February 22, 2010, Maureen Groppe of the *Indianapolis Star* wrote, "Mitch Daniels said today he hasn't completely ruled out running for President in 2012, but added, 'I don't expect to ever make that decision.'" He told reporters, "You won't find me

---

17   George Will, *Washington Post*, February 7, 2010. The column was actually focused on Congressman Paul Ryan and his recently announced budgetary plan.

18   Nick Schneider, *Greene County Daily World*, February 12, 2010.

doing any of the things that candidates do," and, "I've got my hands full trying to do justice to this job [as governor]."[19] Not too bad.

The major one was Dan Balz, writing in the *Washington Post*. His article started out by saying, "Add one more name to the list of possible 2012 Republican candidates for President: Indiana Governor Mitch Daniels. Two months ago, in an interview in his state capital office Daniels explicitly said he was not interested in running for President and dismissed speculation that he might be a candidate. That has now changed. During an interview at the winter meeting of the National Governors Association over the weekend, Daniels said he has now been persuaded to keep open the door to a possible candidacy."[20]

The article went on to say that Mitch basically agreed to listen to get all these well-intended friends off his back. He repeated several of his key phrases such as "survival issues" but made it clear he was only considering such a move from afar and only if no one else surfaced.

Balz expressed the opinion that Mitch was obviously a reluctant candidate but that he at least was acknowledging the fact he was thinking about it. All in all, it was a great piece by a very respected national correspondent.

The next day, February 23, 2010, the *Indianapolis Star* led with the headline, "NO, NO, NO, NO, NO, Maybe." The article at first indicated that Mitch had changed his mind on the subject of running for president, but then later in the article quoted Mitch as saying they shouldn't over read his remarks.[21]

As our friend and former colleague, Dennis Thomas, said after reading all of this, "Net net, probably as good a transition from 'heck no' to 'heck no maybe' as could be achieved."

That was not good; and it caused the phone traffic among our group to increase. The primary problem—we were getting ready to organize a series of residence dinners where we were asking important, busy people to come talk with the governor (at their own expense). Although the initial signals

---

[19] Maureen Groppe, *Indianapolis Star,* February 22, 2010.

[20] Dan Balz, "Indiana's Daniels Reluctant but Open to White House Run," *Washington Post,* February 22, 2010.

[21] *Indianapolis Star,* February 23, 2010.

were good ("I'm now willing to listen"), the statement, "I don't plan to do it, and I don't want to do it," was not helpful.

It was picked up by multiple media outlets with headlines but also became fodder for many blog posts and newspaper columns, many of which were quite positive.

In *Politics Daily*, Jill Lawrence wrote, "If Mitch Daniels ends up with a national career, it will be because he's the anti-Palin: all substance and, aside from his motorcycle habit, no flash." She went on to conclude, "Talk of reason, compromise, civility and responsibility by an even-tempered, deliberative politician who is steeped in policy? Does Daniels remind you of anyone? He reminds me of President Obama. If Republicans want to make a real go of 2012, they ought to draft Daniels."[22]

Mona Charen, writing in *National Review* said, "Mitch Daniels might challenge Obama in 2012; the GOP would be lucky to have him. It is great news for the country, if not for him, that he has at last relented and agreed to keep the door open—if only a crack. The most glaring contrast aside from philosophy (between he and Obama) is Daniel's wealth of experience and record of governing success."

After repeating our phrase, "running to govern not just to win," she concluded, "Surely Hoosiers would release him from his promise (not to run for anything else) if he asked—if we all asked."[23]

* * *

With all these stories and more, we learned two things. First, we needed to try to get Mitch to have a better answer to the question of whether or not he was a potential candidate (more on that later). Secondly, we realized his skin was not so thick. Every story was carefully analyzed by him, and even the generally good ones were torn apart if any small negative was mentioned. Both of these issues demanded some attention.

---

22   Jill Lawrence, "The Case for Keeping Mitch Daniels on the GOP Short List for the White House," *Politics Daily*, February 24, 2010.
23   Mona Charen, "The Anti-Obama," *National Review*, February 26, 2010.

Residence Dinners

The most innovative idea to come out of the Arizona meeting was the residence dinners. We faced the reality that Mitch was the governor of a state. Therefore, his time was limited in terms of out-of-state trips and other activities not directly related to his day job. As we were discussing this dilemma and all the things we needed to do, Bob Perkins suggested we get people to come to him.

Having lunch or dinner with a governor, in the residence of the governor, is not something most people do every day, or ever. Nevertheless, to receive the most benefit, we needed to organize these events effectively, which meant having some "rules of engagement." In early February 2010, I sent the following memo to our group entitled "Residence Dinners—Rules of Engagement." In part, it said:

> As we attempt to broaden our base of knowledge and contacts, the idea of bringing people to Mitch in a unique setting and efficiently using his time is an excellent one. Here are some "rules of engagement" to consider:
>
> - The wording of our invitation, whether in person or in writing, needs to be consistent. One approach would be:
>
>> While Mitch remains focused on being governor of Indiana, he is very concerned about the direction of the country and our

ability and willingness to make the hard decisions on key issues that are really survival issues for the country. Specifically, the growing budget deficit, dependence on foreign oil that is both an economic and national security issue, job creation, and national security as it pertains to dealing with radical Islamic terrorism coupled with modern technology.

To help him think through some of these issues and others, Mitch is asking a few people to come to the Governor's Residence in Indianapolis over the next few months to have dinner to discuss them. He is interested in listening to people who know something about these issues to get their ideas on solutions, and to give him feedback on some of his ideas that pertain to solving these problems.

- We need to have some organizing principle around each dinner, i.e., either a subject matter—energy, healthcare, general economy, bank regulation/reform, homeland security, etc. Or a like group of people—Wall Street, Small Business, Academics, etc.

- We need a host (if we are unable to come ourselves) that will help us invite the appropriate number and type. The perfect number is probably six to ten, although the dining room can take up to sixteen.

- We need to emphasize to our potential guests this is not a fundraiser. We're not looking for commitments, just an honest discussion about the right way to resolve difficult issues, survival issues.

- We need a list of specific names of who will be invited to attend. The list of subject matter, hosts and specific guests should be forwarded to me as soon as you have them.

* * *

That was the basic thrust of the memo. Like most things, the hardest part was getting started, having the first dinner to show how it could work and how it could be beneficial. Many times, Eric and the local people, particularly Al Hubbard, had to be the host due to time constraints and the ability for others in our group to attend (although everyone in our group attended at least once, and in my case, multiple times). The expense of the dinners was covered by private funds.

The format was to meet in the living room for cocktails with a brief, informal discussion and introduction to the evening, followed by dinner in the dining room around one small table. We actually developed a sample script so no matter who was hosting, they would have some idea of the setup. It read:

> We very much appreciate everyone taking the time and making the extra effort to come to Indianapolis tonight for this discussion—and that's what we want to make it—a discussion about some serious issues facing our country.
>
> As you know, there is a great deal of speculation about 2012, and Mitch continues to be a part of that speculation. As he has said, and as you will hear directly from him, this is not something he has ever sought or even considered a possibility.
>
> But he too is concerned about the future of the country and in particular about what he considers "survival issues" that must be faced with honesty and thoughtfulness. As he has repeatedly said, regardless of what happens between now and 2012, we need to get the "what" right, notwithstanding the "who" factor.
>
> He has said his focus right now is getting the Indiana

legislature to go Republican in November[24] to enable him to propose one more significant reform agenda. However, he is then willing to listen to what people have to say and keep an open mind as to what 2012 might bring.

So, tonight is one step in helping to get the "what" right—what are the survival issues and what are some real solutions in dealing with them?

Since these "survival issues" are really Mitch's findings and approach, we thought we'd start with him laying them out for you. He then wants not only your reaction and feedback, but also your specific ideas and help in figuring out what to do about them.

So, let me turn it to the governor to start the discussion.

The dinners proved to be hugely successful. We had people who heard about them and actually requested to be included. The range of people and issues discussed was quite broad, and as we progressed, we learned how to do them better and better.

Some of the attendees and subject matters included:

- A small group from Oklahoma, including the outgoing president of the American Petroleum Institute, Larry Nichols, chairman and CEO of Devon Corporation, to discuss energy issues
- One that focused on financial issues and included Robert Steel and Craig Stapleton (Bush Ambassador to France) from Greenwich, Connecticut; Bill Hybl (El Pomar Chairman) from Colorado; and others
- Well-known veteran fundraisers with Republican Party experience, including the DeVos family from Michigan and the Haslam family from Tennessee
- A dinner built around political strategy and social media that included veterans Eddie Mahe, Fred Maas, Jeff Hunt, Dennis Thomas, Stan Anderson, and Joe Allbaugh

---

[24]   Of 2010

- A group of Goldman Sachs executives brought together by Dina Powell from New York to discuss global financial issues and concerns
- One that included previous major fundraisers from the McCain campaign and key people from Illinois and New Hampshire, such as Greg Wendt from San Francisco, Phil Handy and Ron Gidwitz from Chicago, Steve Duprey from New Hampshire, and old friends Tom Korologos and Ann McLaughlin from Washington
- A fundraising group that included Mercer Reynolds (Bush 43 Chairman), and several former ambassadors
- A "social truce" gathering of some evangelical leaders including Marc Nuttle, Tim Gelogline, Rick Joyner, Dick Fox, and Ken Blackwell
- A dinner that focused on biological and technological terrorism issues and included Tom Higgins, George Nethercutt, Ian Brzezinski, Joel McCleary, and others
- A business leaders dinner that included people from different parts of the country such as Craig and Barbara Barrett (Arizona), Harlan Crow (Texas), Jon Hammes (Wisconsin), Warren Stephens (Arkansas), Harry Clark (New York), and others

One particular dinner in July included two people who met with Mitch prior to dinner and then provided him with specific correspondence that was very helpful in the decision making process. They were former Missouri senator and UN ambassador John Danforth and Jack Oliver, a former RNC finance director now living in St. Louis and considered one of the best fundraising experts in the Republican Party.

Al Hubbard later commented he didn't think he'd ever heard a more articulate plea than what Senator Danforth had to say to Mitch in terms of his need to run. He was, in Al's words, "persuasively eloquent," saying Mitch was the best person in the country to present a clear contrast to what America was becoming and an alternative. In writing a memo to Mitch on July 19, 2010, Senator Danforth said in part:

> Americans deserve a clearly presented choice on the role of the federal government in the country's future. The 2012

election should be a referendum on competing ideologies: on one hand, a growing country and a contained federal government; on the other hand, a growing government and a stunted country. In sum, the campaign should be a contrast between the vision of Reagan and Obama. In recent speeches, the President has characterized 2010 and 2012 as a 'choice' between two futures for America. Republicans should actively join the debate.

You are the best person to present an attractive alternative to Obama ... emphasizing substance over style. Yours would be an issue-based campaign with one central theme: an expanding America versus an expanding federal government. Would you win? I think so. But as you were quoted in the *Weekly Standard*, "You can only do the kinds of things we were trying to do if you don't really give a damn ... about winning an election." Whether you win or lose, you would give Americans a clear choice about their future.

* * *

We did nearly a dozen residence dinners between April and August, and in each case, the feedback was overwhelmingly positive. In most cases, they were very helpful in terms of issue education for Mitch and in trying to urge key political and fundraising personnel to "keep their powder dry" until a decision could be made. Also, the feedback from each dinner was both illuminating and, at times, quite helpful. Examples included:

- "Very productive use of time. Great discussion on immigration, education, and entitlements."
- One questioned the social truce, saying, "If we're not careful about articulating the message, it could come off as money matters more than morals."
- "The governor appeared very engaged and interested in our expertise and perspectives. If he goes, I'll be there."
- "Your comments on cutting the defense budget need to be preceded

with a description of your vision for the role of the United States in the world. Otherwise you sound like an OMB director in charge of foreign policy."

- "You need to be more direct in addressing whether or not you will run. You were too coy."
- "Super impressed; handled the issues extremely well, just the right amount of listening and talking. I love your nonpolitician approach."
- "On the presidential question, I wonder if he is giving himself enough time. The quest for finances and support on a national scale can be grueling. If he wants it, he needs to give himself enough time."
- "The notion of a social truce is incredibly appealing. It will resonate with many independents, a key voter group in the New Hampshire primary."
- "I came away from our dinner inspired by you, your record, and your approach to governing. One concern I have is the potential timeline you shared—some key talent may be locked up by then."
- "Very much enjoyed the dinner and issue discussion. However, I expected the discussion would be more directed at political strategy. Guests like me need to be encouraged to be part of a developing team and some call to action/engagement is needed."
- "Very much appreciated being included in the dinner. Mitch is smart and authentic and has a real shot. The race has a good chance of centering on his strong suit, economic issues."

As the dinners progressed, Eric observed Mitch had become much more direct and to the point, by saying, "We have a plan, no one else out there is running on our type of issues, and it's not too late."

As we concluded July, we determined we would take August off and begin planning for another series in the fall. Mitch wanted to wait before scheduling more, but we proceeded to plan the types we still felt necessary to do. We wanted one focused on foreign policy, more fundraising types, and others focused on women leaders and defense issues. We also wanted to continue our efforts to talk to veteran political types, including former Bush leadership (Andy Card, Josh Bolten, Karl Rove, and the like).

The foreign policy focus was one of the most important because we still hadn't focused on the articulation of a "worldview," and we had numerous people who were able and willing to meet, Condi Rice, Stephen Hadley, Will Ball, and Stephen Friedman, among others.

Additionally, we planned to organize some dinners around Indianapolis Colts home games just to add some different incentives.

The biggest need in terms of the dinners, as articulated by more than one attendee in the first several events, was the lack of a call to action. So, after discussing this both with our group and with Mitch, I sent out a sample one-page "close" for which the host would be responsible. It read:

> People have asked, if I am interested in what we have discussed tonight, what can I do?
>
> Whether Governor Daniels ultimately becomes a candidate in 2012 or not, his approach to the "survival agenda" for the country is an important endeavor. The work to develop real substance behind the various policy issues that make up the survival agenda will enable whoever is the candidate to have a differentiating approach to solving the nation's most critical problems.
>
> If you are interested in helping promote this agenda in addition to keeping in touch with the governor's own decision-making process there are three things you can do:
>
> 1. Contribute to the Aiming Higher PAC. There are two important elements to this effort—taking control of both house and senate in Indiana to enable Governor Daniels to initiate a reform agenda in 2011 in the areas of education and economic growth—an agenda that could be a model for the country; and secondly, major policy groups are being formed with Mitch to develop detailed policy ideas and recommendations for the "survival agenda" for the country. A portion of this PAC funding will go to pay travel expenses for these groups.

2. Provide us with your e-mail and mailing address to enable us to keep you informed as to Mitch's travels, speeches, and articles that will keep you updated on his activities and progress.

3. Help us expand the group of interested people. We are holding a series of Residence Dinners to discuss the survival agenda, both from a policy perspective and a political one. If you have people you think might be interested in discussing these issues, let us know who they are and either come yourself and bring them with you, or we will invite them to an already scheduled dinner.

This new "close" produced immediate results. We had lists of well over a hundred additional potential invitees. Our intention at that time was to continue to schedule these dinners well into 2011.

— Additional Travel and Events

I n addition to the residence dinners strategy, we knew Mitch could
be in Washington for several other reasons, and we put together a
schedule for New York and Los Angeles we hoped to implement in
the first quarter of 2010.

New York was important both for continued policy discussions with
significant people and to try to neutralize major fundraising types and see
people we thought wouldn't be inclined to travel to Indianapolis for dinner.

Tim Ryan, at the time the president and CEO of the Securities and
Financial Industry Association (SIFMA) and a close friend of Mitch's,
offered to host a breakfast of politically interested and experienced business
leaders. Following the breakfast, Tim said Mitch was perceived to be
smart, appropriately evasive, authentic, folksy, and obviously competent.

There was a dinner at Goldman Sachs, a meeting with a group of
conservative press leadership, a session with Ken Mehlman (former Bush
campaign manager, RNC Chair, and now with KKR) and invited guests,
and a dinner with Woody Johnson (owner of the New York Jets, and a
major Romney fundraiser who ultimately stayed with him).

In Los Angeles, Jim McGovern, former secretary of the Air Force and
now a very successful businessman and close friend, organized a lunch and
dinner of major business people and potential fundraisers, including former
California Governor Pete Wilson. "A breath of fresh air" was one comment
following the dinner, and the response according to McGovern was
extremely positive. "Flawless" was how Jim described Mitch's performance.

Brad Freeman (a close friend of George W. Bush) and his partner,
Ron Spogli (Bush Ambassador to Italy), hosted a meeting of friends and

heavyweights for Mitch to meet after lunch. Due to poor planning and awful but normal LA traffic, he was late, and therefore, the session didn't get started very well and was cut short. The feedback was not as good from this session: "Very impressive but didn't sway me from supporting Mitt."

The Los Angeles trip also included a meeting with a group of young adults, very inspiring and supportive, and a breakfast with an impressive and eclectic group organized by David Martin, the immediate past president and CEO of YPO International. Mitch was also the featured speaker at a GOPAC lunch of heavyweights at the Reagan Library that was very well received. Every group with whom he met raised the question of his running for president, and all encouraged him to seriously consider it.

All these events were prior to our realization we needed to ask them for something—some type of close or call to action, which we later corrected.

Several Washington, DC, trips were on the schedule, and most were associated with previously scheduled events, the National Governors Association and an Aiming Higher PAC event.

* * *

One particular dinner in Washington was a very special one. It was held after numerous residence dinners and ample discussion with Mitch on how he should address certain questions. On June 7, he attended a small dinner party at the home of columnist George Will, an event that had been in the making for six months. Will was a major fan of Mitch's, and his wife, Mari, worked with Mitch in the Reagan White House and was an equal advocate. The George Will "off the record" dinners had become famous in political/Washington circles, and we were anxious to see how this developed and the subsequent feedback.

The attendees (along with spouses) included:

- **Michael Barone** (columnist and well-known political pundit)
- **Cleta Mitchell** (prominent FEC attorney and conservative activist)
- **Charles Krauthammer** (*Fox News*)
- **Kimberley Strassel** (*Wall Street Journal* columnist)
- **Fred Hiatt** (editorial page director, *Washington Post*)
- **George and Mari Will** (hosts)

Feedback was most interesting and very positive. From a close friend who was in attendance came this: "Mitch was terrific in every way that you know already. He said, 'I'm not looking in the mirror and seeing a president every day' … But, he agreed 'to consider it and he is open to it and will see what happens going forward; that there are survival issues at stake in the next couple of years and he's willing to consider running.'" It was perfectly fine and reasonable.

We also heard feedback from another participant who said Mitch was a natural politician, good at explaining and connecting to people. This person loved his pragmatism and honesty and believed he would sell very well to the American public. During the dinner, Mitch listened to concerns about both tax increases and energy policy in terms of some of his current thinking, as well as a suggestion that he work more on national security issues. The group generally agreed with him on social issues in terms of the necessity of prioritization.

Feedback from George and Mari Will was equally as positive.

* * *

As time went on, we tried to have a conference call every month with Mitch and the group. In March, we scheduled a call with an agenda that included:

- Message—reaction and feedback to the survival issues phrasing, run to govern, adult conversation, and social media truce approach. What new "vocabulary" is needed for such issues as impact of the debt, etc.? What are concrete ideas for the subject of job creation"? What do we do about Mitch using the "Don't Want To" phrase?
- Update on policy initiatives (Hubbard); Residence Dinners (Cogman); social media strategy (Perkins and Powell)
- New people to contact; names suggested by others with whom we have talked the past months
- Social truce strategy discussion
- Future schedule—LA; Washington; Media interviews; Next call

The results of that call indicated that calls and visits were proceeding on schedule and reaction to the survival issues approach was overwhelmingly positive. It was reported that Newt, Haley, and Mike Huckabee had people stirring the pot, but most thought, in the end, none would actually go.

From our meetings in Arizona, Washington, and New York, a few suggestions came forth relevant to how the conversation flows:

- Crisper, more focused answer on the great success to date in Indiana—here's what we've done and how we did it. Leave plenty of time to ask the participants their opinions on issues in which you seek more guidance and information.
- As a part of the issue discussion, also emphasize the "can do" aspects of dealing with these survival issues; there is light at the end of the tunnel.
- Somehow bring it to a conclusion with some type of call to action—importance of giving to the PAC; providing Mitch with suggestions on how best to continue to define the "what"; any additional information on the survival issues discussed that would be helpful as we continue the adult conversations.

The policy initiatives led by Hubbard were moving along, a timetable of two to three months was set for these teams to get together and develop some ideas for Mitch to review and discuss. The importance of framing the issues from a communications standpoint was also discussed.

Residence dinners were proceeding very nicely. We needed to fill April dates (May dates were already completed) so we emphasized we needed everyone's help to add people.

The social media strategy meeting was scheduled in Indianapolis with Perkins, Powell, and others. A set of recommendations was due out of that first session to then begin looking at alternative ideas for social media utilization in multiple aspects of the effort.

A number of new people were discussed to add to the contact list. Hubbard suggested everyone focus on making at least one call a day to someone, particularly those we wanted to neutralize relevant to future fundraising. So far, that effort was paying off. Many people who had been contacted by Mitt and others were willing to stand pat until decisions could be made.

The social truce strategy was reviewed. So far, we'd had a very positive reaction from some leading evangelicals, who indicated they understood the issues of terrorism and the debt were the most important on which to focus. We needed to bring a few of these people to dinner to discuss this further.

It was suggested we needed to research fundraising amounts in 2008 to have a sense of what it would take to compete state by state. Charlie Black said it was important to focus on how much we would need to raise to get us through Florida on the primary calendar, and he indicated he would be ready with a presentation on that element when we next met.

Momentum Continues
———— Driven by the Media

A s 2010 proceeded through the spring and summer, media attention through articles, interviews, and just plain speculation continued to drive the story. Awareness of Mitch was increasing with a sense of significant momentum.

On March 1, 2010, Ross Douthat, *New York Times* op-ed columnist, wrote an op-ed entitled, "A Republican Surprise." It started out by saying:

> Set a group of plugged-in conservatives to talking about presidential politics, and you'll get the same complaints about the 2012 field. Mitt Romney? He couldn't make the voters like him last time … Sarah Palin? She'd lose 47 states … Mike Huckabee? Better as a talk show host … Tim Pawlenty, Jim DeMint, Bobby Jindal, David Petraeus? Too blah, too extreme, too green, and stop dreaming …[25]

The article then went on to say that, when you mentioned the name Mitch Daniels, everyone perked up. No one knew if he could win, but many believed he would make the best president of all those previously mentioned. It went on to compare his wonky, balding stature with the incumbent president but indicated that, in the minds of many, a Daniels vs. Obama contest would be a very competitive race.

---

[25] Ross Douthat, op-ed columnist, "A Republican Surprise," *New York Times*, March 1, 2010.

Charlie Cook, the well-known and highly regarded Washington political pundit, commented to a friend on Daniels' refusal to shut the door on a run, indicating that he was exceedingly well versed in national politics.

On May 10, 2010, Julian Zelizer, in a special report for CNN.com entitled, "Governor Daniels: GOP's Best Hope for 2012?" said:

> Conservative pundits are in love with a candidate for 2012 and it isn't Sarah Palin. If you ask many top Republicans their favorite pick for the presidential campaign, they will answer Indiana Gov. Mitch Daniels. Daniels could help Republicans reclaim the mantel of fiscal conservatism. His second potential virtue is executive competence—he has a strong record in the Governor's mansion.[26]

On June 2, 2010, in *US News and World Report*, columnist Paul Bedard in "Washington Whispers" said:

> It's still not too late for Republican presidential hopefuls to get into the 2012 primary race. The big presidential buzz remains with Indiana Gov. Mitch Daniels, a two-term budget slasher who was former President George W. Bush's first budget boss. He seems to pick up support daily. Alabama Senator Jeff Sessions says he likes the Hoosier because "he can explain how we got into this mess and how we'll get out."[27]

Philip Klein, in an article for "Political Hay" in the *American Spectator*, said:

> One recurring theme in American political history is that presidents who fall out of favor tend to be succeeded

---

26   Julian Zelizer, "Governor Daniels: GOP's Best Hope for 2012?" *CNN.com*, May 10, 2010.

27   Paul Bedard, columnist, "Washington Whispers," *U.S. News and World Report*, June 2, 2010.

by candidates who exhibit opposite attributes. Carter-Reagan; Bush-Obama. With lofty rhetoric (Obama) now being followed up by incompetent governance (Obama), by 2012, the electorate may warm up to somebody boring who knows what he's doing. Therein lies the potential appeal of Mitch Daniels.[28]

In another *US News and World Report* article writer John Aloysius Farrell said:

> Mitch Daniels in 2012! He is an independent voter's dream: a sensible, practical guy who wants to get in there and fix the stuff that's broken, and doesn't really care what you do in your bedroom at night. And he has a sense of humor! When he was the country's budget director, they played on the phone when they put you on hold, "You Can't Always Get What You Want."[29]

Numerous other stories, articles, and blogs appeared throughout the spring and summer, nearly all positive and encouraging. *Bloomberg*, *National Review*, the *Weekly Standard*—all did lengthy and very laudatory pieces on Mitch and his record as governor that kept his name in the forefront of potential candidates for 2012.

In early summer, Tom Bell suggested we consider "slowing down a bit." He said he felt like we were picking up momentum almost too quickly, and he was guessing it was not sustainable. My response was in general agreement, but we were already heavily booked until August with multiple residence dinners and other activities. In terms of "public" interviews, particularly television requests, slowing down in that regard was fine with me, and that was what we attempted to do.

* * *

28 Philip Klein, "The Grown-Up," *American Spectator*, June 11, 2010.
29 John Aloysius Farrell, "Mitch Daniels in 2012-Much Better than Palin, Paul and Angle," *U.S. News and World Report*, June 16, 2010.

Other interesting items during the summer included a couple of interviews and interactions with Mitch's wife, Cheri. She did an online video interview with the *IndyStar* on June 27, 2010, where she assented to the possibility of a presidential run. That got everyone breathing a little easier.

When asked the question, "So if the Governor came home tonight and said, 'I've decided I am running for president,' how would you react?"

Cheri responded, "I would be surprised. Obviously, there's been a lot of hype about all of that. And do I think he would be a good candidate? Of course I do. I think he's one of the smartest politicians around. But I also know that he would rather encourage somebody else to do it."

Additionally, Mark Lubbers was with the family at their annual July 4 sojourn to the Greenbrier, and he reported that in his view, "Her change in attitude is real and pronounced" (relevant to a presidential run).

Mark went on to say, "She was decidedly unhappy several months ago when the first round of stories hit. Now, however, she seems more interested and engaged in politics than I have ever seen her—which is not a lot—but to be out of the negative range and into positive territory is a huge move. The subject of a presidential run came up in conversation several times, and Cheri never once seemed uncomfortable with it or negative about it. Go figure."

Again, we were intrigued by that report and certainly pleased, but admittedly not yet convinced.

On June 30, Mitt Romney called to invite Mitch to dinner at his home on July 10 during the National Governors meeting. Mitch declined because he wasn't attending the meeting, but this was one of two personal invitations Mitch would receive from Mitt over the course of the year to visit him in his home. Obviously, the media reports and other feedback were getting back to Romney, and he wanted to see if he could obtain any insights from Mitch as to his plans.

Toward the end of the summer, Stan Anderson, veteran Washington insider and friend of many of us for years called to talk about Mitch. He had attended one of our residence dinners and currently was working for Tom Donahue at the US Chamber as a senior advisor. He asked me if there was a plan, and I attempted to fill him in on the various activities in which we were engaged. He asked if he could send a proposed action plan for the next twelve months and I said, certainly.

The principal strategic message he proposed was one of emphasizing the important contrasts between Mitch and Obama. His memo to me on July 26, 2010, said in part:

> The polls suggest—and the November elections will demonstrate—that Americans have lost confidence in Obama, not simply because they increasingly oppose his policies (which they do) but because they believe he does not have the leadership skills to move the country forward. There is also a competency issue argument beginning to take hold. As a successful, two-term governor, Mitch has the opportunity to reinforce doubts about Obama while promoting his own record and experience.

Stan made several suggestions regarding scheduling, including some foreign travel (he thought Mitch should visit the Indiana troops overseas during Thanksgiving and take a trip to Israel as soon as possible). Other ideas had to do with press interviews at Republican governors meetings and National governors meetings, where ample national press was always in attendance.

He made suggestions on what events to attend early in 2011 in Iowa, New Hampshire, and South Carolina, and other recommendations on speeches and organizations to appear before. Many were not possible due to Mitch's ongoing gubernatorial duties, but serious suggestions from a veteran operative such as Stan Anderson added to the continuing momentum.

Thin Skin
—————— (and Occasional Humor)

I n every presidential campaign, events and just plain weariness begin
to take their toll. With Mitch as time went on, certain episodes made
us wonder among ourselves if he really had the temperament to both
make the run and then hold the office.

The fact he had done it twice in Indiana for the top job certainly gave
us hope it could be done. But, as we often said relevant to other issues,
running for president was different than anything else. Nearly every article
written about him personally had phrases such as "balding, wonky, short,"
and the like. These always provoked commentary.

On February 25, 2010, Jonathan Martin in *Politico* wrote an article
entitled "Mitch the Knife" that Mitch didn't think much of, particularly in
terms of what was left out. Most of us thought it was a great article. Mitch
said, "Same old, same old. Never a word about sense of humor. Never a
word about stump skills. This is just another reason I'm *not* doing this.
Who'd ever vote for the person described here?"

Mark Lubbers responded to Mitch:

> This is an un-presidential reaction. The article was
> fabulous! As for stature comments, I won't argue with you
> because you are incapable of understanding this is a plus.
>
> As for charisma discount, by the time these know-
> it-alls, including opponents and their chattering class

consultants figure out that their assumptions are all wrong, it will be too late for them.

My advice is if you cannot enjoy this predictable tripe, then your skin is too thin to be president. If not for the fact that the country really does need you, the whole thing is a giant pain in the ass anyway!

Mitch responded the next day, saying, "Yeah, I knew you'd say that. It's just fun to provoke you."

In the spring, I reached out to Mitch about a *New York Times* article. "When the *New York Times* starts saying something nice, I start to worry. Wow, some article. You probably don't like the balding, wonky part, right?"

Mitch responded, "Can't argue with the truth. But 'wonky' strikes me as a bit unfair!"

On October 9, 2010, Michael Barone, writing in a Townhall.com column, asked the question, "Can Skinflint Mitch Daniels Win the Presidency?" All in all, a good article actually, but some descriptive words clearly got under Mitch's skin.

Mitch's immediate response to the group was, "Short, bald, ugly, humorless, zero voter appeal ... the image is now burned in nicely. Clearly the answer to Michael's question is 'no way'!"

Charlie Black, upon reading Mitch's e-mail, quipped, "Glad we settled that. Do you have Palin's #?"

Once again, Lubbers weighed in: "You are WAY too sensitive (closely related to the concept of thin skin)! These stupid comments about the absence of central casting looks are a backhanded condemnation of this shallow perspective—a way for bright print reporters to castigate TV and mass media and their progeny, thus builds a base of psychological support among best and brightest commentators."

(None of us were completely certain we understood that, but we generally got the point!)

The *Courier-Journal* ran an article by Lesley Stedman Weidenbener in which she commented on Mitch's recent appearance on *Fox News Sunday*, where he again answered the question about running for president.

She said in part, "Daniels is at his best when he's smart but self-deprecating, strong and maybe a little acerbic. He's at his worst when he's irritated and accusatory. The latter certainly doesn't go over well with reporters in Indiana, and it would likely be worse with the national press corps and probably the voters."[30]

* * *

Over a two-year period, hundreds of e-mails from friends, former colleagues, and even strangers urged Mitch to seriously consider running for the nomination. He would almost always pass these on to me, sometimes the entire group, along with his comments. More often than not, his comments, while grateful, expressed his attitude about the race.

To a well-known Washington veteran who urged his candidacy, he said, "You're the guy I thought I could count on to tell me why it is a stupid idea, that I should completely forget about!"

To our old friend, Dennis Thomas, former Reagan deputy chief of staff among other things, who wrote to say, "You have got to do this!" Mitch responded: "You need to read *Newsweek*, where you will learn that I am not just too short and too bald, but also 'stiff' … the first two disqualifiers, sure, but that last one I have trouble getting. But we never see ourselves as others see us."

Occasionally, old friends who were veterans of many press wars due to their experiences in the White House and other places would offer some friendly advice. One case in point was when Ari Fleischer, first White House press secretary to George W. Bush, sent Mitch a memo on August 8, 2010, following his appearance on *Fox News Sunday* with Chris Wallace. This was one of Mitch's first major appearances.

Ari, who by that time was in business for himself and, as Hubbard later commented, would have charged him a substantial fee for the advice he was giving him free, sent him a three-page memo entitled "Free and Probably Unneeded Advice." It was a critique of his appearance, and as Ari said, "After watching the interview, my foolish old instincts kicked in, and I thought I would send you my observation of how you did. Since you didn't ask for this, and because it's a weekend, please feel free to roll this up and swat some flies."

---

30   Lesley Stedman Weidenbener, "The Two Sides of Mitch Daniels," *Courier-Journal*, August 15, 2010.

A few of his comments included, "Nothing is more important than the first sentence of your first answer to the first question and I thought you fouled it off when you could have hit a home run."

Ari restated the question, which was, "What should Washington be doing to boost hiring in the private sector?"

"You replied with a lengthy and somewhat heavy answer," he noted, then repeating the answer. "Wow, that's a long sentence. You could have said ..." Here Ari gave a very succinct, shorter answer. "You also need to introduce your fundamental message about the threat of the deficit and debt at the very beginning of the interview, always as part of your first answer," he added.

Ari went on to compliment Mitch on several things he said and the manner in which he said them, before making some other content suggestions. He also said he knew Mitch didn't want to talk extensively about the Bush record, but in Ari's words, "You'll have no choice. I think you need a stronger, slightly longer answer to address it."

He went on to articulate what he termed, "small things" that included:

> You're probably being modest, but don't use the royal "we"—it doesn't sound right. Simply say "I."
>
> When you discussed Social Security, you broke into a little wonk that most viewers don't speak.
>
> In answering one of Chris' questions, you made it sound personal to him, change it to "Washington lives in a world ..." rather than "you' live in a world of secret agendas."

After reading the entire memo, we thought it was right on target. And it came from a well-respected former White House press secretary who had to deal with the pariahs of the press on a regular basis.

Mitch's response was appreciative, saying he agreed with 90 percent. It then detailed several items that he defended vociferously, none of which made much sense to us.

* * *

From time to time, press stories in which the reporter either got it wrong, or simply said things that rubbed Mitch the wrong way would appear.

The other thing that would set him off was when someone took credit for a speech or articles he wrote. The fact was, he personally wrote everything—speeches, articles, op-eds. That was one reason they were so good. Mitch was a terrific writer, and he also was particularly sensitive to the fact that he didn't have "handlers" who did things like writing for him.

After the CPAC speech, which was universally lauded, a comment got back to Mitch that someone said, "Yes, it was a great speech. I wrote it! (This person, among others, had been given a draft to fact check.) Mitch's immediate response was he could hardly recall who this person was and probably couldn't pick him out of a lineup. He said, "Please see he learns I am very disappointed at what he said; I am not interested in any further contact with him. Let me know when someone has delivered that message!"

After some back and forth e-mails counseling "calmness"—we didn't want to risk alienating this person or his large firm—Mitch continued to say, "Risk what to whom? I just want the guy to know I don't like false credit taking, and maybe he'll quit telling people things that aren't true but are demeaning to me."

Someone once said that the problem with Mitch Daniels was he always thinks he's the smartest guy in the room; that's why it's hard to get him to accept criticism. The fact is, in nearly every case, he *is* the smartest person in the room. So, the challenge was to have people involved who had enough personal credibility with him to ensure he appreciated the fact that the criticism was "constructive." It was solely to help him be even better.

Policy Issues

When it came to determining policy decisions, the first and foremost voice was that of Mitch, as it should have been. From the very first meeting in Scottsdale, he came with a set of principles. He had an idea of what was important and the potential pitfalls of having an "adult conversation" with the American people. We generally followed his roadmap in dealing with the myriad of policy issues that would be demanded of any serious presidential candidate.

The whole concept of "survival issues" came from Mitch, as did the contention that running "to simply win" and not "to govern" was no way to run. He stated from the very beginning that, if he was ever to go through this brutal process of running for president, he was going to be honest with the American people about the problems we faced and, in some cases, the sacrifices necessary to solve them.

None of us knew if that was even possible. Could you have an honest discussion with the American people about the absolute necessity of changing entitlement programs (Social Security, Medicare, and others) and the fact we had an unsustainable debt? Could you have an honest debate on revenue increases and spending cuts? Could we seriously review foreign entanglements and the need for even the Defense Department to cut back on spending? Could we convincingly articulate the wisdom of putting divisive social issues lower on the priority list until we got the more serious economic issues solved?

To help chart this difficult task we all, including Mitch, believed we needed solid, up-to-date data. We needed ideas and suggestions from various experts in their respective fields. We needed an organized effort if we were to provide Mitch with a range of policy positions he could then absorb; change, review; and, ultimately, get up to speed on in terms of most major domestic and international issues.

Al Hubbard volunteered (if he hadn't, we would have "appointed" him) to lead this effort. Al was an experienced policy analyst himself, having served in two administrations, the most recent being the George W. Bush White House as the president's chief economic advisor. In that role, he was involved in most major policy decisions of the second term. Most importantly, Al had a current cadre of experts he knew well in nearly every policy area, in addition to being whip smart himself.

The Romney campaign put out a flyer that listed ten issues Americans must address. They included:

- Defeating the jihadists
- Competing with China
- Stopping runaway spending
- Getting immigration right
- Achieving energy independence
- Affirming America's culture and values
- Simplifying the tax system
- Investing in technology
- Extending health insurance to all Americans
- Raising the bar on education

No one could disagree with any item on this list, but very few new proposals or original thinking accompanied it. It was the normal Republican rhetoric. We were determined to raise the bar on the conversation, a determination that was not without risk. We believed the American people had to be told the truth about critical issues. They then had to be willing to help fight for the real solutions. Running not just to win, but to govern—that was the mantra.

* * *

The initial issue discussion with Mitch and the group had two principal objectives:

1. Obtain Mitch's current thinking on each survival issue with participants providing feedback and input
2. Determine any additional individuals to contact for help in formulating opinions and positions

We grouped the issues into three categories, just for the sake of discussion:

Survival Agenda Issue #1—Economic Growth: The Unsustainable Debt

- Deficit Reduction
- Social Security, Medicare, Medicaid
- Other spending challenges—education, defense, etc.
- How to handle the question of tax increases relevant to debt reduction
- Elements of economic growth plan; emphasis on jobs and standard of living

Survival Agenda Issue #2—Radical Islamic Terrorism; Foreign Policy in General

- Homeland Security—how to keep America safe
- China—how to compete economically
- Afghanistan/Pakistan/Iraq
- Iran/North Korea
- Russia
- Need a "point of view" on foreign policy—what is our worldview?

Survival Agenda Issue #3—Dependence on Foreign Oil; Energy Policy

- What is our objective relevant to energy policy?
- Components of a comprehensive plan
- Energy taxes—how to handle

Other Key Issues

- Immigration
- Health care reform

- Education reform
- Impact on U.S of global financial markets
- Financial industry reform—now what?

Social Truce
- How to articulate?
- Emphasis on Mitch's personal record
- Judicial appointments
- Presidential decisions that impact social issues
- Outreach

General Items/Questions for Discussion
- How do you focus on survival issues, but don't get labeled with "only cares about the numbers, not people" tag?
- What is the impact and potential leverage of major Indiana reform initiatives in 2012?
- How can we play to Mitch's strength on fiscal matters with a differentiated point of view?
- What is the answer to Mitch's role in Bush deficits and war funding?

* * *

For several months prior to our August meeting, Al Hubbard had put together a group of experts eager to help Mitch in this process. Al sent out a very complete packet of information to the group prior to our meeting with various papers and commentary by these experts on a range of issues. They included:

- A summary of Congressman Paul Ryan's plan for economic growth
- Medicare analysis by Jim Capretta, former health policy person under Mitch at OMB
- Social Security by Chuck Blahous, former social security guru in the Bush White House
- General thoughts on economic growth by Eddie Lazear, former Council of Economic Advisors chairman and professor at Stanford

- Tax reform ideas by Harvey Rosen, former CEA chairman and professor at Princeton
- Impoundment proposal by Jeff Rosen, former general counsel at OMB
- Regulatory moratorium ideas by Jim Connaughton, former chairman of the White House Council on Environmental Quality
- *The Bush budget vs. the Obama budget* by Keith Hennessey, former national economic advisor to President George W. Bush
- *Spending is the Problem* by John Taylor, former Treasury official in the Bush Administration and now professor at Stanford
- Energy policy by Eddie Lazear and analysis of alternative energy by Marcus Peacock, former deputy EPA administrator
- Immigration reform by Joel Kaplan, former deputy chief of staff to President George W. Bush and the lead negotiator with Congress on immigration in 2007
- Health care, included in Congressman Ryan's economic growth paper
- Financial regulation by Marc Sumerlin, former deputy director of the National Economic Council, and Larry Lindsay, former national economic advisor and member of the Federal Reserve

Al had done a terrific job gathering together real experts, and we continued to develop data that provided us with the tools to develop some thoughtful differentiation on these various issues. In addition to these specific papers for our August meeting, Al also lined up additional people with whom we communicated on a regular basis for assistance in the various issue formulations. They included:

Current Budget Deficit
- **Steve McMillan**—former deputy OMB Director
- **Austin Smythe**—formerly at OMB, now chief policy person to Congressman Paul Ryan
- **Tim Muris**—former chairman of the Federal Trade Commission
- **Glenn Hubbard**—former CEA chair and currently a professor at Columbia University

Medicare
- **Bob Carroll**—former Treasury official, now head of Tax Foundation

Energy
- **Bob McNally**—energy expert in the Bush White House and now energy trader for Paul Tudor Jones

Tax Restructuring
- **J.D. Foster**—former OMB official with Mitch, now at Heritage Foundation

As in every presidential election, economic issues were front and center and most important to the American people. The appeal of Mitch Daniels related directly to this priority. He was known as a fiscal discipline champion, both in Washington and as governor of Indiana. He had proven you could take a state with a billion-dollar debt and turn it around, without increasing taxes.

The basic tenets of an economic growth initiative that all of the above "advisors" agreed upon, the long term solutions, included:

- We have to control spending.
- We have to limit the deficit.
- To control the deficit, we have to fix social security and Medicare.
- Higher taxes mean slower economic growth.
- We must reform our tax system so as not to punish savings and investment.
- We need to open up foreign markets with more free trade agreements.
- Human capital is critical to a successful economy—education reform.
- We need to fully fund basic research and development.

In the short term, the consensus was we were much better off giving stimulus dollars to the people and letting them decide how to spend the money rather than the wasteful Obama programs. Furthermore, we needed to provide certainty to business on taxes and regulation.

Mitch continued to discuss his ideas for economic growth through television appearances, speeches, and op-eds in carefully selected publications. His common sense "adult conversations" and his experience as a governor who had actually done something about economic growth contributed to the positive response he continued to receive.

On September 8, 2010, Mitch penned an op-ed for the *Wall Street Journal* entitled, "Time for Emergency Economic Reform." He began by saying:

> Ronald Reagan enjoyed telling of the elderly Blitz victim rescued from her demolished London flat in World War II. A fireman found a bottle of brandy under the ruins of her staircase and offered her a nip for her pain. "Leave it right there," the matron ordered, "That's for emergencies."
>
> A look around the American economy suggests that it's time to break out the brandy. By any measure, growth is anemic—alarmingly so for this time in what is supposed to be a recovery period. The administrations' wild foray into trickle-down government spending has clearly failed. Funneling borrowed billions to government workers hasn't stimulated anything where it counts, in the private sector.

Mitch then went on to suggest half a dozen specific ideas for an emergency growth program that he urged Congress and the administration to consider. He concluded by saying:

> With or without Democratic help, Republicans should step forward with these—or superior—ideas. A stagnant, impoverished America will not be a greener or safer or fairer place. Grown-ups make trade-offs. Pass the brandy and then let's get busy.

* * *

As we looked at major policy areas, two categories—economic issues and foreign affairs—demanded additional work and attention.

Economic

On the economic front, there were two primary "red flags" with which we needed to deal, and discussions on these continued throughout our entire journey.

One was the charge that, during Mitch's time as OMB director, budget deficits soared after President Clinton left them a surplus. Joe Scarborough made certain comments, basically reiterating the Obama attacks that still blamed all the economic woes on Bush.

This was an issue we debated internally over the summer. How do we respond to these attacks when tied directly to Mitch? Should he respond or should we get surrogates? Or do we just leave it alone?

The general consensus was we shouldn't leave these negative, and in many cases, incorrect statements out there, but surrogates would be better to carry the message than Mitch himself. However, he needed to be better prepared to answer the questions that would surely come during television and other media interviews.

Hubbard got Keith Hennessey, Joel Kaplan, Steve McMillan, and others to think about the proper answer, backed with facts. The challenge was to not get too complex with the answer.

Much of the rising debt was the direct result of the recession and fiscal policies designed to combat sluggish growth. The trillion-dollar surplus touted by Clinton and the media was a fantasy, concocted by budget projection models that assumed the revenues produced by the dot-com bubble economy would continue forever.

The fact was Mitch came to OMB as a known quantity—a budget cutter with fiscal discipline nicknamed "the blade." Both Democrats and Republicans on Capitol Hill vilified him because he opposed their spending habits. Then 9/11 happened, and the world changed. Most of the rest of the time he was there as OMB director was overshadowed by doing and spending whatever it took to secure the country. Then he departed.

My point in a message to our group was:

> The relevant issue is, what did Mitch do when he was in charge of a government himself, in other words, Indiana? Then, we tell the story. The record of Mitch Daniels in

terms of fiscal discipline and getting government under control versus what is going on in Washington today, there is no comparison. That should be our narrative. It also has the added benefit of being true.

Additionally, the charge that OMB under Mitch projected the cost of the Iraq War to be much less than what actually happened was also misleading. OMB was asked to project costs for three to six months, which it did accurately. But war is inherently unpredictable, and conditions on the ground after the actual fighting was won were far more challenging and proved to be much longer lived than anticipated.

Charlie Black reminded us all that we must not be put in a position of taking ownership of Bush's eight-year fiscal record. We did need to set the record straight on Mitch's time at OMB, but other good surrogates could deliver that message.

The other ongoing economic issue we continued to debate internally with Mitch was the overall subject of tax increases. Here the old issue of "nuance" was again in play.

An article on December 2, 2010, in the *Economist*, entitled "Vote for Agony: Cutting Public Spending and Raising Taxes May Not Be As Politically Suicidal As It Seems," quoted a Harvard study that had mixed messages but reinforced the concern of many in our group. It examined the impact of cutting spending versus raising taxes on elections. As Bob Perkins pointed out, the key takeaway was, "In only 20% of elections in the countries that slashed spending did the government lose power, compared with a 56% rate of being booted out of office for governments which chose to raise taxes. Voters evidently dislike tax increases much more than abhor spending cuts."[31]

To which, Charlie Black responded, "Has always been true and always will!"

Mitch, in numerous interviews and speeches, continued to leave the door open for possible tax increases. In his mind, that was part of being truthful with the American people and having an "adult conversation."

We didn't disagree with the notion you needed to present hard truths,

---

[31] "Vote for Agony: Cutting Public Spending and Raising Taxes May Not Be As Politically Suicidal As It Seems," *Economist*, December 2, 2010.

but Al Hubbard and his bevy of experts were not at all convinced you couldn't fix our problems without a tax increase. Certainly, you wanted to carefully explain (which was Mitch's position) that spending cuts, reform of systems, and more efficient government had to come first. However, in all probability we believed you could succeed without additional taxes that clearly were a barrier to economic growth. Al asked his experts to develop a data based analysis on why we could succeed without additional tax burdens, and that was all in the works as we proceeded.

The other major tax increase issue had to do with energy taxes. Mitch didn't come from an energy producing state and, therefore, hadn't experienced all the intricacies of energy production and its impact on the economy. One of the first groups invited to the residence included people to discuss this issue. This particular issue had the potential to be a problem with an important element of our traditional constituency. I was determined to get people in front of Mitch to make certain he thoroughly understood the ramifications of additional energy taxes at any level.

* * *

Foreign Affairs

Although Mitch had traveled extensively, worked in the office of Senator Richard Lugar (foreign affairs expert), served in the White House, headed the Hudson Institute, and held leadership positions in a global corporation, he was not known for his foreign policy expertise as compared to his fiscal discipline reputation on domestic issues.

From the beginning, we suggested he get fully briefed on the global situation since this would obviously be an area on which he would be expected to have opinions and knowledge. He'd need to answer the question Charlie Rose had put to other candidates in the past, "What is your worldview?"

On June 8, 2010, an article in the *Washington Examiner* by Ben Smith entitled, "Daniels Avoids Foreign Policy," went on to say it "wasn't clear whether or not he has thought these issues through, or whether he views foreign policy as anything more than a cost-control issue."[32]

---

[32]   Ben Smith, "Daniels Avoids Foreign Policy," *Washington Examiner,* June 8, 2010.

At one of the early residence dinners, attended by old friend Tom Korologos, Washington veteran and, most recently, ambassador to Belgium, he followed up with an e-mail to Mitch that read in part:

> Great dinner and great seeing you again. Very impressive analysis of the domestic scene, which you have at your fingertips. However, there is a better way to answer the foreign affairs question. You said you weren't into foreign affairs much and you really hadn't focused on it, etc. This is obviously something that will come up more and more in the presidential process. Here's some advice on how you might respond:
>
> "I worked for Senator Dick Lugar as his chief of staff for many years. He has been a member of the Senate Foreign Relations Committee for decades, many of those as Chairman. I also was Director of OMB in the White House where foreign affairs experts from Presidents to Secretaries of State and Defense surrounded me. In the private sector, of course, we dealt with foreign countries virtually every day. Also as Governor I have been on a myriad of international trade missions promoting Indiana exports and working with multi nationals to come and do business in Indiana with some great success. A great deal of expertise in that area has rubbed off on me. My nutshell views are …"

From there, Tom outlined potential comments on economic growth as a security issue; free trade; support for a strong defense; turning away from the Obama administration's constant rhetorical attempts with rogue nations; and support for our allies, including Israel, in the fight against global terrorism.

He then suggested Mitch see Henry Kissinger,[33] Dick Allen (Reagan's National Security Council director), Richard Haass (Council on Foreign Relations), former Secretary of State Condi Rice, and others. He offered to set up meetings.

---

[33] He later would, in New York.

Mitch told Tom his remarks and suggestions were "spot-on" and he'd try to incorporate them in future remarks. He also noted he had a session scheduled soon with former Bush NSC director Stephen Hadley and indicated the other names he mentioned were people he admired greatly. He would certainly take him up on his offer to facilitate.

Other people we suggested Mitch talk with included:

- **Stephen Friedman**, former Goldman Sachs chairman and first national economic advisor to George W. Bush and the most recent Bush chairman of the Foreign Intelligence Advisory Board
- **Brian Gunderson**, former chief of staff to Secretary of State Condi Rice
- **John Bolton**, former United Nations ambassador and close friend

All of these people were well versed on the global stage and, in some cases, with different points of view on foreign policy.

* * *

Another issue that remained a bit of a puzzle and deserved special attention as time went on was that of immigration. The topic was heating up and becoming a decisive issue even among Republicans. It was also important due to the increasing political realities of the Hispanic vote, which was increasing in numbers and increasingly Democratic. Several had the opinion that comprehensive immigration reform with a path to citizenship was not possible until you clearly defined how you could secure the border first and foremost.

* * *

Of course, the final issue that would grow to become a major issue in the campaign was health care reform, both in the primary as a criticism of Romney's effort in Massachusetts and in general with Obamacare as the primary target. We never got to the point of debating either, but Indiana, through Mitch's leadership, had health care reform that could have been presented as a workable alternative to Obamacare.

Grace-Marie Turner, a health care expert and conservative columnist, remarked to a friend that it was impossible for Romney to win on this issue due to his own plan in Massachusetts that was a state version of Obamacare. She later wrote a number of articles praising Mitch and his approach to health care reform.

* * *

As time went on, policy preparation and discussions continued. We had general agreement on most things, and Mitch was genuinely interested in getting more information and briefings from the experts on a myriad of issues. The residence dinners proved to be very useful in this regard, and individual meetings in Washington and New York continued to be scheduled.

Mitch was well grounded in his own beliefs. He was smart beyond belief on nearly every issue. And he had great political instincts on most things. The challenge with Mitch continued to be a balance between strongly held beliefs and a bit of nuance from time to time, all related to "doing nothing to deny the options" in terms of a presidential run.

Mitch would say more than once, "I'm not about the politics." But the fact is, if you thought you could do the job as president (and he said he did) and if you wanted in your heart of hearts to *be* president because of what it would enable you to contribute (and he said he did), then you had to be "about the politics." After all, it was the top political job in the world.

People

The remarkable thing about a presidential race is the diversity and, at times, randomness of the people who come out of the woodwork wanting to help or simply to offer an opinion. That is particularly true, perhaps, when you have a reluctant candidate at first and people are genuinely interested in encouraging that individual to run. In the case of Mitch Daniels, the range of people who wanted to engage with him was extraordinary. The reasons for this were many.

Mitch had had a varied and multi-dimensional career—he'd been a lawyer, chief of staff to a well-known US senator, a White House staffer to President Ronald Reagan, president and CEO of a think tank, a senior executive with a Fortune 100 company, and cabinet member to another president and had twice been elected governor of Indiana. He was well known in Washington political circles, with mainstream media, and in corporate America. He literally had a personal network of friends and colleagues across the country.

Additionally, people were hungry for new leadership and for a winning candidate for president who could take on the incumbent, with whom they had little regard. The idea of someone "new" with a record of achievement focused on the biggest problem facing our country—fiscal discipline, or lack thereof—was very appealing.

Once word got out that Mitch was "willing to listen," even though he constantly denied interest in running, people by the hundreds, significant people, wanted to be involved.

The initial group that gathered in Scottsdale remained the same throughout the duration of the process. At times, we considered adding people, and we did add hundreds of people in various ways. However, the original group stayed the same from beginning to end. At one point, someone commented that perhaps Mitch needed more experienced top-level advice. If we had continued the pursuit, I would have been the first to agree. But Mitch was never one for many consultants, particularly anyone he didn't know.

Outreach was necessary as much as anything to neutralize people (specifically major contributors and fundraisers) to allow time for Mitch to make a decision. It was also important to reach out to new people interested in someone fresh and different. The necessity of trying to do better with young people, Hispanics, and women also was a factor in reaching out.

The people who contacted us ran the gamut from total unknowns to the rich and famous. We tried to keep up with each and every contact. Mitch was very good about personally responding to nearly all of these people in one way or another. The residence dinners were a great vehicle, and his willingness to be heavily scheduled when he was able to get out of Indiana was very productive.

A diverse, interesting, and, at times, unique group of people was gathering around the cause.

A female producer for a leading radio show in Los Angeles wrote in an e-mail, "I must tell you a little secret. I'm really a Democrat, but I have to say I love Governor Daniels. I think he is a rock star who should run for president. And now that you told me he rode in on his motorcycle—that was just icing on the cake. What a cool dude!"

A group of young professionals, all from well-known families who had participated for years at the pinnacle of American business and politics, had formed a group in New York determined to find the best candidate to run in 2012. It was spearheaded by Tim Reynolds, son of Mercer Reynolds (Bush national finance chairman and ambassador to Switzerland), who was the director of corporate affairs at Highstar Capital. He invited Mitch to meet with his group and became an important advocate.

Former International Paper CEO and chairman of the Business Roundtable, John Dillon, through the efforts of friend Dennis Thomas, came to Indianapolis for a personal meeting with Mitch and to attend a residence dinner. He sent Mitch a message the following day that said,

"Mitch, I understand some of the considerations associated with a decision about moving forward, but as you mentioned in our discussion, 'someone has to do it' and frankly I do not see the combination of management skills and leadership in any of the current Republican candidates. You could possibly successfully take on the mammoth job of righting the United States of America. I would be pleased to participate in any way that would be helpful in your deliberations."

Mercer Reynolds, in addition to his former position with Bush-Cheney, was probably keeper of the best rolodex in the country in terms of potential fundraisers, state by state. He offered his help and his rolodex. We literally had a list, state by state, of the best talent available. With the help of Mercer and others, we began contacting all of them, and many came to the residence dinners.

From time to time, we'd hear from Jeb Bush, who Mitch kept trying to agree to run himself, and he would pass on comments of support from some key individuals. We heard the same from Karl Rove, a number of suggestions of people to call that had expressed interest in Mitch.

And, of course, we heard from CEOs from across the country—hundreds of major business leaders who urged Mitch to run on behalf of the country.

The Youth and Hispanic Vote:
—— Could We Get Them Back?

P art of our discussion at our first meeting in Arizona was the kind of coalition that could be put together for any Republican candidate against Barack Obama. Specifically, who could Mitch appeal to that would truly be differentiating?

The Obama coalition in 2008 made great strides among women, Hispanics, and young people, among others. Most people thought we had a great opportunity with Hispanics and young people in particular.

Hispanics posed a problem for any Republican due to the immigration debate, but it was always felt among the party leadership the Hispanic population should be ours because this group shared our values much more than they did the Democrats'. Jeb Bush and former George W. Bush Commerce Secretary Carlos Gutierrez teamed up to form the Hispanic Leadership Network that attempted to restore the Republican Party's standing with this fastest growing segment of the electorate. It was the first major outreach effort by the Republicans who believed it must change its tone toward Hispanics to have any chance of winning back the White House in 2012.

We believed Mitch had some particular areas of strength to which the Hispanic population would respond positively. He had achieved some major education reforms in Indiana and was on record as saying he had one more big push if he could win back the state house in 2010. He had always been a champion of small business, and his record in terms of economic growth was a model for the nation. These were issues important to the

Hispanic community. Additionally, he actually spoke some conversational Spanish and had a small group of Hispanic leaders with whom he met regularly in Indiana.

* * *

The greatest potential of support for Mitch, however, was the youth vote. The Pew Research Center had published some data that was very hopeful. The Democratic advantage over the Republicans in party affiliation among young voters, including those who "lean" to a party, reached a whopping 62 percent to 30 percent margin in 2008. But by the end of 2009, this thirty-two-point margin had shrunk to just fourteen points.

Mitch's major focus in terms of survival issues was the debt being left to the next generation. We believed, if correctly communicated, this could be a serious effort to attract young people to the campaign. In a well-publicized and highly lauded commencement address to Butler University graduates, Mitch called his own generation "a selfish one" that was leaving a legacy of debt that was unsustainable.

Mitch had said more than once, "For the next generation, our message should be, 'we're spending money on ourselves and passing the bills on to you. We don't think that is right. We're the party and the candidate that is about the future, therefore we care about you.'"

In a swipe at Obama's change slogan, Mitch would say, "We want change that believes in you. Not change that believes in government as the answer to everything, and that paying for it can be absorbed by the next generation."

His overall pitch continued to include a plug for Republicans to direct themselves "almost entirely to the young people of this country." In Indiana he said, "The GOP is the party of purpose, arrayed against Democrats who are reactionary, negative, and everything we must not be, as we address national events."

So, perhaps it shouldn't have been, but it was a complete shock when we woke up one morning in October 2010 to find a group of students at Yale University, completely on their own, announcing a nationwide "netroots" movement to draft Mitch Daniels for president.

The organizer, a senior named Max Eden[34], said on the newly formed website, www.studentsfordaniels.com, on October 1, 2010, "We believe Mitch Daniels is the best man to ensure our future economic security, that a draft committee is most definitely in order, and if that committee comes from students it will create a powerful narrative."

Eric Holcomb immediately reached out to Max and his group to thank them, keep them informed, and encourage them within the boundaries of our "listening to people" regarding the presidential race.

The interesting thing about this group we later discovered was they were all former Obama supporters. Eden described himself as an "enthusiastic voter for Obama in 2008," but in his words, "We are uniting behind Mitch Daniels because his candidacy will give us a new hope for solving two of the greatest issues my generation faces, the degradation of national political discourse and the drastic rise in the federal debt."

Max Eden went on to say on the website and subsequent direct mail pieces:

> Governor Daniels has gone out on a political limb by suggesting that we must declare a "social truce" in order to fix the economy and tackle the debt. We are all welcome to our social opinions, but when the Chairman of the Joint Chiefs says that the national debt is the top threat to our national security, it is time to declare a truce in the culture war and do what needs to be done to cut the budget down to size and get our economy producing jobs. Between his remarkable fiscal credibility and his serious tone, Mitch Daniels is what my generation has been waiting to see out of a Republican presidential nominee.

Awesome was all we could say. Max's words reinforced our belief that the fiscal crises and the unsustainable debt issue, Mitch's issue, could be a defining issue in getting back the youth vote of the nation.

As the year progressed, the Yale contingent spread to more than thirty campuses, including Cornell, Purdue, Harvard, Hanover, Emory, and

---

[34]   Like many of the interesting young people who voiced their approval, Max was not someone we knew at the time.

Georgetown. They produced a fabulous YouTube commercial, followed by a television spot for use during the Super Bowl they hoped to fund. Additionally, they planned to attend the CPAC conference in February 2011 with a massive "Students for Daniels" presence.

On December 31, 2010, Mitch sent a message to Max with a New Year's greeting that said the following:

> I figured it was about time I checked in personally to tell you and those who have associated with you how much I appreciate the interest and confidence you have shown in me. Not at all clear that life will permit me to try the great adventure that many are urging, but I promise you that if we do, we won't bore anyone. We will speak to and about young people constantly, and it will be a more direct conversation than the American people have had from their presidential candidates in a long time. It might be the most interesting campaign in memory for the two or three months before it blows up!
>
> Anyway, Happy New Year and please pass that on to your colleagues.

Max responded by thanking Mitch for taking time to write and said, "Our generation is hungry for just the kind of direct, candid, and forthright presidential campaign that you speak of. I look forward to seeing you and hearing you speak at C-PAC in February."

When Mitch did speak at the CPAC conference on February 11, 2011, he had a private Q&A session with around fifty members of the Yale-led student initiative just prior to his speech. The *Yale Daily* was present and later reported on some of the questions and answers.

Mitch started the session by saying how uplifted he was at the whole endeavor started by them. "You are motivated by the right reasons," he told them, "and a very legitimate concern—the most important one of our time—the inequity and unfairness of the raw deal you are going to be handed if nothing changes. There is an excellent chance I do not run for any other office—it was never in my contemplation. But, I have decided to take seriously all the people who have urged me to consider a presidential campaign, and I promise you your little exercise here has been more motivating to me than even the big shots that have come around with the same idea."

He then answered questions for nearly thirty minutes, addressing issues from where he would cut the budget to why he thought he could do the job.

The final question by one student was, "Should you decide to run, what credentials that you have do you believe will make you the most qualified in the race?"

Mitch answered, "I get asked about what I did before becoming governor that was most important. They always think I'm going to say something in government. It wasn't. It was my business years. Those were the years I learned how to make ends meet, how to get large numbers of people to pull together successfully.

"In the current federal context, you look and there's nobody who has even run a lemonade stand. I'm serious. That's a serious defect, and I think it shows up in their policy. They gush on and on about diversity, but not when it comes to thought or private sector experience."

As the session was concluding, one person spoke up. "You're our only hope, probably all of us in this room agree, so will you please run for president?"

Chants of "Run Mitch, run!" filled the room. And Courtney Pannel, Class of 2011, presented Mitch with a T-shirt modeled after the Shepard Fairey-designed poster that featured Barack Obama and the word, *Hope*—this version featuring Daniels's face and the word, *Solvency*.

* * *

Later in March, following the Gridiron Dinner where he was the featured Republican speaker, Mitch appeared on *Meet the Press* in Washington. A "Students for Daniels" group from George Washington University met him outside the studio, and he spent some time with them answering their questions and thanking them for their encouragement.

The following week, a student who'd established "Wake Students for Daniels" at Wake Forest University received an e-mail indicating a new chapter at the University of Southern California had also been formed, using social media. The student made a strong case for the utilization of social media should a campaign get underway, emphasizing the point that a strong social media presence was going to be a prerequisite for any candidate in 2012.

On April 18, 2011, Lauren Noble, a student at Yale, wrote an article for StudentsforDaniels.com entitled "A Time for Choosing Mitch Daniels." She said, "Gov. Daniels is a compelling candidate not simply because he is a truth-teller willing to state hard facts (as he did in his speech at C-PAC), but also because he has a long record grounded in principle and characterized by competence. The conservative movement needs a leader who will do more than reject; it requires a leader who can rebuild. Simply put, he is a candidate who could restore the Republican Party's ability to do arithmetic and make it stand for the extraordinary aspirations of ordinary people once again."[35]

---

[35] Lauren Noble, "A Time for Choosing Mitch Daniels," *StudentsforDaniels.com*, April 18, 2011.

Crises within the Campaign

In every national campaign, crises develop that were either unexpected or whose intensity was underestimated. In hindsight, many of them could have been avoided or at least mitigated. But in the heat of the moment, they often take on a life of their own. How you deal with these crises reveals a great deal about the candidate, the team, and the manner in which the candidate would govern if elected.

In the Mitch Daniels case, five stood out as one reflects on the nearly two-year effort. Most of them, other than the one relating to family opposition that was known from the beginning, grew out of statements by Mitch that were either misinterpreted or unfairly characterized. Of course, simple mistakes on our part also played a role.

Crisis Number One: "I Don't Really Want to Run"

Perhaps the one crisis that kept coming back over time, even after we thought we had resolved it, was how Mitch answered the question on whether or not he was seriously considering a run for the presidency.

Some of this, particularly in the beginning, was due to his own personal ambivalence. He truly never did see this in his future, and he had to be convinced other people were serious about wanting him to do it. Mark Lubbers said from the very beginning, "He wants to be drafted." Our response was, "Great, let's get people to draft him." But at some point he had to acknowledge that he, himself, was truly and sincerely interested.

The other ongoing issue was the family. In some cases, we believed some of Mitch's off-the-cuff remarks, which were always picked up by the press, were directed at them. His reluctance was to ensure the family that "All is okay; I haven't lost my senses. I'm not really serious; I'm just responding to people who want to float my name."

We had multiple conversations with Mitch on this subject, both as a group and individually. Our stance from the very beginning was to adopt Eddie Mahe's approach: "Do nothing to deny the option." Mitch intellectually bought into that, but it was always difficult for him to actually abide by it.

As previously indicated, the first major element of this crisis developed during his February 2010 trip to Washington to attend the National Governors' Conference, where he had multiple interviews with the media. This was a normal activity notwithstanding the presidential question. Those interviews then prompted the local press to talk with him, resulting in a headline in the *Evansville Courier-Press* on March 7, 2010, that said, "Gov. Daniels Says He Won't Run for President," along with a Mizell Stewart editorial the same day in that paper, entitled, "It's a Shame Daniels Won't Run."[36]

All of us immediately came forward with recommendations on how better to answer the question. One example put forth by Rick Powell and Tom Bell was, "I want my position to be clear—I currently have a job, a very important one I take seriously, and I owe it to the people of Indiana to keep my focus on the challenges and opportunities we have in this state. I am concerned about our country and as we get closer to a national election, we'll see what develops. I'm hopeful a strong Republican candidate will emerge; I'm willing to listen to what people have to say."

We all agreed there is some charm to people who aren't overly ambitious for the job. However, we were concerned that ambivalence can feel contrived if overplayed. The phrases "I don't want it," "I've never wanted it," "I don't plan to do it," and "I don't expect to do it," that were said in these interviews, were a serious problem. We were out trying to fill residence dinners, an event that people paid their own way to attend. When these phrases were seen in print, people wondered why they were

---

[36] Mizell Stewart, "It's a Shame Daniels Won't Run," *Evansville Courier-Press*, March 7, 2010.

coming. This was definitely not in keeping with the strategy of doing nothing to deny the option.

On March 7, 2010, after seeing the Evansville article, I sent Eric and Mark an e-mail. "Do we have a problem here, or is it just in-state reporting?" I asked. "We have a lot going on that should stop if that headline has any validity. Should I call him?"

The consensus response was that neither was certain, but both speculated Mitch was just trying to make peace at home. Both suggested we do nothing and see if it happened again.

The only positive thing to come out of this first episode was the language Mizell used in his piece. Along with the title ("It's a Shame Daniels Won't Run"), Mizell said his first meeting with Governor Daniels (Mizell was new to Evansville) was different than any he'd experienced in twenty plus years of covering and following state and national politics in places as diverse as Ohio and Florida.

"When I walked into the conference room I was simply stunned," he wrote. "No state trooper keeping watch, no deputy press secretary to take notes, no staffer tapping away at a Blackberry. The Governor met with us for an hour sans notes, took every question, and was very comfortable with the give-and-take with the assembled reporters and editors."

He added that while it might seem simplistic, that meeting had told him everything he needed to know about Mitch Daniels. He wrote:

> He may not always be right, but he'll call it the way he sees it. He's confident enough to stand on his own two feet. He may not inspire a great deal of passion but he doesn't trade in extremes just to get attention.
>
> His track record demonstrates that he respects authority when he's a worker bee and wields it when he's an executive, like any one of us might in that position. Someone will naturally hold that against him at a national level, but it's a quality working-class Hoosiers respect.
>
> He's got more executive experience than anyone— and I do mean anyone on the scene—but it doesn't matter if the price you have to pay is parading yourself like a peacock for two years in Iowa and New Hampshire.

All told, that's why Mitch Daniels is not going to run for President. And that's too bad.[37]

On March 26, 2010, *Politico* ran an article by Anne Schroeder Mullins, "Will They or Won't They?" It was a compilation of all the statements potential Republican candidates were making in what *Politico* said was, "perfecting their non-response responses to queries about the race."

By a good margin, those attributed to Mitch were the most negative:

"I really don't plan to. I really don't much want to." (To the *New York Times*)

"I've been as clear as I know how. I said in the same conversation, I don't plan to do it. I don't expect to do it, don't really want to do it. I'm not doing any of the things that people who want to run for that office do." (To the *Evansville Courier Press*)

"No, my mind is on the problems of our state. We have got our hands full and that's what we're working on." (*Fox News*)

"This is the only public office I've sought, or ever will." (*Star Press*)

"No. There's only one way you can spell it." (*Herald Bulletin*)

"If these people are still around, and still not fully satisfied with the field, and if I don't see anybody who's raising what I think of as the survival issues for the country, I guess I'd listen if it's not too late, which it might well be. I've told people if it's too late, so be it." (To *Foxnews.com*)[38]

As we continued to wrestle with just the right combination of words, participants at the residence dinners also contributed ideas and feedback. One said, "We understand why he is cautious right now, but do you have to be so definitive in saying I don't want to do it and can't see myself doing it? This clearly sends a mixed message that confuses people."

Ibid.

Anne Schroeder Mullins, "Will They or Won't They," *Politico*, March 26, 2010.

Another attendee, following a dinner where that was a concern, said, "Did I just waste my time here?"

Those comments and others are what caused us to develop a better close and call to action.

On March 23, Mitch posted on his Facebook page (something he rarely did), "To all those writing to urge a venture in national politics, tks, but our commitment is totally to our duties here in IN. I confess to being dejected about Sunday's further impoverishment of the next generation[39], and massive invasion of personal freedom but think my best contribution is to keep working to protect Hoosiers from even higher taxes than those Washington just imposed."

In a subsequent phone call with Bob Perkins on another subject, when this posting was raised and read to him, Mitch indicated it sounded a bit more negative than he meant it to be. It was Bob's view that he didn't mean to signal anything, just a Freudian slip.

That prompted me to set up a conference call of the group, minus Mitch, for Saturday, March 27. In a pre-call memo to the group, I said:

> In the past few weeks, there have been a dozen meetings in Los Angeles and New York, involving over a hundred people (individuals with money, brains, and influence), multiple phone calls, numerous interviews and countless phone calls—all relating to Mitch Daniels and the potential for his involvement in 2012.
>
> By and large, the response has been overwhelmingly positive. We've covered the positives in previous reports, so now come a few of the negatives—actually only one real negative consistently voiced—"why does he keep saying he doesn't want to do this, he can't see himself ever doing it, he wants to find someone else to do it, etc. etc.?"
>
> And then last night, the Facebook page!
>
> In the next sixty days, we have another one hundred people who are either going to come through Indianapolis for residence dinners, see him in Washington, or otherwise

---

[39] Mitch was referring to the signing by President Obama of the health care reform bill into law.

invest their time and effort to continue to promote this idea of 2012. When they see things like the Facebook page, or read headlines in the paper that say, "Daniels says he's not running for President," or hear him end an event by saying, "I really, really don't want to do this"—then we are going to begin to have a serious credibility problem. Most importantly we are completely abandoning the principle of: "Do Nothing to Deny the Option," which is what I thought we were operating under.

That is what we need to discuss Saturday morning in our brief phone call, just among us. Are we overreacting, or is this as big an issue as I think it is?

He has stayed on message brilliantly in every other aspect (*his* message!)—the survival agenda, the social truce, focus on Indiana and 2010 to get the legislature back for one more major reform initiative, and an interest in putting together the best minds in the country to help him develop some solutions to the critical problems facing our country. All of this is received with great enthusiasm, but we are at risk of losing it. This is due not only to his continuing negative comments on running, but also because we have no effective "close" in answering the question he always gets from these groups: "Well, how can I help?"

Therefore, as we think about this prior to Saturday's call, here is one "close" concept drawn from comments most of you have expressed in the past forty-eight hours.

And then I outlined our language and ideas in terms of a close and an answer to the question of running. The core of the answer to running was expressed like this:

I have never seriously considered running for president, never planned to do so, never thought it was even a possibility. But, just like you, I am concerned about our country and the unsustainable debt that is being run up by the current administration without any concern for the next generation and the terrible burden it is placing on their shoulders. So, I am interested in having an adult conversation with our fellow citizens, helping to come up with some real solutions to real problems, and somehow contributing to the effort to turn our country around. What form that contribution might take, I have no idea, but I'm willing to listen to what others have to say and will keep an open mind as we go through this year.

The outcome of that call was a general agreement that we had to get Mitch to understand the problems being created in terms of his statements vis-a-vis our "do nothing to deny the option" strategy. I was elected to call him and give him the message.

On March 30, at 1:30 p.m., I made the call.

I told him we'd done extensive follow-up with people in New York, Los Angeles, Washington, and other places with people who were following all his interviews and comments with great interest. I indicated his Economic Club speech in Indiana had been universally lauded and that we had already discussed the very positive feedback from the New York and LA meetings.

Almost as relevant, I told him, were the reactions we were getting from people regarding Romney. No one thinks he can do it—same old spiel, same old stump speech, refuses to admit Massachusetts health plan failures, and on and on.

But, I said, we have a problem. I told him of our group conference call early Saturday morning and that I'd been tasked with calling him to talk about this problem; I was speaking for the entire group.

So, I started:

If you really down deep in your soul don't want to do this, won't ever really seriously consider it, for all the legitimate reasons there are not to do it, then you need to tell us now.

Because we're to the point where we are now involving hundreds of people who are going to come to Indy and other venues not only because they are interested in you personally and care about what is happening to their country, but because we're all using our relationships to get them there.

When they read online or in the paper or hear others repeat things, even if they are repeated in error, that you "really, really don't want to do this," and "No means *no*," and "I've run for the only office I'm ever going to run for"—then they ask themselves, "Why am I coming to this event, or spending my money to have dinner with him, or otherwise engaging with this effort?"

Even if you don't say things like you did on Facebook, even then, if we don't have some kind of "close" or call to action when you end these dinners and various events for them to do something, we're missing an opportunity to at least keep in touch with all these people in some way.

We know you haven't made up your mind. We know in the end, you may choose not to do it, all of which is perfectly fine. But this "internal debate" needs to be just that, internal, not for public consumption. Because when it gets into the public domain, it directly impacts the goal of "doing nothing to deny the option."

If this thing happens, it will be because there is a genuine draft. Saying things like the Facebook page and other closing comments when people ask you about this idea is the surest way to choke off the draft.

You don't have to commit to anything. You just have to consistently say, "I'm keeping an open mind."

I then gave him our idea of the precise language he could use as we closed out a dinner or meeting or to answer a question from a reporter about 2012:

I have two things on my agenda. These are my current job and working for the people of Indiana, specifically working to get a Republican legislature in 2010 to enable us to do some major reform initiatives in 2011 and my concern for the future of our country and my belief some Republican needs to run on what I call the survival agenda. And, I'm interested in helping to find the solutions to our survival issues and, once we do, finding the right person to run on that agenda.

Some people have suggested that person be me. I'm not sure that is the right answer, but I am willing to listen to what people have to say as we proceed through this process. My main concern at the national level is getting the "what" right—and that is what I'll be contributing to in the next nine months, so no matter who ends up leading this effort, he or she will have real solutions to the real problems that are now confronting our country.

I then said, "And, stop right there!" If we were in a dinner or at one of our meetings, I told him to have Eric or the host say something about keeping in touch through e-mail and other forms of communication.

After all was said and done, he agreed with all of our points and liked the language. He wanted me to assure the group he had been "suitably chastened" and heard the message.

* * *

On April 3, 2010, Mitch was interviewed on C-SPAN, and Jonathan Martin of *Politico* reported, "Daniels offered two new twists to his usual pooh-poohing of the prospect of running for President." The article read:

> First, he suggested he'd make up his mind after this November, when control of the Indiana House will be decided. "I don't think I'll have a different answer, but ask me in a year," Daniels said.[40]
>
> Second, he hinted at one factor those close to him have said all along may ultimately be a factor in why he doesn't run: his wife isn't enthused about the idea.[41]

---

[40] It wasn't a great answer, but it was better.
[41] Jonathan Martin, *Politico*, April 3, 2010.

Later Mitch joked about his recent "cracked the door open a little bit" statement to the idea of running. He said that Cheri told a local reporter that, when he got home that night, the door might not be cracked![42]

After all this—the interviews, the group phone call, and my long conversation with Mitch that seemed to go very well—we thought we had pretty much put this behind us. We could go on to whatever the next crisis would become. But, alas, it was not to be.

* * *

The next element of this dilemma developed in terms of the necessity of actually giving people a timetable. This was particularly important in our effort to neutralize people for a time, specifically key fundraising types who were now getting more and more pressure from Romney and Pawlenty to sign up. The idea was to make this part of the "close" or call to action when we were in a residence dinner or meeting. Giving people a definitive timetable for making the decision would help us convince them that Mitch was seriously open-minded and was willing to listen. To do otherwise was becoming misleading to people, and that was a concern in the feedback we were continuing to receive following various dinners and meetings.

Adding to our angst was a preview that Mark Lubbers received of a *Chicago Tribune* article that ran on Sunday, May 16, 2010, by John Kass. The article, which primarily focused Mitch's attitude about the new phenomenon, the Tea Party movement, was in many ways a great one. Kass said what separated Mitch from other Republicans was his attitude toward the populist Tea Party movement.

From Mitch's perspective, he simply believed that the Tea Party needed to be authentic and independent from either party. He felt as if the Tea Partiers had a constructive role to play in the process, and he appreciated what they were trying to do, particularly in their focus on the federal debt.

---

[42]   This was a reference to when he made that statement to the press during a Washington trip and it immediately was picked up by the Indiana press while Cheri was being interviewed live on a radio show. That was her comment on the air. Someone called me with that report, and I was talking to Mitch later that day. He had not heard the comment. When I told him, he laughed and said, "Well at least she hasn't lost her sense of humor yet!"

If he had stopped there, it would have been a home run, but he didn't. The interviewer, John Kass, asked the inevitable question about running.

Mitch said, "It's not happening. People who run for President have to do it nonstop for years. And that's another good reason not to."[43]

As I said in a confidential memo to our group the next day:

> A fabulous article greatly diminished by a completely unnecessary statement. This is the type of article I would have sent to every person we've seen in the past few months. Some of you may think we could send it anyway. I don't. Most every person who we've seen has gone away confused, mostly negative in thinking he's not going to do it in the end, but willing to give it some time and somewhat buying the "what" development spiel we're touting. If they see this, it just reinforces their negative thoughts.

Several key people around the country reacted immediately upon seeing this article. Eddie Mahe fired off an e-mail to Mitch that same day urging him to be careful about such statements and suggesting a better way to handle the situation in an interview. He said, "'It's not happening' just simply sounds too definitive. The only thing that was missing to send the signal that it's for sure a No Go would have been if you would have added—'PERIOD!'"

Once again, after talking with several in our group, I sent a message to Mitch with our concerns and actually attached a new draft statement for him to consider as we continued our dinners and meetings. It said:

> My position is simply this: I'm flattered and frankly humbled by all the calls and encouragement to think about 2012.
>
> I won't compromise my duties to the citizens of Indiana because we still have a great deal of work to do, and I am particularly focused on getting Republican

---

[43] John Kass, "The Un-Obama doesn't Run with the GOP Pack," *Chicago Tribune*, May 16, 2010.

control of the state House in November so we can advance another significant reform agenda.

But my concern for the future of the country is real, and I'm taking seriously the challenge ahead of us. I'm willing to listen to what people have to say and give serious consideration to people's encouragement.

And I'll make a final decision sometime in the spring of 2011.

If you are so inclined, you can help—by sending me your ideas on the various issues we face and how we might solve them with innovative and creative solutions.

And by "keeping your powder dry" until we can have time to make our decision.

Regardless of the ultimate decision, I believe what we are doing now to develop the "what" will be a valuable contribution to whomever is our standard-bearer, and I very much appreciate your willingness to lend a hand.

Charlie Black followed this up with his own e-mail to Mitch that said, "Just remember what one of my preachers told me years ago. You are obligated to tell the truth, but you are not obligated to say everything that is on your mind."

Amen.

* * *

The following week, the group had another conference call to discuss, once again, how we would get this point across to Mitch. We decided Tom Bell would go to Indianapolis this time to sit down with Mitch one-on-one and have this conversation—in other words, stage an "intervention." The specific topic was this—Are you seriously in this to consider a run, or should we all go do something else? The reason this was important right now was we had two very important dinner groups coming to Indy, full of major fundraising types, including a key person from New Hampshire. The next week was a Business Roundtable appearance and dinner at George Will's home.

On Sunday, May 23, I sent an e-mail to Tom in preparation for this important sit-down. It said in part:

> Not that you need this, but since it is on my mind, here are some thoughts on paper as per our conversation yesterday.
>
> Why it Matters: The purpose of the residence dinners was twofold—to help better educate Mitch on aspects relating to the various survival issues, with perhaps some innovative ideas and solutions, and to neutralize key fundraisers and political players across the country who are interested in 2012.
>
> I believe we are achieving the first goal—so far some very interesting, informative tutorials on complex issues and more to come. Regardless of who is the ultimate nominee, this will enable him to significantly contribute to the overall effort.
>
> We are at great risk on the second goal, both by what he says at the dinner or doesn't say and what he continues to say in interviews.
>
> People at this level want to know he is at least "listening" to what other people have to say about who the best candidate would be, and that there is a process/timeline that has an end game, i.e., "I'll make a decision by May 1, 2011," or whenever. If they depart these dinners (as more than one has so far) saying, "What a smart, capable, experienced leader—too bad he's not running," then we've failed. And the problem with that failure is it becomes viral; these people talk to one another, and before long many others who will never have an opportunity to come to Indianapolis will basically decide he's not running and commit to others.
>
> It just isn't that hard to prevent. No one is asking for a commitment right now (at least most aren't); all they want is some signal he will listen to what people have to say, go through a process, and let them know a decision is forthcoming by a certain date.

I then restated the "message" we had written regarding Mitch's answer to the question of running and when he would make a decision and concluded by saying:

> This allows people to leave the dinners or finish reading an article with the idea there is a process unfolding that has an end game, and will be a valuable contribution no matter what ultimately happens. It enables us to keep in touch with people by continuing to communicate with them by sending articles, and allows us to expand the residence dinners (and press interviews) into the fall to include even more people important to the cause. And it doesn't compromise him one bit in terms of "misleading" people. It is honest, straightforward and does nothing to deny the option. Hope this is helpful.

* * *

On Friday, May 28, Tom met with Mitch at the residence. They had a long talk, and Tom expressed our concerns and floated some additional language in addition to our message that was crafted to see if Mitch was comfortable with it and understood the importance of it.

The primary addition was the phrase "I haven't decided to run for president, but I haven't decided *not* to run either. What I have decided is I want to inject myself into this conversation because I am very concerned about the direction of our country." Tom indicated Mitch liked the approach and promised he would use it. Tom told him that we could handle the rest by telling our guests he is open-minded; we are building the team; we hope they will wait and help us in the interim, and we'll have a decision by April or May.

Tom's final comment to me was, "In my view, he is still in the boat."

* * *

On June 1, after a residence dinner, Eric sent all of us a message:

> Met briefly with the Governor after all our guests left. He wanted to make sure everyone knew he repeated (word for word, I believe) what Tom met with him about. Hubbard did a great job of setting the stage at the outset. My proudest moment of the night was when Mitch said: "You want me to keep my options open, you keep your options open too!" The meeting was the most encouraging we've had if you were a guest, and our key person from New Hampshire said he was "keeping his powder dry and wasn't going anywhere."

Al Hubbard, who served as host on June 1, also sent a message with his evaluation. He said:

> Great evening—even Mitch seemed to like it! The real shocker was when Mitch said he would decide by the end of the year![44] And when the group kept questioning his strategy, he explained that he believed he could be successful with a late start and money would not be a problem; he was confident the dollars would be there. He also responded to a question about "fire in the belly" with a commitment to work 24-7 if he decides to go. He was by far more forward leaning than ever. Never before has he tried to defend a late start other than to say it was necessary.

* * *

This was an issue, a "crisis," that never really completely went away. We got through the summer and all our planned activities without any further disruption. Mitch generally followed the script in our meetings and various press interviews (although we cut back on those significantly, on purpose).

---

[44] That timetable was later moved back, of course, which was fine.

As he became more aware and got more interested in the fact that this really was a possibility, he more readily accepted the language and truly, in fact, did nothing to deny the option. That is where we wanted him to be—no commitment but no words or actions that would deny the option.

It didn't always work. On August 25, 2010, a headline in the *Louisville Courier-Journal* read, "A Daniels Denial on 2012 Run." Said the paper, reporting on Daniels' comments during a meeting with its editorial board, "Daniels said he is not interested in the post, is not raising money for such a campaign and has not spent much time outside of Indiana. He said all are proof that he is not running."

The Louisville article did, of course, initiate other follow-up articles, one from Asher Smith of the *Huffington Post* that compared Mitch to the Fred Thompson candidacy of 2008. It simply said, "Mitch Daniels doesn't want to run for President, he simply wants you to ask him again."[45]

On September 19, we hosted a group at an Indianapolis Colts game. After spending the evening with Mitch and hearing him talk, the group came away thinking the probability of him running was much lower than they'd previously believed.

Lubbers sent an e-mail to me the following morning. "The air is starting to come out of the ball," he said simply. "It was fun while it lasted. My judgment is if we were to go forward he would have had an even money bet of getting the nomination."

All of this, of course, caused yet another phone call between Mitch and me, and we had it on Tuesday, September 21. I shared the conversation later in the day with the group:

> Just finished a conversation with Mitch and wanted to give you the high points. I don't want to put in an e-mail any detail on the family situation so happy to talk with you individually. The bottom line is that it hasn't changed (the family opinion on running) except perhaps even more adamant.
>
> He expressed the belief if we had actually planned all that had happened in the past nine months, we couldn't

---

[45] Asher Smith, "Meet Mitch Daniels, 2012's Answer to Fred Thompson," *Huffington Post*, August 27, 2010.

have planned it better in many ways (I did remark that, in fact, there was a bit of planning that went on, but I get his point!). The attention and interest built over time has been quite extraordinary in his view and I didn't disagree at all. It simply reinforces our view the country is scared and concerned and desperately looking for a leader to help change it.

He believes he is still following the advice, 'do nothing to deny the option.' I told him directly he often doesn't recognize the negativity that comes through his statements. Case in point, the game last night. He thought it was a great event, which it was, but my e-mails indicated people came away having a great time but believing he wasn't a candidate. That is the norm, not the exception, particularly in the past two weeks.

I believe he is truly conflicted. He doesn't see anyone else getting any traction, understands there is a real opportunity here, has great concern for the country— but simply isn't there in his own mind even if the family situation was different.

I told him we thought we should stand down until after the November election[46] in terms of public outreach—no residence dinners in October, no other major network exposure—a focus on Indiana, which is what he has said he wants to do. I said the only activity we need to continue to strongly ramp up is the social media effort because that will be valuable to him no matter what. And, he can certainly continue to talk to people individually as he will be doing in New York, on policy matters particularly in the foreign affairs area. He agreed with this approach. He has a very full schedule between now and Nov. 2 so this will enable him to focus on all those activities and hopefully have some time to think through what ultimately has to be a very personal decision.

---

[46] 2010

We agreed to get the group together in two weeks for a phone call to compare notes, and that phone call happened on October 1. We determined we would meet in Indianapolis in December, and a decision would have to be made at that time, not a public one necessarily but an internal one.

Several expressed the opinion that he didn't want to say no because he now saw it as a real possibility, but the family attitude was a major issue.

We discussed finances, reviewed a memo from Travis Thomas, and talked about having Laura Bush call Cheri. We discussed whether or not we should have people send him e-mails to encourage him to run. We decided that was a good idea but only after Election Day, November 2. Mitch had indicated publicly that, once we passed that date, he would begin to make his decision.

The time when a decision had to be made was fast approaching. We wanted Mitch to know what people thought, people he knew and respected. The question was, would it make any difference?

Crisis Number Two:
The Social Truce

One of the very first things Mitch said when we sat in my living room in January 2010 was that he wanted to "call a truce" on the primary social issues of the day—abortion, gay marriage, prayer in schools. In his words, "A truce is not surrender." A truce, to him, was just a recognition that the country was facing true survival issues, and we needed to make certain they were our priority before everything else. He wasn't trying to change anyone's mind on these issues or talk anyone into changing his or her positions. He just wanted to initially focus the people of America on the fact we were going bankrupt, with an unsustainable spending spree.

The group unanimously agreed on the approach. For some, who were more personally liberal on some of these issues, it was a no-brainer. They probably didn't even agree with Mitch on some of his positions. Regardless, the idea of not making the very divisive topics of abortion and gay marriage front and center issues had great appeal.

For others in the group who generally agreed with Mitch on his pro-life stance, in particular, this concept was also completely accepted. It was a matter of priorities as far as we were concerned. We felt most Americans would welcome a campaign that didn't get into the divisive, emotional issues so many on the political fringe wanted to discuss to the exclusion of what we considered more important issues in the current environment.

It was my particular view, as I expressed in that January meeting, that Mitch might be one of the only people who could get away with this idea. Many people thought that Rudy Giuliani and others over the years lost their nomination chances due to their stance on these social issues and their unwillingness to bend. I thought Mitch, because he was personally in sync with most Republicans on a majority of these issues, could be the one to pull this off. He didn't generally disagree with those who promoted most of these issues; he just wanted to put them on hold while we solved other problems he considered to be critical to our survival as a nation.

Was I wrong! While his stance on the social truce was embraced by many independents, Democrats, and even Republicans, it caused a firestorm with many on the religious right and numerous interest groups who rely on these issues for their livelihood. It also caused some consternation internally on how we handled it. We could have done a much better job, but again, it was a learning experience as we progressed.

The first inkling of a potential firestorm came in reaction to the *Weekly Standard* feature article on Mitch by Andy Ferguson on June 5, 2010. Tony Perkins, president of the Family Research Council, in writing in his newsletter, challenged Governor Daniels to retreat from his stance that abortion should be put on the back burner until the nation overcame its fiscal woes.

Perkins said, "I support the Governor 100% on the call for fiscal responsibility, but nothing is more fiscally responsible than ending the taxpayer funding of abortion and abortion promotion. Without life, there is no pursuit of happiness. Thank goodness the Founding Fathers were not timid in their leadership; they understood that 'truce' was nothing more than surrender."

Others would expand the issue to ask questions about how this translated into his support of the Hyde Amendment or the Mexico City Policy or his appointment of Supreme Court Justices.[47]

I immediately called Cleta Mitchell, expert FEC attorney and longtime friend since college, but importantly, in this context, an insider with the conservative crowd. We would talk often on this subject as it unfolded, and she did yeoman work on our behalf to get people on the right to understand our position. She believed our position was "dicey, but doable if a lot of groundwork is laid, and if you get the language right." Her initial

---

[47] The Hyde amendment bans the use of certain federal funds to pay for abortion with exceptions for incest and rape. The Mexico City Policy is an executive order that bans federal funds to overseas groups that perform abortions.

point of view was we could "do it" (call a social truce for the time being) but we shouldn't "say it" that way.

She had three suggestions for Mitch:

1. Call Tony Perkins to say you would like to talk with him personally so he would understand your point.
2. Invite a group of social conservatives to a meeting to lay out your point of view.
3. Appear at some meetings this year and hold social conservatives close in Indiana, including them in your efforts to take control of the state house and senate, which is one of their target states.

We basically did none of the above.

As time went on, more and more columnists jumped into the fray. The *Washington Post* online edition had an article by Aaron Blake that listed the biggest vulnerabilities of each GOP presidential hopeful. For Mitch Daniels, it was the social conservatives.

Blake wrote, "The Governor has built a solid record for himself and is a popular early dark horse pick for political observers, but that's with economic issues front and center. Social issues still matter in the Republican presidential primary, and Daniels has got some work to do on that front. Daniels remains suspect to many social conservatives."[48]

Some friends tried to walk a fine line between support and basic disagreement on the subject. David Keene, leader of the American Conservative Union and longtime friend of Mitch, said:

> Indiana's Mitch Daniels has been recognized as the nation's best governor. He's also a heckuva politician, but the kerfuffle over his recent comments on whether social or economic issues should be at the top of the Republican and conservative issues agenda proves that a poor choice of words can befall even the most adroit politician.
>
> However, whether or not he runs for the presidency is no reason to condemn a principled conservative with a

---

[48] Aaron Blake, "The Biggest Vulnerability for Each GOP Presidential Hopeful," *Washington Post*, November 24, 2010.

virtually unassailable record simply because of a poor and easily misunderstood choice of words.[49]

And, Jim VandeHei, editor of the hugely influential *Politico* newsletter, sent a message to one of our group suggesting Mitch and his social truce "debate" should be written up for the smart set (meaning his readers) because people want to know more about where his head is on this issue. He went on to say that he had been reading the social statement fallout, and it seemed to him that it was important to put this into context before it became conventional wisdom. He asked to let him know if there was interest in doing so.

* * *

Some positive media stories and a number of allies came to the forefront.

Curt Smith, leader of the Indiana Family Institute, sent a letter to his membership and released it to the public on June 11, 2010. In part he said, "I have known Mitch Daniels for nearly 30 years and he is deeply committed to his Christian faith. He, of course, supports the Mexico City Policy and the Hyde Amendment policies. His record in Indiana speaks for itself. Above all, he walks the talk."[50]

Some political leaders like Governor Haley Barbour and Congressman Paul Ryan joined Mitch directly in supporting the idea of a "social truce." They indicated because of the downturn in the economy and the real issue of "fiscal conservatism and economic liberty," Republicans should agree to disagree on pro-life issues for the time being.

On October 19, 2010, commentator and author Dick Morris suggested in an online column of *The Hill* that the new Republican right was built around the Tea Party—in other words, economic issues rather than social issues. He said, "There is still a litmus test for admission to the Republican Party. But no longer do abortion, guns and gays dominate it. Now, keeping the economy free of government regulation, reducing taxation and curbing spending are the chemicals that turn the paper pink."[51]

---

[49] David Keene, "Addressing GOP's Agenda," *The Hill*, June 14, 2010.

[50] Curt Smith, *Indiana Family Institute Newsletter*, June 11, 2010.

[51] Dick Morris, "The New Republican Right," *The Hill*, October 19, 2010.

Charlie Black responded to that message when seeing it, saying, "He's right about what's going on this year but the social issue folks won't go away and must be taken into consideration in 2011–2012."

He was right about that fact, and some in our group still failed to grasp the intensity and importance of it.

In addition to Cleta Mitchell, the other person we turned to for advice and counsel on this issue was Oklahoma attorney Marc Nuttle. Marc was a friend of many years and now a veteran political operative, still very active in the evangelical community (he was Pat Robertson's campaign manager when he ran for president in the 1980s).

Marc had some very interesting points of view and had committed to help Mitch. He said the conservative and Christian movements were quite fractured now and un-unified, each following their own agenda. He brought leaders such as Rick Joyner, Ken Blackwell, and Dick Fox to the residence for one of our dinners and the discussion was quite useful. The message from Nuttle and his colleagues in a subsequent e-mail to me was:

> The truce problem is ours, not Mitch's. We have to ultimately be the counter to the old right that has a narrow, tactical view of the world that is incorrect. Economic freedom is a moral value, too. Our challenge is to galvanize the unorganized—that is really what the Tea Party is all about. Reagan was in no way a born again Christian nor was anyone around him. But people gravitated to him and his message—they were allowed to define themselves based upon what he was saying. People don't want to follow the already defined 'right to life person' or the 'Christian Right person,' even though they may be Sunday church-attending, God-fearing people. They want to define themselves but follow the person they think will change things for the better.

In the midst of this, I had sent Mitch a note that included this:

> On the overall subject of the "social truce" phrase, you have said that truce doesn't at all mean surrender, and I

think that is always a good phrase to include. But, here's a parallel thought from Cleta Mitchell. At the George Will dinner when you answered the China question, you basically said you didn't worry about China militarily, you worried about them economically from the standpoint of our economy (due to our unsustainable debt) being so weak they would one day own us. The point being we have to get the fiscal issues right first, or we won't have to worry about anything else.

It's the same concept as social issues—get our economic house in order first—our primary survival issue—and then we'll focus on other important things like foreign affairs, education, and social issues. Her point being we shouldn't just say social issues are going to the back of the bus—all issues need to be secondary (other than homeland security perhaps) to the primary one of economic growth and recovery. Framing it somehow in this context would resonate better with most "thinking" social conservatives.

* * *

The real firestorm came later on June 8, 2010, when Mitch was meeting with a group of reporters at an event hosted by the Heritage Foundation in Washington, DC. He was being questioned on his proposal for a social truce. Mitch said, "We face a genuine national emergency regarding the budget and maybe these things [various social issues] could be set aside for a while. But this doesn't mean anybody abandons his or her positions at all. Everybody just stands down for a little while, as we try to save the Republic."

John McCormack, a columnist with the *Weekly Standard*, seeking to clarify whether Mitch simply wanted to deemphasize these issues or actually not act on them, asked the question: "As President, would you issue an executive order to reinstate Reagan's Mexico City Policy your first week in office?" (Obama had revoked the policy during his first week in office.) Mitch replied, "I don't know."[52]

---

52 John McCormack, *Weekly Standard,* June 8, 2010, in a press briefing.

The responding noise was loud and ugly.

Tony Perkins, in his Family Research Council e-mail newsletter, *The Washington Update*, on June 10, 2010, said, "That's astonishing. Not only is Gov. Daniels noncommittal about his role as a pro-life leader, but the Governor wouldn't even agree to a modest step like banning taxpayer-funded promotion of abortion overseas (known as the Mexico City Policy) which President Bush did on his first day in office with 65% of the country's support."[53]

Other blogs and articles used the Mexico City Policy answer as an excuse to attack the entire social truce positioning. It became the basis for attack by the right-wing extremists, but also more moderate "thinking" social conservatives who couldn't understand why Mitch wouldn't commit to overturning the policy like every other previous Republican president.

According to others supporting Mitch but with experience on this issue, the Mexico City Policy was a "big deal." It had become a mini-tradition, according to former Bush aide Joel Kaplan, who said it was the first thing a Republican president changes and the first thing a Democrat changes.

The truth of the matter is Mitch didn't know what it was (nor did any of the rest of us until the storm broke), and as he said later, "The answer should have come easily, but the whole question caught me totally blind and off guard. All my mistake."

On Sunday, June 13, Mitch wrote, "Okay, with a day to think about it, I, of course, support the Bush policy. Reinstating it (the Mexico City Policy) is not inconsistent with a general truce." He asked that I let Cleta know he favored the policy and thought it should be reinstated, pointing out an *IndyStar* article that morning which finally told the story correctly.[54]

His answer ultimately got through with various communications and meetings with people at a couple of residence dinners, but the entire episode taught us a few lessons and revealed some potential problems down the line.

The most pressing issue once the Mexico City "I don't know" answer hit the airwaves was to clarify our position. Because that answer was being

---

[53]   Tony Perkins, *The Washington Update*, June 10, 2010.

[54]   He used a press conference with the Indiana press corps to answer the question about the Mexico City Policy, so he could give the correct answer.

used to attack the entire social truce concept, in my view, it needed to be addressed. I suggested such to Mitch and the group in a quick e-mail.

His immediate response was:

> I'll listen but I'm not inclined to say a word. I'm not a presidential candidate and not required to act like one, let alone respond to every one-horse "blogger" with a pet issue. Now that I've had a minute to think about it, I surely would reinstate the policy, just as I'd support the Hyde amendment policies here. But they can ask me questions like this if I ever become a candidate … for now I was just making a general suggestion about what most threatens the nation's future and what we have to find a way to come together on.

My immediate response back to him was:

> Mitch, I get that, but the fact that the social truce "idea"— your idea—is such a brilliant one, and an innovative one, is not something we want hijacked just because they have gotten a wrong impression. And, make no mistake, this is not just a blogger—this is a network that has reach and influence and who, frankly, for the most part will be in your corner or [that of] whomever else you would support.
>
> I have several other e-mails today that I haven't shared (which I will) making the same point, specifically about the "Mexico City Policy." Many people like Nuttle, Cleta, Ken Blackwell and others have been calling Tony Perkins to tell him he's not correct but all he has is the "I don't know" statement.
>
> This is the new communications environment in which we live, unfortunately, and once it is out there with no truth setting, it can mushroom into an unnecessary problem. Frankly, knowing your true position on this just gives you added credibility for your social truce approach."

His response back to me: "So you tell 'em."

As I shared this communications trail with the rest of our group, others begin weighing in—some helpful, some not, but all pointing out we had some attitude problems with which to deal.

That same day, one of our group weighed in with his comments to me saying I should just let it (the idea of a clarifying statement) go. He said, "This isn't the new communications environment. This is Tony Perkins taking the opportunity to aggrandize himself and his cause at Mitch's expense. There is nothing at all 'new' about those tactics. It's what he is paid to do. When the time is right, we can let Right to Life or some other rival group announce that Mitch, of course, would reverse the Mexico City order. But caving into these obnoxious tactics in the first inning is something Mitch doesn't do."

This was not helpful, and after conferring with Charlie Black who agreed with me, I responded to our colleague, "I've already let it go; I have no standing to reply to anyone. And, with great respect I will tell you that you are dead wrong in your analysis."

As I told Charlie later, this attitude was a serious problem, and ensuring it didn't rub off on others was important. Al Hubbard, in his own words a liberal on social issues, clearly understood this type of attitude was ridiculous. The point was not about tactics or kowtowing to any interest group or individual. The fact is Mitch made a mistake, as he said himself, and we needed to be smart enough to deal with it. Additionally, the communications environment *had* dramatically changed. Everything was instantaneously on the airwaves, and we had to be ready to deal with it.

Finally, on Sunday, June 13, after the press conference and other communications had been transmitted, I had this final communication with Mitch:

> I'm not sending this to the "group" because I don't want to escalate this any further. But, as I will always strive to do with you, I want you to have my unvarnished, honest point of view.
>
> The people that comprise the "social conservatives" group are in reality a diverse group. A majority of them, probably a vast majority, will be very supportive of

your efforts, primarily because of your personal beliefs, historical record both as Governor and before, and an increasing awareness of the importance of "survival issues" as defined by you.

We need these people. Whether it is to elect a Republican House in Indiana in 2010 (as you probably know, Indiana is one of four states designated as a priority by Focus on the Family), or elect a Republican president in 2012 (you or someone of your choosing)—this is a core of our constituency that along with the growing segment of "independents" which also takes several forms is vital to any success we desire at any level.

Even having said that, it doesn't mean we'll always agree with them on every aspect of their agenda. With certain elements we'll probably rarely agree in terms of priority. But, on things we do agree, such as the Mexico City Policy, it is senseless to get in a battle that was simply a misunderstanding, regardless of who was to blame. In today's communications environment, and it is different than any we have ever previously known, once a negative gets "out there," it is very difficult to keep it from continually raising its ugly head. It is much easier to immediately correct it and move on.

The social truce concept has tremendous appeal to a broad range of people. But, like anything else, it is important to determine the best way to articulate it. I believe we learn more about how to do that as we progress. The difference between you and, for instance, Rudy Giuliani, who also tried to deliver this message, is simply your own personal beliefs and record. That provides you a credibility that can't be manufactured, it is real. And with people like Marc Nuttle, David Keene, Cleta Mitchell, and George Will and a host of others who really understand the politics on a national scale, they will accept this as a critical component of a successful campaign.

Finally, the fact is, as Cleta stated, survival issues take

priority over many things—education reform, certain foreign policy initiatives, other important issues, not just social issues. It is simply a matter of bringing focus to what must happen first to enable work and progress on the many other things that ultimately will need addressing. It doesn't change what you believe in your heart, it just brings an orderly, prioritized focus to what has to happen first.

Hope you are having some down time today—enjoy your Sunday.

Mitch responded shortly thereafter by simply saying, "Agree. My value add here might be to say what needs saying, and as Charlie put it, if it's not acceptable, better to find out now."

However, this "crisis" was never about candor; it was about responding with immediacy and willingness to admit a mistake, correct it, and move on. It was another step in our learning experience.

* * *

Toward the end of 2010, Mitch participated in a Fund for American Studies "Town Hall Call" where he answered questions and talked about the world. I listened in on that call and sent him the following message: "Great job on the Fund call. Your answer on the social issue question where you start out by reminding everyone of your own positions [something we kept urging him to do] was right on target."

He responded, "Thanks. Practice makes perfect ... or at least 'improved.'"

The social truce noise would die down as time went on, but it never went away. In 2011 when Mitch was preparing to give a major speech at the CPAC conference, the subject was regularly revisited by the media, wondering if he would talk about it in front of this group. The speech did make reference to it, but not in those words, and his positioning of his point of view was much better delivered and received, although still not by everyone. Opponents in the primary saw a chance to drive a wedge, and they continued to take it.

In preparing for the CPAC speech, Trent Duffy, who we were talking with about a formal position if a campaign developed (as press and communications) offered some advice. He was concerned anything Mitch said on the "social truce" at CPAC would overshadow all his other very positive messaging points and would detract from his ability to contribute to the debate.

He suggested George Will, who was introducing him, could help a great deal by pointing out his pro-life record in Indiana. Trent also believed Mitch should handle the issue head-on. He even suggested that he say he had been "misinterpreted, that actions speak louder than words, that maybe he chose the wrong words, but judge me by my record in Indiana." In Trent's words, "If your objective is to contribute to the debate, you've got to lance the boil."

Mitch wouldn't go as far as Trent had suggested, but he did rephrase some of his language to make it more compatible with some, although conservative talk show hosts like Rush Limbaugh still criticized him. George Will was a tremendous help, praising Mitch's speech in a column the next day, saying it was nice to hear an adult conversation without pandering or rancor.

Cleta Mitchell, while praising the speech unconditionally, did say regarding the continued social truce controversy in an e-mail to me on June 10, 2010:

> The social truce was and is a bad "advance notice" from Mitch and was and is a totally unnecessary and destructive diversion. It muddles the waters and injects rancor and divisiveness where none need be. And it will kill the opportunity to get out of the starting block if we don't fix it right away, in my opinion.
>
> And, actually, it is quite the opposite of "an adult conversation." It is more in the nature of "I want it because I want it no matter what."
>
> I deal with this stuff and these people every single day. Mitch can say whatever he wants about the social conservatives and think whatever he wants about a "truce" and he can wish whatever he wants about what he would prefer on this topic. But the bottom line is this social truce

notion has been unnecessarily damaging and diversionary and divisive.

It can and should be fixed if this is going forward. The sad thing is it has the opposite of the intended effect. It diverts attention from the very things Mitch wants to focus on.

This advice and concern continued to be a subject of conversation between Cleta and myself up until the day Mitch made a final decision. If we had gone forward, it would have been an issue that needed a strategy and commitment to fix. Mitch wouldn't have needed to change his position or withdrawal the point; rather we'd have implemented a range of activities that emphasized Mitch's record and personal beliefs, coupled with new language to better articulate why prioritizing was important.

Mark Twain once said, "The difference between the right word and almost the right word is the difference between lightning and a lightning bug."

Crisis Number Three:
————— Stimulus Flip-Flop

I n August 2010, another episode developed that brought into question (a) whether or not "thin skin" was a real issue with Mitch and (b) how to handle a situation where a change in a policy position was questioned by the media.

The issue was federal stimulus money for Indiana. In February, Mitch signed onto a letter at the National Governors Association meeting seeking additional stimulus funds to run the state's Medicaid program. On *Fox News Sunday* with Chris Wallace in August, he denounced a new $26 billion stimulus bill that was expected to pass Congress the following week, a bill that included the money he had sought in his letter.

The contrast in those two positions ignited substantial political backlash from Democrats, who argued Daniels was more interested in his national appearance and potential bid for president than taking care of Hoosiers.

The headlines read, "Did Daniels flip-flop on stimulus money?"

In subsequent radio and press interviews, Mitch defended his position, but in doing so incorrectly described the letter he signed. Ultimately the staff issued a clarifying statement, saying he signed it to be a "team player."

His response was not timely. Therefore, the story built up negative momentum and the response seemed defensive, "thin-skinned and just plain wrong" in the words of Mark Lubbers. Lubbers continued, "By yelling at the reporter on day two, he guaranteed himself a second front page story and got himself in a news story that says he lied."

The media then kept the firestorm going with additional articles in the *Washington Post, US News and World Report,* the *Huffington Post,* all the local newspapers, and numerous television talk shows.

It also raised questions on whether or not Mitch had staff willing to stand up to him and tell him when he was wrong.

My communication with our group was basically this, "The challenge is to get a clear, concise, thoughtful response that both takes care of Indiana (his most immediate goal) and speaks to the larger problem nationally." A statement was put out eventually, and after a period of time, things cooled down and the subject was dropped.

Al Hubbard, Bob Perkins, Eric Holcomb, and others weighed in on the longer-term issue of staff support and staff willingness to tell him when he was wrong and should admit a mistake. In a presidential race, this could become a real issue.

Mark Lubbers sent Mitch a note saying he agreed 100 percent with the view expressed in a local newspaper column. It said reporters would have quickly and easily given Mitch a pass if he had admitted signing the letter was a mistake.

Obviously, this was a concern for the group. Mitch's attitude about outside advice and his approachability in terms of staff telling him the truth was not an insignificant issue. It all died down, but the long-term ramification was still a matter with which to deal if we were going to go forward.

Crisis Number Four:
Press Leak

Every organization, from the White House to a national campaign to a major corporation, worries about the public leaking of confidential information. Nevertheless, it happens. In terms of the presidential planning and activities on behalf of Mitch Daniels, we'd had a remarkable run of no leaks on anything.

That changed on September 1, 2010, when the *Washington Post* ran an article by Chris Cillizza, later picked up by others, on the "Inner Circle of Mitch Daniels." They were actually doing a series on all the potential presidential candidates' "inner circles" and, because of all the buzz surrounding Mitch, included him in the series. It said in part:

"So, who is Daniels relying on to make up his mind about a bid? While he is famously independent when it comes to his campaigns, Daniels does depend on a group of informal advisers for guidance."[55]

He then listed fourteen people, literally half of whom I had never even heard of, never mind talked or worked with, and he left out two of our group all together. Charlie Black, once this broke, did send us an e-mail saying Chris (whom he knew well) had called him for clarification of some names he already had in terms of their occupation or relationship to Mitch, but he had no idea where he'd got the information.

The article created virtually no interest. Other than the fact these names leaked, no one actually thought much of it, except Mitch.

---

[55]   Chris Cillizza, "Inner Circle of Mitch Daniels," *Washington Post*, September 1, 2010.

The problem really came ten days later on September 14, 2010, when Jonathan Martin of *Politico* published a lengthy article on the residence dinners entitled, "Daniels Makes White House Move." His opening paragraph read, "Indiana Gov. Mitch Daniels has been holding a series of private dinners with top Republican business leaders, policy hands and donors from around the country since this spring, an indication that he's thinking more seriously about a presidential bid than he publicly lets on."[56]

He then went on to describe in great detail the dinners, their purpose, and certain people who had attended. He interviewed a couple of attendees, former Congressman George Nethercutt being one, so it gave us some indication of which dinner he was specifically referencing. All in all, the article from our standpoint was quite fabulous. It said all the right things with all the right disclaimers. In many ways it was a terrific and accurate accounting of exactly why the dinners were being done.

This article, of course, prompted others, including one the next day, September 15, in the *IndyStar* with the headline, "Is Indiana Gov. Mitch Daniels setting the table for '12?"

We never found out the source of the story, but the fact is, we never tried to keep it a secret. We never told any of our guests to keep the dinners confidential, and we invited literally hundreds of people over the span of six months.

Following the article, we had numerous e-mails to various members of the group from people wanting to be included in future dinners. Former Tennessee Governor Don Sundquist sent an e-mail saying he wanted to be invited; a former chief of staff to a Bush cabinet member said the same; others sent e-mails saying what a brilliant leak this was.

But not everyone liked it, specifically Mitch. He immediately sent an e-mail to our group saying, "This is incredibly disappointing to read. I don't know who it is that feels it necessary to show how plugged in they are by running their mouth off about all this, but please stop. One more of these and I'll save everyone a lot of trouble and announce I'll never run. I can't think of anything less helpful."

We didn't know if his main problem was Cheri and the girls reading about this in the paper or what. I'm not sure he ever told them what we

---

[56] Jonathan Martin, "Daniels Makes White House Move," *Politico*, September 14, 2010.

were doing (which we had continually encouraged him to do), but he was obviously not pleased.

From the standpoint of the members of our group, we thought it was a very positive story. On September 14, Mark Lubbers responded to Mitch:

> Aside from blowing our cover, which has been remarkably long-lived, I don't see much problem here. This story affirms what you have said publicly—and when asked about this I would say—"As I've said, I have friends who are urging me to do this ... and they have friends who they have arranged to come see me. For better or worse, that's what leaving the door open a crack entails. The dinners have been interesting—good exchange of ideas among people who can help the direction of our party regardless of who runs. And as I've told everyone, it is the ideas that we bring to the American public that matter as much as the person who is our nominee."

Lubbers went on to say:

> If pressed—as you will be—I would counter with—"As should be plain from columns I've written and the handful of speaking I've done out of state, mostly at various think tanks, I intend to be involved in the life of my country, as should anyone who has knowledge and experience on the issues now before the country. That is a matter of patriotic duty, not political ambition."

I sent a confidential message to Lubbers, saying, "This is a perfect story if we just won't screw it up. I just talked to Eric, suggesting that we need a statement. The press is going nuts trying to get more information and we need to make this a positive story, which it can be."

Later that day, the governor's office released the following statement to the local Indiana media:

You all have asked for a comment from Gov. Daniels about the story that was published by *Politico* this morning. Here is a statement from him:

> I've said I have no intention or plan to run for president. That is true.
>
> I've said I'm not taking any of the steps or going to any of the places that a presidential candidate would go. That is true.
>
> I've said that many people have asked to visit with me about a candidacy and about reconsidering my disinclination to run. That is true.
>
> I've said that my priorities and my attention are firmly fixed on my duties here in Indiana. That is true.
>
> I've said I've made no final decision about running for president and won't for months and that is true.
>
> The *Politico* article and other recent stories confirm the truthfulness and accuracy of each of these statements.

The response of the group to this statement was immediate and unanimous:

"Precisely the wrong response—defensive, snarly and cynical. This was an opportunity to turn a very positive story into something even more positive. I'm not sure he is up to this."

"At some point, his attitude could become such a hindrance that, even if he were prevailed upon to actually make the race, the core attitude could get in the way at some point when he was confronted with a key decision as to alternative courses of action. This could end up leaving us vulnerable to a less than desirable nominee, or four more years of what we have now."

"Tuesday's statement and the further unfortunate comments in this morning's paper make it totally clear Mitch is not running. Out of courtesy to and respect for the group I think he needs to pull the plug. His statement was terrible. It was excessively defensive, petulant, pissy, and most importantly, completely non-presidential."

Bob Perkins did weigh in with this:

In reading all the clippings and messages, I'd like to slow up the "lynch Mitch" feeling I'm sure we all have. I have no idea what is going through his head, but I think we have done a great job in getting this process started. My view is we shouldn't push that hard between now and Dec. 13[57] to make it more perfect. Yes, he could be more on message, and for sure, he needs to be less thin-skinned and more willing to take a punch now and then. But, we are on everyone's radar screen today and we weren't a year ago. We're moving the ball forward.

Eric Holcomb, in reading all our statements, suggested some remedies that included stopping everything until after the November elections to enable the staff to slow down his schedule. He said, "Ignoring all my suggestions, you're probably right. He needs to be told all these comments by the group. Who talks to him?"

I was again nominated. I agreed to call Mitch since I had already scheduled a call with him previously to follow up on his trip to the Greenbrier, where he was going to be with Cheri and all the girls. Supposedly he was going to discuss the subject of a presidential run.

I was going to suggest to him we cancel the October dinners and do nothing else until after the November elections, when he then needed to make a personal decision. Would we stop or would we meet in December; that was what he needed to decide.

Tom Bell was out of the country for all of this on a cruise with his family. But I contacted him on September 16 to ask his opinion. I said:

I know you're getting e-mails, but it's probably hard to see all the attachments that have been flowing. I was going to call Mitch today but could wait until you return for all of us to talk. This is going nowhere.

The *Politico* article was nothing but positive, but all Mitch could do was rant that there was a leaker in our group, which I totally dismiss. We've had 150 people

---

[57] Our next scheduled meeting

through the residence and another 150 we asked—as Charlie said, "I'm shocked it hasn't gotten out already and who cares if it does?" The article accurately described what they were and in no way violated his "haven't made a decision yet" position. What it has done was to cause multiple people to call or write and say—"I want to come!"

He has to make a decision. This doesn't alter our public timetable whatsoever, but he has to make a personal decision on whether or not he wants to do this, and whether or not he wants to pull out all the stops to convince Cheri. Confidentially, George W. Bush has said he'll talk to Cheri and have Laura talk to her but only if he has made the decision himself to do it. That is exactly the right position.

I'm fine with waiting until after the election in November for him to do this, but in the meantime I think we should put our efforts on hold—no dinners, no other aggressive outreach. Every time I talk to someone now to encourage their involvement I feel like I'm playing them. Every other person in our group feels this way. Perkins is probably the one who feels the least adamant, but he generally agrees.

I'm just asking for a quick response. If you disagree with me, tell me. Should I go ahead and talk to him or wait? I told him I'd call him when I returned from my trip to see how the Greenbrier session with Cheri and the girls went, so I have a reason to call. I assume it didn't go well, but don't know. Let me know what you think.

Bell responded immediately:

Don, I would talk to him about how he feels about our efforts thus far, remind him that we can't expect our Indy dinners to be a secret, but not draw any lines in the sand. I agree we should just wait until after November and you should make that suggestion to him.

I think I would say something like "we have made a lot of progress; now let's just wait until after November and then you can tell us if you want to continue the process or give it up. If you want to continue we will form a draft committee and prepare for your ultimate decision. If no, we will all go back to our normal lives. Your call." My bet is he will want us to keep going and if he does we can negotiate some new rules with him."

Generally, that is what was done. I did talk with him, and we agreed on the post-November strategy. There was no movement with the family. We punted until after the election.

Cheri and the girls—Meredith, Meagan, Melissa and Maggie

As Mitch said, "It's hard to believe that family life could be much better than it is now"

Mitch and Cheri at the Indiana State Fair, a favorite event

The last gubernatorial campaign - victory night 2008

Mitch on his Harley—a preferred mode of transportation

RV One and Mitch went to cities and towns across Indiana

Another "home stay" for Mitch as he visited Indiana citizens

Retail politics at its finest -- pouring coffee for constituents

As Governor, Mitch continually listened to the citizens of Indiana

*Mitch honed his conducting skills first with the
Newton/Jasper Community band*

The youth of America were a target of Mitch's message on fiscal discipline

Mitch and the Ball State crowd

Education reform was a priority for the Daniels Administration

*Mitch's Kids - A partnership between state
government and the Boys and Girls Clubs*

Augusta National - the first meeting to discuss a presidential run - Daniels, Bell, Cogman and Black

Cleta Mitchell, partner with Foley and Lardner LLP, election law expert extraordinaire

Spontaneous signs began appearing urging a Daniels candidacy for president
(photo by RP Gentry)

Speech by Indiana First Lady, Cheri Daniels, to the largest
Indiana state republican party dinner ever held
(photo by RP Gentry)

Mitch with his long-time mentor, Senator Richard Lugar

*Mitch, as President of Purdue University, doing what
he loves most -- being with the students*

THE GROUP

Tom Bell, Atlanta, Ga.

Charlie Black, Washington D.C.

Don V. Cogman, Scottsdale, AZ

Al Hubbard, Indianapolis, In.

THE GROUP

Eric Holcomb, Indianapolis, In

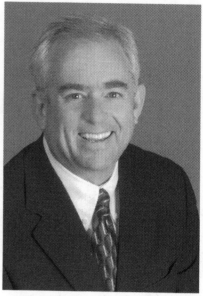

Mark Lubbers, Indianapolis, In

Bob Perkins, New York, NY

Rick Powell, New York, NY

Crises Number Five: VAT
— Comment at Hudson Institute

The first job out of the White House in the mid-eighties for Mitch was to return to Indiana and become president and CEO of the Hudson Institute. Tom Bell had been the CEO but was in the process of moving on, and he recruited Mitch, who was looking for a way to return to the private sector and to live in Indiana.

As a result, the Hudson Institute and its founder, Herman Kahn, had always been close to Mitch's heart. In October 2010, Mitch was the guest of honor at a Hudson Institute dinner in Washington, DC, where he gave a speech, highly covered by the press given the presidential buzz.

In the speech, Mitch (who described himself as an acolyte of Kahn's and that he marveled at his creative thinking) recited from Kahn's 1982 book, *The Coming Boom*: "It would be most useful to redesign the tax system to discourage consumption and encourage savings and investment. One obvious possibility is a value added tax and flat income tax, with the only exception being a lower standard deduction."

He also suggested support for increasing gasoline taxes. Kahn wrote, in a passage Mitch read from, "One fully justifiable tax would be on imported oil. Any large importation of oil by the U.S. raises security problems. There are, in effect, external costs associated with importing oil that a tariff would internalize."

"Now maybe that transgresses some philosophical viewpoint of yours," said Daniels to the crowd, "but, to me, that's an interesting point today, just as valid as the day he wrote it."

The next day, October 15, 2010, the headline in *Politico* read, "Daniels Open to VAT tax and Oil Tax Hike." The article was written by James Hohmann.

The firestorm was just beginning.

In a brief interview after his speech as reported by Hohmann in his October 15 article, Mitch downplayed the significance of his comments. He stressed he would support a VAT "only under the right circumstances," reiterating his desire for it to be paired with a flat income tax. "If you think the paramount problem for the country is the debt, and we'll never get on top of it without really robust growth, one of the things you want is a very different, more pro-growth tax system. And, a quarter century ago, Kahn was writing about one. That's all. There are other ways to get at it. The point here is—think about solutions, think about outcomes."[58]

Of course, those comments didn't make it into most articles and certainly not into any headlines. The response was loud and disruptive:

On October 17, 2010, an article in *The Atlantic.com's Daily Dish* by Andrew Sullivan said "Indiana Gov. Mitch Daniels has now managed to alienate prominent social and fiscal conservatives."[59]

In another article in *Politico* by James Hohmann, Americans for Tax Reform President Grover Norquist said, "Absent some explanation, such as large quantities of crystal meth, this is disqualifying. This is beyond the pale." Hohmann reported that 154 House Republicans signed a letter strongly opposing a VAT and that even fiscal conservatives who defended Mitch as one of them said it was a bone-headed move if he was seriously considering a run for the nomination.[60]

A veteran Republican consultant (and supporter of Mitch for president) said, "It is painful to say this, but my sense is that this comes close to taking him out of the ball game."

Another supporter suggested, "Remember, you can't get hurt for what you don't say! Mitch may be right on tax reform, but any talk of increasing

---

[58]   James Hohmann, "Daniels Open to VAT tax and Oil Tax Hike," *Politico*, October 15, 2010.

[59]   Andrew Sullivan, "The Heresy of Mitch Daniels," *The Atlantic's.com Daily Dish*, October 17, 2010.

[60]   James Hohmann, "Mitch Daniels Takes Hit for Tax Talk," *Politico*, October 17, 2010.

them is a no-win proposition and should not be uttered. I'd suggest criticizing the tax code, saying let's reform it and then start fresh with a lower, fairer tax policy, coupled with government spending reductions to get the nation fiscally back on track."

Another wrote, "Just spent an hour with Rich Lowry (*National Review*) walking him back from the ledge. These people are desperate for a competent and compelling 2012 candidate, when one shows up who appears in their view to be flawed, they over-react."

* * *

The e-mail traffic among the group was intense. On October 15, I sent a message to them initially that said:

> I just finished listening to the Hudson speech on C-Span. I have to say, one of the best I've heard from Mitch. Absolutely incredibly well delivered with great content. Literally a few sentences of "nuance" on the VAT with a slightly different word-smithing and it would not even have made the news. The oil tax, perhaps another issue— that could have been done better or even left out—but the rest of the speech was truly exceptional. I would refer people to the tape and encourage them to listen, with his "clarifying" remarks in print. Let's discuss tomorrow on the call.

After two days of nonstop media onslaught and Mitch's response to Grover's comments which was, "I have no time for self-important types who never have cut anyone's taxes or anyone's budget or done anything in the real world," I sent another message to our group:

> Here's my take. Once again, we ignore the possible nuances that would make this a better story. Nuance is not in Mitch's vocabulary, which is dangerous in my view. I'm not talking about changing his opinions, I'm talking about nuances. Why can't you say—"A VAT to me makes

a great deal of sense, if and only if, it is a replacement not a supplement, to our existing tax structure, specifically our income tax and some downward alteration to capital gains." He said it later, after the speech, but I guarantee you that part will not be reported by anyone. I've already seen one follow-up article and it made no mention of it—just the headline—Daniels supports VAT tax and Oil Tariff.

Oil Tariff—why mention it at all in this setting? It is a complicated subject, only relevant (if even then) as a part of a much bigger energy independence strategy, and it gets a good portion of our constituency riled up.

* * *

The idea of an op-ed by Mitch trying to clarify his position(s) and quell the uprising was suggested. We thought we could probably get it into the *Wall Street Journal* or some other publication.

A member of our group communicated to Mitch and the rest of us that he thought we should attack Grover Norquist. I frankly thought his reasoning and conclusions were flawed from beginning to end and, again, not helpful in getting Mitch to understand this was a crisis of his own making that we needed to fix.

Mitch actually started the process by writing a draft op-ed and sending it to all of us for our comments. We went back and forth, some thinking it much too defensive and others believing we needed to at least say something, even if more limited. He entitled it "A Learning Night in Washington," and it dealt not only with the issues at hand, but also the "gotcha culture" of Washington, particularly the online media.

All of us had multiple comments and suggestions, notwithstanding our concern that maybe no response was the best response. I initially said my instinctive reaction to the draft as written was that it served no useful purpose except to make us all feel good.

However, after reading several redrafts, the idea of getting on the record with clarifying remarks about the consumption tax did have some merit. I suggested if we ever got to the point where we were having to conduct this discussion in the more formalized setting of a campaign, we could point to this article as affirmation that, once again, the Washington media was doing its thing in missing the point.

On October 19, I sent Mitch the following message with my thoughts:

> I listened to the entire tape again last night, the best I've ever heard you speak. Thoughtful, exceptional in both content and delivery, a sincerity that really came through as you made your points. I believe a few very simple "nuances," not "political-speak" but merely clarifying nuances to make certain your position is clearly understood would have prevented much of the uproar, but we'll save that debate for another day.
>
> I would send it. I still believe it is a bit too defensive, and I think it needs a few more sentences on policy that emphasize what I think is your true attitude about a consumption tax (a replacement not a supplement, and much more along the lines of Harvey Rosen's proposal). However, the real point of the Op-ed is going to be the provocative suggestion that "Washington" needs to be willing to listen to new ideas to solve the survival problems we face as a country.
>
> I appreciate the value of one of our colleague's comments, but I disagree with his paragraph that seeks to further and more directly demonize Norquist and others. Simply not necessary, the point is made. Making him and others the target doesn't do us any good in the long run. We're giving him more credit than he is due, this isn't about him.
>
> It is a well-written piece. I can imagine David Broder or George Will, for instance, would reaffirm their belief there is at least one Republican with an intellect who is thinking about solutions to real problems.

The initial draft was greatly depersonalized, focused more on policy, emphasized the need for an "adult conversation" on key survival issues such as these, and took out certain elements that appeared to be "whining." Mitch was actually more concerned about the "twisted nature of political discourse" than the legitimate arguments about what kind of tax, but the fact was, tax increases were the headline.

The final paragraph of the rewritten article (written almost entirely by Mitch himself, as usual) said, "The task of our time is to rescue the American project from the perilous fiscal corner into which we have painted ourselves. An occasional evening on which we set aside 'gotcha' politics and explore options could be helpful. We'd be well advised to take counsel of the old British saying, 'Now that the money has run out, we must begin to think.'"

August Strategy Meeting

As the summer of 2010 concluded, we determined it was time to get the group and Mitch together again in person for a strategy discussion and update on activities. The November off-year elections were just three months away, and we had been telling people we wanted to wait until those were completed to make any significant decision on whether to go or not.

If the GOP in Indiana were successful in winning both houses of the state legislature, it would mean an all-out effort by Mitch to achieve one more significant reform initiative for the state. This would be a significant achievement that could possibly be replicated nationally with very positive national publicity and implications. Additionally, it was important to Mitch to fulfil his promises and responsibilities as governor, and doing so would soften the blow if in fact he chose to resign early for a presidential run.

Prior to our meeting, which was to be held in Indianapolis, Tom Bell was asked to call Mitch to prepare him for one of the main reasons we wanted to gather, a decision on taking the next step, meaning the formulation of some type of formal "draft" committee. Tom reported back that Mitch agreed a decision was needed and indicated a generally positive response.

The August meeting started with dinner on August 3 in the home of Al Hubbard. Each time we got together, I put together an agenda and invited everyone to contribute ideas. I stressed from the beginning it was just a guideline, but we found without one, things would simply ramble and get out of hand. We met again the next day, August 4, all day in the residence.

The discussion agenda for dinner included:

A review of the past six months
- Residence dinners
- Out-of-state trips
- Press coverage
- Ongoing communications with attendees

Social media strategy
- 2010 utilization/2011
- Staffing/investment

People needs
- Iowa-New Hampshire-South Carolina-Florida
- Press
- Policy coordination
- Social media
- Finance director

Timetable/activities/needs
- September to December 2010
- January to May 2011

Major concerns
- Staffing
- Timetable
- Issue reconciliation

Much of the dinner discussion centered around bringing people up to date on the various activities and a general discussion of where we thought things stood in terms of Mitch and the family.

* * *

The next day was the real meat of the meeting, and the agenda included multiple items on which we needed to make significant decisions.

The agenda included:

1. Current thinking—Mitch

We tried to start every meeting when we got together in person with Mitch giving us his current attitude—had anything changed in regards to the family and his own attitude about running?

We also received intelligence from Charlie and others on what they were hearing, particularly from other potential candidates. Romney was telling everyone that Mitch wasn't running. Pawlenty was trying to use the social truce idea as a wedge, particularly in Iowa, and was considered the second choice of many if Mitch didn't run. Gingrich was supposedly announcing in February. Palin, Thune, Huckabee, and Haley—no one thought they were going. Santorum, Bachman, and Paul weren't even mentioned.

It was reported many funders and fundraisers wanted to commit, if not to Mitch, to someone. These were people who wanted to play in the big leagues and be a part of something from the very beginning.

It was reported the Bush leadership, Josh Bolten, Andy Card, and others didn't think Mitch was going to do it but would very likely be with him if he said yes.

A discussion ensued regarding the memo Senator Jack Danforth had written, with most being in agreement with his approach of contrast and civility.

2. Media/press

We reviewed the past six months and talked extensively about the future frequency and type of interviews. Bob Perkins, in particular, mentioned the importance of talking to some of the major blogs, including *RedState* (Erick Erickson), *Drudge Report*, and *Breitbart.com*.

Politico was mentioned, and Rick Powell said they apparently were interested in receiving more information. It was becoming the major inside-the-beltway political newsletter with a substantial audience and needed to be addressed at some point.

We discussed our response to the multiple requests coming in from high-profile programs such as *60 Minutes, Good Morning America*, and *Fox News.* The conversation focused more on whether or not to accept any of those invitations right now than it did on the substance of what would be said. The general consensus was to continue toning down the major national press appearances almost entirely until after the November elections but take advantage of certain strategic opportunities as they developed.

3. Social media initiative

Bob Perkins, Rick Powell, and Eric Holcomb discussed various elements of social media, the importance of it, and the timing of doing certain things. Jeff Hunt had prepared a memo outlining specific things to be done now relative to Indiana that might be a good foundation for later expansion. Rick also brought some materials to demonstrate what the rest of the political world was beginning to embrace relative to social media.

The problem here was Mitch; he wasn't a true believer. He generally capitulated to our suggestion this was something we needed to do. We got the go-ahead to do certain things, but I could tell he wasn't convinced this was a major priority. We missed some real opportunities in this regard, as did the Republican National Committee and every other Republican candidate at the national level.

Social media was becoming the language of the young and, more and more, of all ages. We wanted to test some techniques, build a following, and strategically use various channels in the Indiana state elections to show what could be done. It was a minimal effort that didn't even approach what could have been done, simply because we needed Mitch to champion it. He simply wasn't there yet.

4. Issue discussion

A good deal of time was spent going through all of Al Hubbard's materials and the very thorough analysis he and his team of experts had produced. Each issue was dissected and various approaches discussed in terms of how to communicate certain positions.

5. Out-of-town calendar

The general agreement was to slow out-of-state activity until after November, but several things were already on the calendar in New York, Washington, and Los Angeles. We talked about individuals to see in each place and small group gatherings to put on the schedule between other major events already scheduled, primarily for the Aiming Higher PAC fundraisers.

A major discussion was held on whether or not Mitch should make campaign appearances on behalf of gubernatorial candidates between now and November, specifically in Iowa, Texas, California, South Carolina, and Florida.

All were clearly justified. In Iowa (the first primary contest), the incumbent, Governor Terry Branstad was a close friend of Mitch's. As for South Carolina and Florida, a successful governor such as Mitch would be a natural person to go to those states and lend a hand. In Texas and California, he would also be welcome as a successful governor telling his story. Both of these states were important for us in terms of future fundraising help.

Basically, Mitch downplayed them all. He was particularly adamant he wasn't going to step foot in Iowa. He said all it would do was increase speculation he was a presidential candidate (to which we said, yeah?), and he steadfastly refused to go. All of us believed Mitch's participation was an easy, appropriate, very helpful activity in some very key states, but he wouldn't budge. We believed it was a missed opportunity.

I don't know if Mitch's decision not to campaign in the gubernatorial races was another example of his insistence on doing things differently from other presidential candidates (all of the other candidates were actively campaigning for these candidates), or if he was preventing another issue between him and Cheri. Ultimately, he did very little campaigning, except for states that had minimal strategic value for the future.

6. Residence dinners

We reviewed all the past dinners and attendees and talked about how we were keeping in touch with them. We discussed future dates in 2010 and future invitees. Our plan was to hold off until after the November elections.

7. Communication

We discussed what to do on a regular basis in terms of keeping in touch with all the people we were seeing and all the people who were constantly contacting us to say they wanted to become involved. List maintenance, which was in Eric's hands, was also reviewed.

8. Timetable

We reviewed the calendar in terms of the remainder of 2010 and the first half of 2011. We needed to determine our primary objectives for both time frames. Particularly in 2011, we needed to understand Mitch's availability due to the legislative session and the time requirements necessary to complete his reform agenda in the state.

9. Miscellaneous

Every campaign for national office devoted time and resources to researching the opposition, but we needed to do the same type of research on Mitch himself. We knew the opposition would be doing it, so to enable us to get in front of any potential issues, it was important to undertake such an exercise. Eric had someone doing preliminary work, but it wasn't progressing particularly well. Charlie said he had a person who could do this and agreed to investigate costs.

Mitch had contracted to write a book, and we discussed the timing and utilization of it. He indicated he would send a draft to a couple of us for review and comments. This was an opportunity to have a current narrative of his principles, beliefs, and record of achievement. We all agreed it deserved some attention and focus.

As with all our meetings, we needed to schedule well in advance, so we discussed when and where the next meeting should be held. Everyone thought this was necessary, and a preliminary date was set to again meet in Indianapolis in December.

Cleta Mitchell had given me a brief memo on the alternative types of draft committees that could be established with the FEC. There was ample confusion on what could and should be done. Basically, once one spent five thousand dollars or more, he or she had ten days to file the appropriate paperwork, except for the testing-the-waters approach that required no filings.

The latter, it was obvious to us, was the best mechanism for us. It enabled us to provide an avenue for people to contribute funds and encourage Mitch to run. This approach was relatively unknown; clearly the easiest (requiring only an address, chairman, and treasurer); and didn't even need to be officially or publicly announced. Money raised could be used for polling, travel, research, receptions, and other similar activities.

Cleta had recommended we set the committee up outside of Indiana; all of the business was done electronically anyway. Details needed to be worked out, but the major issue was getting Mitch to agree to this approach. He wanted to think about it and talk with me again the next week.

10. Major concerns/needs

Much of this discussion centered on staffing and specific states in which we needed to be concerned. We discussed:

- **John Dillon** as potential finance chairman—John was former chairman of the Business Roundtable and retired CEO of International Paper.
- **Travis Thomas** as finance director—Jack Oliver's number two, Travis had Indiana connections through his wife.
- **Rob Engstrom** or **Nick Ayres** as potential campaign manager—Rob was with the US Chamber, and Nick was with the Republican Governors Association; Nick, in particular, was a hot commodity, who we believed would be with Haley if he ran.
- **Cleta Mitchell** as legal counsel

We ended this meeting with a great deal of positive feelings among the group and Mitch. If one would have asked each participant, as I later did, if he thought Mitch was moving in the direction of ultimately saying he would run, the near unanimous opinion would have been yes.

There were, of course, "conditions," but everyone expected a big win in November in Indiana, and most thought it would give Mitch an opportunity to finish his task for the state and build on that momentum to go the next step. No one was clear on what role Cheri and the family would play, but we were generally optimistic the family issue was manageable. We still had a good deal of work to be done, but between August and Election Day in November, overt activities did start to slow down. Press speculation, however, continued at a rapid pace.

* * *

On Sunday, August 15, 2010, Jack Colwell, the Dean of Indiana political reporters, writing in the *South Bend Tribune* said, in part:

> Mitch Daniels is going for President. How far he intends to go and whether he could go all the way are other questions. But Indiana's governor gave the "go" signal in his *Fox News* interview with Chris Wallace. Daniels told Wallace that he would keep an open mind about running for President, a step far beyond the past approach of scoffing modestly about any such possibility.[61]

On August 19, 2010, a lengthy profile of Mitch, complete with a picture of him riding his Harley, appeared in the *Economist*. It traced his evolution as a successful governor into a potential presidential candidate and concluded by saying:

> Mr. Daniels still insists he is unlikely to run for president. But he has a familiar post-partisan sheen, not unlike a certain former Senator[62]—though he is more conservative, shorter and much balder. He likes to talk about a "programme of unusual boldness" that unites the parties and sets America back on track. "Supposedly we are not capable of making decisions like this," Mr. Daniels said, grinning as he smacked a stubborn bottle of ketchup, "but somebody has to try."[63]

Tim Hefferman, writing in *Esquire* on September 14, 2010, said:

> It's a big day in American politics with eight of the nine remaining states holding their primaries for governor and Congress. *Politico* reports that Mitch Daniels is now openly laying the groundwork for a presidential run.

---

[61] Jack Colwell, "Daniels Giving all the 'Go Signals,'" *South Bend Tribune*, August 15, 2010.

[62] A reference to President Obama

[63] "Mitch Daniels: The Right Stuff," *Economist*, August 19, 2010.

And I think it means we have just met the party's 2012 presidential candidate. Daniels is, among other things, the only inarguably successful politician in serious contention.[64]

In another lengthy profile, this time in *Newsweek* (again accompanied by a picture of Mitch on his Harley), reporter Andrew Romano asked the question: "Indiana Gov. Mitch Daniels is small, stiff and unimposing. So why is he attracting legions of fans?"

He went on to say:

Part of the reason Daniels is attracting Republican interest is that his record of competence and fiscal restraint represents a refreshing change of pace. Highly regarded *New York Times* columnist David Brooks said there is emerging a new Republican type, what he called the "austerity caucus." He said, "Mitch Daniels, the governor of Indiana who I think is the most likely to win the GOP presidential nomination in 2012, is the spiritual leader."[65]

And, finally in a bold declaration on September 10, 2010, columnist Matthew Tully said:

All signs point to a Daniels bid for president. Governor Daniels isn't ready to announce his candidacy. No politician wants to be seen as overly eager. So, today, I'm going to do it for him: Gov. Mitch Daniels is running for president.[66]

This was followed on September 16, 2010, with an article by Chris Sautter in his weekly briefing on Indiana politics outlining why he thought Mitch wouldn't run. "More likely is that Daniels walks up to the edge

---

[64] Tim Hefferman, *Esquire*, September 14, 2010.
[65] Andrew Romano, "Responsible Rider," *Newsweek*, September 10, 2010.
[66] Matthew Tully, "All Signs Point to a Daniels Bid for President," *IndyStar*, September 10, 2010.

but holds back from running for president to avoid being soiled by the process," he said.[67]

So, the media was right where we wanted them—confused; divided; and, frankly, without a clue.

[67]   Chris Sautter, "Why Mitch Daniels Won't Run," *Howey Politics Indiana*, September 16, 2010.

August to November
———————— Election Day

Mitch had been working on a book for some months regarding his vision for America and concerns about the survival issues. He had been thinking about this before any talk of a possible presidential run, and therefore, his first paragraph started out by saying, "Most books such as this were written by someone getting ready to run for President but that is not the case in this instance." We, of course, had him change that first paragraph.

He sent the draft manuscript to several of us, and we each had comments and suggestions. All in all, it was a brilliantly written book. However, as one of our group said, "Someone else with political and policy antennae needs to review the manuscript to make sure there are no unintended bombshells. Knowing Mitch, there will be some *intended* bombshells, but we ought to at least discuss these with him."

I made several suggestions, mostly dealing with "nuance." For certain, I was thinking about the book in terms of a potential presidential run. I said I thought the first paragraph needed to be changed for obvious reasons and suggested it read something like this (most of these were his initial words):

> Books are written for many reasons. I'm offering these thoughts because, for the first time, I am desperately alarmed about the condition and direction of the American republic. I'm not that interesting a person. I dislike intensely the self-absorption that has characterized

my generation and the politics of personality that have contributed to the deep predicament in which our nation now finds itself. So, if you're looking for biography and personal revelations, try *Wikipedia*.

I told Mitch my suggestions were minor, and obviously this book had to be his thoughts and his words. I thought it was a brilliant, thoughtful, and compelling piece of work. I believed if many people could ultimately read it, they would see what a great president he could be.

* * *

The social media work, led by Perkins, Powell, and Holcomb, continued into the fall. The goal was to double the e-mail list, substantially increase Mitch's fans on Facebook, and conduct a training session on the basics of social media for the staff.

* * *

Another message came from the Romney camp, this time through old friend, Ron Kaufman, asking Mitch and Cheri to spend a couple of days with Mitt and Ann at their "cottage" in New Hampshire. Ron indicated to Mitch that he thought it would be worthwhile for Mitt and Mitch to spend a little time together. The invitation was politely declined again.

* * *

In mid-September, *Fox News* anchor Bret Baier came to Indianapolis to film a lengthy interview with Mitch, to be aired on Fox after the November 2010 election. It lasted more than an hour and I received an audio download that enabled me to listen to the entire interview, which went very well. Jane Jankowski, the governor's press secretary remarked, "Baier is so good; I said to myself he would make a really excellent presidential press secretary."

Al Hubbard had contacted Travis Thomas, and a conversation was arranged with Mitch. Travis was receptive to being finance director; as Jack Oliver's number two in the most recent highly successful Bush campaign, he was considered by many to be the best possible person for the job in the country. Travis was currently working in Texas with a communications and public affairs firm, Public Strategies, and would want to return to the firm after the campaign. He had a strong interest in Mitch, and only Mitch, in addition to the fact his wife was from Indianapolis and her family still resided there.

Travis prepared a lengthy and thoughtful memo on campaign finance operations with some initial thoughts. We were enthusiastic, and Travis's willingness to come on board provided another reason for us to prepare a specific timetable for a decision on whether or not to go. We needed to be able to tell Travis something, or we'd lose him.

* * *

Two other conversations between Mitch and myself during this time frame were important and had significant implications. The first one had to do with the formation of the testing the waters committee.

At our August strategy meeting, I had handed out a one-page description of how a testing the waters committee might work—we entitled it "Mitch for America." The basics were:

Objective

Establish under federal election law guidelines a "testing the waters" entity to ascertain interest in and support for a Mitch Daniels for president campaign. This is fundamentally a mechanism to assist Governor Mitch Daniels in making a decision whether or not to be a candidate for president of the United States in 2012 and to provide individuals interested in his candidacy a place to express that support.

Methodology

Create a Mitch for America bank account, initially at Wells Fargo Bank in Scottsdale, Arizona. Obtain an EIN tax number from the IRS and name Don V. Cogman as Treasurer. Establish a mailing address, designate a staff person to handle receipts and correspondence, and develop a 180-day plan for implementation. (A small firm in Alexandria, Virginia, that Cleta Mitchell had used before could handle the accounting very reasonably if desired and could even be listed as treasurer).

Designate a spokesperson (Cogman or Perkins are the least conflicted with current jobs) to handle initial press inquiries as to the purpose of the entity when this becomes public. (We won't announce it but have to assume it will become public.)

Procedures and protocols

This effort is to be initiated by interested individuals, not Governor Daniels. However, the governor will be notified of our actions and be aware of its existence. If Governor Daniels makes a decision to become a candidate for the presidency of the United States, this entity will be converted to his official campaign committee, as prescribed by FEC regulations, and all contributions will be counted toward primary contribution limits. If the decision is not to run, donors to the committee will be refunded their contributions on a pro rata basis after expenses.

Contributions can be expended for travel expenses, survey research, fundraising, and other activities as prescribed by FEC law and regulations. No funds can be expended for general advocacy of the potential candidate. Current maximum contribution allowed—by individuals only—is $2500.

Timetable

This effort will be initiated *no earlier* than November 3, 2010, by establishing the bank account. Solicitation of contributions will commence by November 15, 2010, through personal contact, direct mail to internal lists, and small functions in various locations (without the participation of Governor Daniels). Additional details to be formulated.

* * *

In mid-August after our strategy meeting in Indianapolis, Mitch and I talked about the testing the waters memo and proposal. He had wanted a few days to think about it and called me with his comments, which I reported to our group in a confidential memo:

> Generally he was okay with it. He believed we covered most of the key issues correctly. He wanted to move the start date past Nov. 15. He actually preferred January because he believed once we set it up, it would become public and bring all the pundits out of the woodwork. As he said, that doesn't mean we can't do things to get it ready.
>
> He was still very concerned we spend as little as possible so we could return as much as possible to donors if he doesn't do it.
>
> He would like a letter from me or someone basically saying what this is and what it isn't, something that memorializes the purpose in print to actually give out to people who inquire.
>
> He indicated he would use this as an excuse to talk to Cheri, maybe even that evening. I emphasized our willingness to talk to her to back up his credibility, that he didn't start this, we did.

The reasons we liked the idea of a testing the waters committee were threefold: One, it raised the conversation with Mitch to a new level. He knew this was a serious effort that needed a decision, even if that decision was private and not public for a period of time. Secondly, it finally gave us a mechanism in which interested people could participate. It indicated a seriousness to key people we were still trying to keep neutral, so they wouldn't commit to Romney or others. Finally, it prompted the necessity of the serious discussion with Cheri and the family we had been urging Mitch to have for months, with real data that had not been discussed previously.

Al Hubbard and I were aware that if we didn't show a great deal of money raised, the failure to do so could be used by the media to paint a negative story. The truth was we didn't have to file anything anywhere under this scenario. I knew Mitch would not be comfortable with a full-blown fundraising effort if he hadn't made a decision yet, particularly with his attitude about wanting to send 95 percent of the money back if he didn't run.[68]

* * *

The second significant conversation with Mitch at this time came on August 20, 2010, very early in the morning, around 6:20 a.m.

He called to relate his conversation the previous night with Cheri. He had my document on the testing the waters concept. He'd used it to start the conversation, with the goal of trying to ascertain her feelings on a potential run for the presidency. He had indicated yesterday morning when we'd talked that he and Cheri hadn't been together, just the two of them, in the evening for over a week and that last night might be an opportunity to have the conversation.

I asked, "How did it go?"

"It depends on what side you're on," he responded. "For your side, not very well."

Fundamentally, Cheri had asked, "When are you going to tell them you aren't going to do it?"

The one bit of good news was she didn't think Mitch himself was planning this or that this was some type of self-promoting effort. That his wife might think this was all his doing had been a concern for Mitch from the beginning. She believed people were genuinely coming to him

---

68   Al pointed out at the time that this was totally unrealistic; it takes money to make money. I agreed.

and asking him to do this for the sake of the country. But she said that was not the way she saw spending the rest of her life.

She wanted to be able to go to Starbucks in her sweats and meet her girlfriends and go shopping and do things normal people do. She had set her mind about what a candidacy would mean—if Mitch ran and won, the rest of her life would be consumed with all that goes with being in the White House. She admitted she'd thought the same thing about him running for governor and that she'd overreacted to that idea; but this was different.

"She didn't say I don't *want* to do this," Mitch told me. "She said I *won't* do this." That was the most dramatic line he said, and it resonated with me.

I responded that every First Lady I'd ever read about, most recently Laura Bush but also Michele Obama, had had the same attitude and opinion when talk of her husband running for president first arose, but each of them had come around. Did he think Cheri might also do so?

He didn't know, but he was willing to see how it might play out when we knew more about other candidates.

Cheri was to be with all the girls at the Greenbrier house the next week, and obviously, this would be a topic of conversation. Mitch said he would try to talk to a couple of the kids himself before that week.

I asked about the possibility of having Laura Bush (in addition to some of us) talk to Cheri at some point. Mitch was fine with that at the appropriate time. He actually thought having George W. Bush himself talk to her first might be the way to go. The fact was, Mitch said, while Cheri loves her country like everyone else, the whole "doing this for the sake of the country" was not going to be a sellable argument.

He said he kidded her about all the good things that would come from being in the White House (I'm assuming he meant Camp David, Air Force One, and so on), but her reaction was that none of the perks made up for all the bad things.

I told him I believed Cheri's refusal to consider a run was double pronged. Clearly she was concerned about the actual campaign—what doing it and living through it would mean. But I was convinced she was also concerned about having to relive the divorce scenario. None of the group believed the divorce was in any way a defining issue, but just the idea of the media rehashing it was a concern for the entire family.[69] However, Mitch didn't think it was the second part that was weighing on her mind. They had been through all that with the governor's campaigns. While the scrutiny would be more intense this time, he didn't think this was the primary issue with her.[70]

I said, "So do we just continue to slog forward and see where this goes?"

He replied, "Yes, continue to march. See how the conversation goes next week. See if we can orchestrate continued conversation with her and others in the next few months."

I ended the conversation by saying that, by our December meeting, I thought we needed to have this settled or close to it.

Later that morning, I sent out an e-mail to our group, and by the end of the day, I talked to each member individually to give everyone the primary points regarding the family, as I didn't want to put these in an e-mail.

The next day, September 21, Cheri called Mark Lubbers and left a long message. She said she'd thought the group was local people only, had been surprised to learn otherwise, and didn't realize it was an "organized" group.

She had known Mark for a long time, and she was very direct. "I've told him I won't do it," she said. "I'll vote for him, but I'm not going to the White House."[71] She ended the message by saying that no one could call and talk her out of her position.

We all took that information with a grain of salt. It just reinforced what we already knew, but we still believed there was an outside chance that time and events could impact her decision.

* * *

As we waited for the November elections, Tom Bell sent Mitch an email in mid-October checking his schedule for a possible return to Augusta to

---

69 Mitch and Cheri divorced in 1994 and remarried in 1997.

70 It should be said that I'm not sure he was correct on this. I believe this had to be more of an issue than he acknowledged, although I received more clarity on this subject later in the process.

71 Lubbers thought that was actually a positive comment.

"commune about the future" following the election. Our thought was, if we could get him back down there for a private, serious discussion on whether or not this could really happen, it would be a good way to focus him.

We didn't necessarily believe we needed to make a "public" announcement yet, but if we were going to continue the residence dinners and set up the testing the waters committee (which meant raising money, among other things), then we needed to know what was in Mitch's head. Additionally, if he gave us an indication he was moving in that direction, there were multiple things to do, particularly on the personnel front. Key players, both staff and volunteer fundraisers, were beginning to commit to others, particularly to Romney. We needed to be able to inform people that Mitch was very seriously considering a run.

Mitch responded to Tom's e-mail by saying: "If this were a mere papal audience, a private stock tip from Warren Buffett, or a date with Jane Seymour, I'd have to say sorry, I'm too busy. But for this, let me scour the schedule. Either way, thanks a million."

Augusta still held its magic; and Mitch hadn't yet lost his sense of humor.

Election Day to December

E lection Day was a huge success, both for Republicans across the country and particularly in Indiana. Both houses went Republican with comfortable margins, and Mitch had his majorities to try one more major reform effort on which they had been working for months. Press speculation on what this might mean for a presidential run began immediately.

A Paul Bedard column read, "Indiana's Mitch Daniels Eyeing 2012 Bid," the first of many such headlines. It went on to chronicle his huge win in the state races and indicated he would be making a final decision "early next year."[72]

The same day, a feature article in the *American Spectator* by James Antle III asked the same questions. It focused on his reputation as a budget cutter, wondering if the American people were "ready for a leader who says less is more?"

The article quoted Mitch as saying, "If government spending prevented pain, we wouldn't have pain. Obama's budget leads to disaster." It went on to say that, according to Mitch, the question is whether we are ready to do something about it.

It concluded by saying, "If Daniels runs for President, he will be asking the American people to do something they have seldom if ever done since Calvin Coolidge: elect a frugal candidate who combines government-cutting with a good-government ethic and doesn't look like a commander

---

72   Paul Bedard, "Indiana's Mitch Daniels Eyeing 2012 Bid," *Washington Whispers*, November 10, 2010.

in chief straight out of central casting. As the bills come due, maybe another Coolidge Republican's time has come."[73]

On November 15, 2010, Pejman Yousefzadeh, writing in the *News Ledger*, penned a long article simply asking, "Why Daniels?"[74]

The whole issue of substance versus style was beginning to receive even more attention. More and more articles were beginning to use the language of "survival issues" and "hard truths" and "adult conversations" when describing what Mitch would bring to a national campaign.

* * *

Since Election Day was now past, many people were asking the question, "When is he going to make a decision?"

Mitch told a press conference the day after the election that he was going to ask any person thinking of running for any office in 2012 to just be quiet about it for the next several months. He was emphasizing the importance of focusing on the upcoming legislative session in order to accomplish some significant reforms with his new state legislative majorities. He was asked if that meant he would not be talking about the presidency until after the legislative session was completed, to which he emphatically answered in the affirmative.

One in our group even suggested we consider a strategy of not competing in Iowa, New Hampshire, South Carolina, and Florida and taking on the role of "presumptive front runner," using the people of the defeated candidates to fuel the finances, among other things. His reasoning being we were going to be behind since Mitch wouldn't publicly commit until after the April legislative session was completed.

Charlie Black quickly shut that down. "I respectfully disagree," he said. "Rudy Giuliani would be president today if that strategy worked. We have plenty of time, even starting in April. The first four events will filter the field down to two serious competitors, and the door is closed after that."

About this time, we also got a request from Matthew Bai at the *New York Times Magazine*, who wanted to do a feature cover story on Mitch and his decision to run or not to run. He made a very detailed proposal and

---

73 James Antle III, "Mitch the Knife," *American Spectator*, November 10, 2010.

74 Pejman Yousefzadeh, "Why Daniels?," *News Ledger*, November 15, 2010.

Mitch asked the opinion of the group on whether or not to do it. Matthew wanted to spend multiple days with Mitch, sit in on meetings, talk to the family, and have wide access to fully explore the reasons for making the decision. He would not publish anything until after the decision was made public.

It was an intriguing proposal but one that carried ample risk. None of us, of course, trusted the *New York Times*, but beyond that, we also were very wary of Matthew discussing a potential candidacy with the family. *We* hadn't even discussed it with the family, primarily because we knew of their intense opposition so far. Having someone from the outside enter into that discussion didn't seem like a smart thing to do. We all counseled against it, and Mitch decided to pass.

About this time, other spontaneous movements to draft Mitch began appearing. In addition to the student efforts, a group called Switch2Mitch went live with a new website, complete with a petition for people to sign, T-shirts, and a message to Mitch: "America and the world need you now more than ever." No one in our group knew any of the people behind this effort.

* * *

It had been determined the group needed an end-of-year meeting with Mitch in December, so we scheduled it for Indianapolis on December 13 to 14, 2010. Once again, Al Hubbard hosted most of us at his home, where we would have dinner the night before an all-day meeting the next day at the residence. This meeting was pivotal in the entire decision-making process, and Mitch had promised he would have a conversation with the entire family over Thanksgiving to give us an up-to-date reading.

From my standpoint, this meeting had to be a "go or no-go" session. As previously stated, we didn't need to make a public statement, but we needed to know privately and internally if we were going to do it. So, given the importance of this meeting and several other defining issues we needed to settle, I arranged a conference call just with Al Hubbard and Tom Bell to discuss both the agenda and my primary concerns.

We held that call on November 12. I had sent out a brief agenda with questions/talking points the day before, so each of us could be prepared to come with some opinions. I said we could, of course, discuss anything that was on their minds, but the primary reasons for the call were to ask them briefly about:

- The family—In your view is there any realistic possibility of convincing Cheri (and secondarily, I suppose, the girls) that running is something Mitch should do? And, if they don't budge, is there any way to do it without their participation and/or support? Do you feel an obligation to be completely honest and candid with Mitch on how ugly we think it could get on the personal side?

- Timing—Do you think he must make a personal decision, or even a private one, by the end of our December meeting? The question is primarily asked relevant to the time and effort needed to convince Cheri. It also pertains to putting in place certain finance infrastructure if not actual fundraising and recruitment of key staff (even if the start date is after May 1). What if Mitch wants to put it off—what do we tell people?

- Nuance—Do you think it is possible (or do you even think it is wise and/or necessary) for him to understand that "running to govern not just to win" is admirable, but you also have to "to win to govern?" That means, occasionally, without altering his fundamental beliefs, can he bring some nuance to how he phrases things and positions himself on key issues?

- Is he thick-skinned enough to do this? Who can be recruited that he will listen to on key decisions?

Those were some of the difficult but important questions we would have to ultimately answer. The three of us basically agreed on most of these issues. We needed a decision, internal not public. We needed nuance from time to time. And we had to determine how to deal with the family and staffing issues.

* * *

I had asked Mitch prior to Election Day if we could get people who had an interest in his candidacy and who had an opinion on whether or not he should do this, to send him e-mails with their points of view. Some might urge him to do it, some might say otherwise, but if we were nearing the point where a private decision needed to be made (which we believed we were), then letting people give him one more dose of their opinions might be helpful. He agreed to let us encourage people to do it.

I drafted a letter, approved by Mitch, for each of us to use in sending to our own personal list and to most attendees at previous residence dinners. It said:

Dear _____

Since we have been in communication over the past nine months regarding Mitch Daniels and his potential interest in 2012, I wanted to give you a personal update. As you must imagine, this is not an easy decision for him to make. There are multiple factors at play both professional and personal that will ultimately factor into his decision.

The past few months his focus has been on Indiana recapturing the State House in Indiana to enable him to pursue an aggressive reform agenda in January. Mitch invested a great deal of time and effort in both recruiting a strong slate of candidates and helping to raise the necessary funds to help them be successful. It paid off with a resounding victory on November 2.

Now that we are past Election Day, Mitch will take some time to seriously consider the various options for 2012. As he has repeatedly stated, this is not something he ever contemplated doing, but the truly spontaneous encouragement he receives daily has indicated to him there is a need and a desire for someone with his experience and expertise to seriously consider the possibility.

It is true the political timetable for making this type of decision has changed somewhat from previous years. It isn't necessary to declare as early in the cycle as some have previously done, but we all realize the importance of at least letting people such as yourself know if he continues to be serious about his consideration.

If you have an opinion on what his decision should be, I would encourage you to let him know sometime in the next month or so.[75] If you are so inclined, please give him the benefit of your advice and counsel—whatever it may be—and let him know what you think.

Many thanks for your continued interest. We face some perilous times as a country and I believe the American people are searching for a leader who can help us chart a new course. If you have an opinion, please take a few minutes and communicate it to Mitch.

The response was genuine, thoughtful, and filled with encouragement from across the country. Some of the respondents said:

"Nothing has happened since we first talked to argue against you making this run—and all the things that have happened reinforce why you should. I know that family is an issue, but what's the greater sacrifice—running and subjecting one's self and family to all that goes with it, or not running and possibly having them live in a country and a world that becomes very problematic in terms of economic and national security?"

"I hope you do decide to make the run and share your considerable talents with the country. I am convinced you can win."

"2012 will be a unique opportunity for the right challenger to the incumbent president. I do not see anyone in office or on the horizon of the Republican Party who is more qualified to be president than you—or who would be a better candidate for President—or who would be more likely to be elected."

"Americans must identify the leader to lift the nation beginning in 2013 in a way not unlike President Reagan had to restore the basic values of our country in 1981. Solid, thoughtful, seasoned and resolute executive leadership will be needed. No one would offer that as well as you, Mitch. Add my voice to the growing chorus that urges you to commit to make the sacrifice. America needs your leadership."

---

[75] I included Mitch's personal e-mail address.

"Just wanted to weigh-in on your possible candidacy. I feel uncomfortable asking anyone to take on a difficult task with low pay and high likelihood of disappointment. Nevertheless, you are by far the best qualified Republican and I will be with you."

"Should you decide to embark on this journey, you will have my full support because I believe you can connect with people. You have the depth and breadth of experience and the even temperament to build a team, and you have a record of effectively governing right of center. I am hopeful you and your family determine your calling is to run in 2012."

"I find myself in the category of wanting the next president to be a person of accomplishment, humility, integrity and intelligence, and the experience to understand how difficult the problems America faces really are. In other words, I am looking for a serious person with serious ideas to do a very serious job—and one who loves the country that calls him. It seems to me you fit that bill."

"It will be the first time for me to vote for a Republican for president, but I can tell you that I'd be proud to sit at the family (all Democrats) dinner table next time I'm back home and tell them I'm supporting you with my time and money in a run for the White House."

There were many other messages, and Mitch answered each and every one personally. I believe they had some impact on his own internal decision, one we would hear in December.

* * *

On November 20, 2010, Peggy Noonan published her column in the *Wall Street Journal* entitled: "To Run or Not to Run, That is the Question." I couldn't believe it. It was as if she had been sitting in our meetings listening to all our own questions and concerns.

The subtitle said, "It's only Thanksgiving 2010, but some GOP politicians must decide if they want a shot at the presidency."

I suggested to Mitch he make a copy of the entire article and give it to each family member at Thanksgiving to get the conversation started, which he said he would do.

Among other things, Peggy Noonan wrote, "A lot of potential candidates will decide if they are definitely going to run between now and New Year's—and some of them will be deciding over Thanksgiving weekend. It's all happening now, they're deciding in long walks, at the dinner table, and while watching the football game on the couch. They'll be talking it through, sometimes for the first time and sometimes the tenth. 'Can we do this, are we in this together?'"

In the brilliant and articulate manner for which she was known, Peggy captured the essence of the issue facing Mitch and his family. She noted how hard these conversations could be—not just about the disruptive and often ugly aspects of a campaign, but also about the position itself. She particularly pointed out the burden on the spouse, with adulation one week and derision the next. The whole idea of no privacy, complete intrusion into daily life, your personal life wide open for all to see—she said all the things that Cheri and the family were pondering.

The article concluded with a statement about history that I wanted to underline for Mitch. It simply reiterated the fact that it was disingenuous for a person who knew in his or her heart a run wasn't going to happen to play with this decision or fake it or try to prolong it. That was an issue that constantly challenged each of us in the group, and certainly it was on Mitch's mind daily.

* * *

On November 22, right before Thanksgiving, I sent Mitch my own message. I said since I asked others to send their final thoughts on his momentous decision that I shouldn't neglect my own responsibility to do the same.

I told him I had been rereading the Peggy Noonan column. I remarked that I thought it contained some remarkable insights and thoughtful observations about making this difficult decision, and I listed all the parts I had underlined.

I then concluded by saying:

> Every day I think about this decision you must ultimately make yourself. Right or wrong, I feel some obligation to you personally since we started this just a little over a year

ago, to be completely honest and forthright about what this decision means.

To the country, I think Peggy Noonan has it right. We must have a candidate who has the intellectual heft, the experience that indicates he or she knows how to get the job done, the credibility of a proven leader, the ability to persuade the center. Notice she didn't say they had to be six feet tall with Hollywood looks—people want a real person with real convictions and real solutions to real problems. That definition is the personification of Mitch Daniels.

To the contributors and potential key staff, I also think she has it right. They want to play, for whatever reasons— some personal, some ego-driven, some truly patriotic—and they will only wait so long.

To the family, she was the most articulate. She said, "… but they have to agree to enter Big History, or a candidate can't go." Herein lies the greatest dilemma. Others in our group, for whom I have the greatest respect, have persuaded me that a candidate's spouse and family don't have to do anything at all during the campaign. I'm still not as convinced as they are, but I see the possibility of that working. However I don't think it at all removes the "ugliness" of the process that will still occur. The event of twenty years ago will still be talked about and blogged about and while it may have no impact as an "issue" (which I don't think it will), it will be uncomfortable and even demeaning depending on how nasty the opposition in conjunction with the news media wants to make it. I think we owe it to you and the family to make certain you understand that reality.

I have to admit when we first had our conversation followed by our time in Augusta, I didn't have a complete idea of all the ramifications of a decision to do this. I've read multiple books and talked to numerous people over the past twelve months, and I believe I have a better idea of what a sacrifice this is to the person and the family that decides to say "go."

I also believe I have a reasonable view of the direction in which our country is headed and the fundamental difference between our view of America and that of the opposition. It is concern for our children's children that keeps me from just saying—don't worry about it, let someone else do it, maybe it will turn out satisfactorily. We're at a crossroads—do I believe you can be that leader to make a difference in the future of our country—yes, I do. Do I understand what a sacrifice that is for both you and the family, even if they don't supposedly participate— yes, I think I do. Do I have an answer for you—no, I guess I don't. Because I can make a case for both answers, and whatever you decide, I'm there to do whatever I can to help.

Have a Happy Thanksgiving—should be a memorable one.

* * *

Post-Thanksgiving Call with Mitch

The Monday following Thanksgiving, I had a lengthy telephone conversation with Mitch to see how the weekend went with the family. He said he gave each a copy of Peggy Noonan's column, and the bottom line was "nothing has changed" in terms of their opposition.

He went on to say, "My temperature hasn't changed much either, but nothing has changed in terms of my feeling no one out there is catching on and the country continues down the wrong path. Everyone seems to be pushing back their decision—Mitt, Newt, Haley, etc. What is the drop dead date by which we have to decide; can't we push it back further?"

I responded yes, Mitt and the others have said that, but don't think for a minute they aren't busy doing a multitude of activities. He acknowledged this was true.

"How do you set up a plan that is a total contingency plan?" he asked. "I don't think it is totally impossible, is it? Can we talk to some people in Iowa and other places and ask them—what is their absolute drop dead date?"

He totally bought into the Peggy Noonan article on the need for Conservatives to embrace the center to win. He said, "I'm going to CPAC and say, 'Some of you won't like what I'm going to say, but I need to say it anyway—you have to like the middle'!"[76]

I asked him, "Does any of this matter in the end in terms of the impact on the family? If we put off the decision, can we ask George W. Bush, for instance, to invite you and Cheri to Crawford for a talk?"

He responded, "It might be better to have friends talk to Cheri."

I didn't necessarily agree with that. I had always thought it would be easier for her to say no to us than to the former president.

We agreed to make the December meeting more focused on timing issues rather than nuts-and-bolts tactics. We had to answer some key questions. What is the drop-dead date? How does it impact our ability to attract key staff and prominent volunteer fundraisers? How do we position ourselves both publicly and privately in meetings and dinners?

Our goal was to focus on what had to be done in the coming six months, regardless of the ultimate outcome. We were fast approaching the time when the hardest decision had to be made.

---

[76] I remarked that perhaps we could articulate that a bit differently.

December Strategy Meeting

As we approached the December meeting, we attempted to search out various opinions on the issue of a "drop-dead" date for making a decision. Specifically, as per Mitch's request, we talked to some knowledgeable people regarding Iowa.

One veteran political consultant in Iowa, who wanted Mitch to run, said in his opinion Mitch could wait until May to formally announce. But he needed to talk to key people earlier. He said he needed to raise money that could be spent in June and actually be on the air prior to the August straw poll. In his view, Mitch needed to finish in the top three, but it wasn't necessary to win. He also believed he could "nuance" the social truce issue and be accepted. He expressed the view that 80 percent will vote for who they think can win it all; the remaining 20 percent of true believers will vote for their candidate regardless of his or her potential to win.

A slightly different view came from another Iowa insider and veteran of many presidential campaigns in that state. He said the heavy hitters were already signing up, and he was concerned about "waiting until April" when the Indiana legislative session was completed for Mitch to announce his decision. He didn't say Mitch had to do anything personally, but he believed he needed to let other people, his people, start the process. This meant writing a plan, lining up key people, and getting offices ready to establish. He believed Mitch had the right story to tell but needed time to tell it in order to be successful.

From a Democrat with ample experience in Iowa came the suggestion that Mitch should do what John Kerry did in 2004. He came in late, spent a lot of money, and proved he was a more winnable candidate than Howard Dean, who everyone originally thought would win the state.

Another experienced Iowa person said you couldn't ignore Iowa by not personally campaigning or skipping debates; that strategy had hurt Reagan quite a bit. She suggested Mitch didn't need to go in early, explaining that overexposure hurt people like Howard Dean in the past. She believed Mitch should use the RV and the Harley, in addition to social media and advertising dollars to make up for a late start.

* * *

Prior to our meeting, Al Hubbard had been in consultation with Travis Thomas regarding fundraising and provided us with a lengthy memo. The objective was to take the necessary steps in January to ensure that Mitch was in the best possible position if he decided to run in April.[77]

We had the same type of memo on the initial effort at opposition research on Mitch himself: Reagan years, Bush years, tenure as governor, but nothing yet on the personal issues.

The social media strategy was also presented in a brief memo for testing and utilization during the legislative session in Indiana. The two primary areas of focus were on the education reform initiative and the automatic tax refund proposal. Jeff Hunt was putting together, pro bono, a strategic plan complete with specific objectives, metrics, timeline, and costs for discussion at the December meeting.

We had a final memo from Cleta Mitchell on the various alternatives for commencement of Federal candidacy relative to FEC regulations.

All of this was folded into a draft agenda for the December meeting that was then circulated for comment and any additions or suggestions. After several discussions with various members of the group and a telephone conversation with Mitch, I offered that we needed to alter our approach slightly with more focus on timing and the decision. It was possible our discussion at dinner Monday night would dictate somewhat how we would proceed on Tuesday, but I said we would remain as flexible as possible.

---

[77] At the time we were still under the impression a decision would be made in April 2011.

* * *

Dinner on Monday, December 13, 2010, was held at the governor's residence. The agenda included:

Current Political Environment/Other Candidates—
Led by Charlie Black

Current Thinking/Family—Mitch

Two major areas of discussion:

1. Timing—What is the absolute "drop-dead" date for a decision (private decision on yes or no to a campaign)?
   - Impact on fundraising
   - Impact on fundraisers
   - Impact on key professional staff
   - Impact on key volunteer leadership in five key early states
   - Determination on what, if any, committee to form
   - Personal calls to key people in all those categories above—who, when, and by whom

2. Positioning
   - Conservative/Center
   - Issue positions and how to communicate them
   - Survey research—needed or not?
   - Overall strategic messaging—Why Mitch Daniels?

The December 14, Tuesday morning meeting was also held at the residence and was generally devoted to more nuts-and-bolts issues. The meeting lasted through lunch to nearly two thirty when people had to leave. We had very good discussions on each major topic.

The testing the waters committee was the unanimous selection of the way to go, and I was going to prepare the appropriate materials and memos for Mitch to see and sign off on in terms of the way it would work.

We sorted through some sticky issues in terms of policy and made some key points on nuance and the importance of positioning. I reminded him of what former Democrat Governor Mario Cuomo of New York once said: "You campaign in poetry and you govern in prose." In other words, we all agree on the "running to govern not just to win" approach, but that doesn't negate the need for nuance once in a while.

We agreed to move ahead on social media strategy, but it was clear Mitch was only agreeable because everyone else was adamant it was important. I could tell he still wasn't completely sold on it. I was certain when the time came to spend some serious money, it would be another debate.

We went through all the media requests and punted on most of them for later discussion. The most important one coming up was the CPAC speech, and Mitch was going to write the first draft as usual and give us a chance to provide comments.

There were no major issues regarding the schedule, other than the reality of Mitch having to be in Indiana until the session ended, primarily to ensure that he won his major reform battles. Several of us thought he should accept the many offers he was receiving to visit Iowa and New Hampshire in particular, but he remained resistant.

Our major personnel issues were Travis Thomas as finance director and trying to keep him on hold and someone to handle press and communications. Mitch was interested in a person who worked for him at OMB, Trent Duffy, for the communications position. Mitch agreed to call Trent to ascertain interest and availability. We talked about campaign manager prospects and reviewed some names. What we really wanted was a CEO to manage all the various aspects of a complicated operation.

On the fundraising side, Charlie said we needed a minimum of $30 million to get us through February 2012 and then needed a total minimum of $40 to 50 million to be competitive. He reminded us of the limits. To put it in perspective, we needed twelve thousand individuals at the maximum amount just to get us to the first $30 million. Internet fundraising could be a big boost, but it couldn't be done overnight, and the best people available who knew how to do this were being besieged by other candidates. Charlie reminded us none of this could be done without staff, seed money, and Mitch personally involved. As Travis Thomas had said to us in a memo, once you start fundraising, you have to jump in with both feet because the media will carefully monitor and handicap your chance solely on your bank account, fair or not.

We spent a good deal of time on the importance of setting a deadline for making a decision. We were losing key people, and as someone said, many key influencers—including the Bush inner circle, key media such as George Will, and other major political pundits who had influence—were now saying Mitch wasn't going to run. His indecision was also seen as proof he didn't have fire in the belly.

We talked about January 15, 2011, as being a drop-dead date for at least a personal decision, a date that would come and go as many others. The idea was to make the decision internally, complete the appropriate calls, wait until after the CPAC speech, and file whatever needed to be filed[78] in February.

We then made a list of pros and cons (in terms of running or not) with everyone expressing opinions.[79] The list read:

Pros
- The issue of the day is ours—fiscal responsibility—been there, done that—it is Mitch's unique differentiation
- Ability to attract young people and get them back like Reagan did in 1980
- Competence
- Intelligence
- Ability to connect with the common person
- Sense of humor
- Political instincts
- Business background/experience
- Bush Administration experience (also a negative)

[78] Which we later discovered was nothing if we went the testing the waters route
[79] I think we may have done this when Mitch was not in the room.

Cons

- Obama will get stronger; will be hard to beat
- Social truce cuts both ways; more of a negative in the primary
- Tax increases must be nuanced
- Energy tax; import fee
- Indecision
- Family
- Staff (lack thereof)
- Thin skin
- Bush Administration (also a positive)

* * *

Toward the end of the meeting, Tom Bell asked the key question of Mitch, "So where are you and what are we going to do?"

As previously indicated, to everyone's stunned surprise, the answer Mitch gave was, "Well, I'm at about 80 percent." He went on to say he still had the same reservations about the brutal nature of the campaign, getting through the legislative session with success, and finding time to do all the things that needed to be done. However, he was convinced it wasn't too late and he didn't see anyone else capturing the imagination of the electorate.

He did say the family was still an issue. Someone suggested perhaps one of us could talk with Cheri and let her know that serious momentum was building, that it wasn't just Mitch wanting to do this. Mitch made the comment that I was staying the night, and he, Cheri, and I were having dinner together. It was suggested I be the one to talk with her—that night. Of course, everyone but me thought it a brilliant idea, and that is how the meeting ended.

* * *

As we were breaking up, Mitch asked me to stay behind and meet him in the study. I went downstairs and he closed the door. He said he hadn't wanted to say all of this in front of everyone because the meeting had gone so well and everyone was so enthusiastic, but he believed the family was a serious obstacle, more serious than we had even thought.

We'd all left that meeting thinking this really might be happening. To now hear him give me this message made me sick to my stomach. I asked him what he thought were the best arguments to try to use with her, and he honestly didn't know. I don't think he had ever sat with Cheri or the girls and said, "Look, people really want me to do this and think I *can* do this and think I *should* do this. I now want to try to do this. Won't you let me give it a try?" I don't think that conversation ever took place, so it was up to me to see if I couldn't get that across to Cheri that evening.

After thinking about it for a few minutes, I told Mitch I thought it would be much better if I had this conversation with her by myself before dinner. I said I could say things that couldn't be said if he was sitting right there, and she could do the same. If we really wanted a candid, heart-to-heart conversation to try to bring this to a head, and I think everyone thought that is what we needed, then that was the best way to do it. He agreed, and the only other thing he said was, "I don't want you to make her feel bad about her position; just make sure she understands the family will be the priority in my final decision."

I then called Cheri to ask if she would meet me at the residence for a drink before we met Mitch for dinner, and she agreed to do it. An hour later, Mitch called me at Hubbard's house where I was staying. He told me Cheri had called him to say that I had called her and wanted to have a drink, but "I am not going to talk to him about this!" He just wanted to warn me. That gave me a great deal of confidence!

Tom Bell sent me an e-mail that afternoon (he had returned to Atlanta) saying, "Nice job on the meeting. I think he's there, now just need to move the family. Good luck tonight. I've said a prayer for you. Remind her sometimes God sets our path, we just follow. I honestly think this is one of those times."

I spent the rest of the afternoon literally writing out what and how I was going to communicate our message. I reviewed it with Hubbard and actually practiced my spiel several times as I was working out in the Hubbard gym. At 5:00 p.m., I went back over to the residence. Cheri and I had a drink in front of the fireplace in the living room, just the two of us. Two hours later, already late to meet Mitch for dinner, we finished and left for downtown with the state trooper who was Cheri's driver and security.

* * *

The Conversation with Cheri

This is how the conversation unfolded with Cheri and what I told Mitch the next day. It is pretty much verbatim.

I started by saying, "I know you don't want to talk about it, but let me tell you a story. You don't have to talk or comment. Just let me tell my story and give you my perspective, some of which may surprise you."

To this she said, "Of course, I'll talk to you about it and listen to what you have to say."

So I told her how it had started, with the article by Kimberley Strassel in the Saturday *Wall Street Journal* in September 2009 and the subsequent calls I received from friends asking if I had seen it and wondering whether or not Mitch would ever consider a run for the presidency. Then came my call to him and, finally, our agreement to meet and just talk about it.

I told her of Mitch's insistence from the beginning that a presidential candidacy for him was completely unrealistic, the dumbest idea he had ever heard, never something he had ever contemplated. And I told her how, as time went on, his willingness to at least listen and hear what people had to say and to continue to meet others to get their opinions had increased.

I told her about the unexpected avalanche of support that followed. I emphasized the spontaneous nature of it, comparing it to the Tea Party, and how 99 percent came from outside Indiana. This outpouring of support came from old friends and acquaintances but also from big names, from prominent journalists to governors to CEOs in nearly every region of the country.

I said I thought three reasons were motivating the movement toward her husband:

1. People were scared. The politics and practices of Barack Obama had people convinced he was trying to change the very fabric of this country. If he was given eight years, it might take a generation

or two to ever change it back. We considered it a fight for the soul of our country and for the future of our kids and grandkids.

2. The primary issue for the country was the need for fiscal discipline—getting spending under control and stopping the intrusion of government into our daily life. That was Mitch's issue. He had been there, done that, and had the experience and record of achievement as governor that proved he could do what needed to be done.

3. Mitch was the only one who could win. Every other candidate was flawed in a major way. No one owned the issue of the day like Mitch. If the issue had been foreign affairs or energy dependence or some other area, maybe the uniqueness and differentiation would not have been so apparent, but *the* issue was Mitch's issue.

I told her that, as we talked to people, more and more asked, can we get him to do it? Most knew of the family's reluctance. Almost to a person, each said we completely understand. It is a sacrifice, a burden, and an ugly and sometimes awful process. When asked what his wife thought, we'd say, she doesn't want him to do it. The response was always, what a smart lady!

I told her that, as time went on, I had become persuaded (which I wasn't in the beginning) that, in this day and age, one could actually do things differently. One could do this and let the family basically stay home if that was what they wanted to do. However, certain threshold events had to be attended—the announcement event, the first primary win, and other significant milestones. It was important to say to the press that the family supported Mitch in this endeavor, even though each person had her own life to live and would not be on the campaign trail.

I told her I knew the stories and certain speculations wouldn't stop just because the family was not around. Charlie Black, who had been through this multiple times, most recently with the McCains, said the divorce issue could be handled. One story, one day, and from then on it would be deflected.

I told her about my e-mails, the Yale students, and the message I'd sent to Mitch myself last week. I thought the time was right for Mitch to make this run, and for the first time, we really thought he could win. The country needed him to win, but I knew a candidacy had the potential to have its ugly moments. I hoped he would say yes, but I would understand if he said no.

I said I thought he had come a long way in seeing himself as a president, that it might really be possible. But he had stressed to me that very afternoon that the family was the priority and would come first.

The rest of the conversation became very personal and isn't one that I believe can be shared. But the bottom line was that Cheri and the children were opposed. She believed Mitch would make a great president and understood why people wanted him to do it. But it was a life-changing episode, not just for him but for the entire family. A presidential campaign brought security issues and privacy concerns, not just for a few years but for the rest of their lives. Personal freedom of movement and security just wasn't something the family was willing to sacrifice, understandable when you step back and try to be objective and walk in their shoes.

By the time we ended the conversation, we were already late to meet Mitch. The conversation was very friendly; Cheri apologized to me because she knew her refusal wasn't what I wanted to hear. But she made her stance crystal clear from beginning to end—there was no wiggle room, not an inch.

* * *

We went to dinner, and not another word about 2012 was discussed the entire evening. We had several more months to go, halfway into 2011, before a final decision was made and then made public. But, in my heart of hearts, I knew we were done. I knew that, in the end, Mitch would be true to his word to me. He had stated more than once, "If the family says no, I won't do it."

The rest of the group was not convinced. I think a majority, if not all of them, expected his announcement six months later to be yes. But they hadn't seen or heard the absolute resolve in Cheri's face and voice that I had seen and heard that evening in the residence in front of the fireplace.

I had always believed the reliving of the divorce was the main impediment to getting her to agree to a national campaign. I do believe it played a larger role than even Mitch believed; particularly, I think that was true of the girls. They just didn't want to see their mother deal with the episode again. Nor did they want to relive it. And that was perfectly understandable. However, I also came away from our conversation with the feeling that Cheri's attitude about life being changed forever was equally as important. She really didn't like the fishbowl, and she honestly and truly didn't want to live the rest of her life as the First Lady. That intensity of feeling was real and, again, understandable.

The next morning, I left for the airport very early to return to Arizona, and Mitch was not available to connect with me until that afternoon. I told him up front that I would give him the entire story. When we finally connected, I could tell he blanched at a few things, but he listened until the very end. To me, he sounded resigned to the reality of the situation. I asked him what he wanted to do, and he said, "Let's keep this between us for now." I told him the group was expecting me to call and give some type of report. We agreed I would do so, just hitting the high points with as little specificity as possible.

He basically wanted to keep with the schedule we had discussed at the meeting. We had agreed the testing the waters committee wouldn't be formed until mid-February, and certain things (including that) could be put off even further, using the legislative session as the reason to not make any announcements one way or the other.

I think Mitch was concerned about disrupting the major reform initiatives he wanted to accomplish during the session, and once you make a final announcement, you're no longer on the circuit. He had the book coming out, and that was also a concern, not a major concern by any measure but a factor in the timing of all of these various considerations.

And, as I had said to Al and Tom in particular, "He doesn't want to say no." I had no doubt in my mind that, in the end, he would say no. But I could tell he really didn't want to say no. I believe he knew he could do the job, he felt as if he had a solid chance of winning, and his commitment to public service was real. He just didn't want to say no until he absolutely had to do so.

He was going to have one more follow-up conversation with Cheri following our meeting. On Monday, December 20, knowing he was going to talk with her the day before, I e-mailed him. "Just checking to see if lightning struck on Sunday and a miracle occurred?"

He responded almost immediately, "It may be the season of miracles but not that one. Sorry."

* * *

As we moved toward the end of 2010, the group continued to follow the timeline we discussed at our December meeting. Bob Perkins sent an e-mail suggesting we tell people we were going to set up an exploratory committee after the CPAC speech, a move that was premature in Mitch's opinion and mine. We needed to slow the momentum without giving away too much of our position until we were ready.

Press speculation continued to run rampant. In a *Hill's Pundits Blog* on December 16, 2010, Brent Budowsky said, "We have seen enough of the Republican debates to render a verdict—the big winner is President Obama, because not one of the GOP candidates can both appeal to a majority of Republicans and be seen by the general electorate as credible. The second winner is Gov. Mitch Daniels of Indiana, who may still be called to duty in the Republican campaign."

Brent concluded by saying, "If Newt does not self-destruct soon, and he may, watch for the eyes of the nation to turn to Indiana with a Draft Mitch Daniels movement getting serious."[80]

On a special Christmas Eve Fox News *Special Report*, panelists Stephen Hayes and Charles Krauthammer both singled out Mitch as a man to watch. Hayes identified the Indiana governor as "perhaps the true Tea Party candidate—someone willing to speak the hard truths about the need for entitlement reform."

Krauthammer counterintuitively found "Daniels' lack of charisma appealing—as an antidote to our overdose of hope-and-change."[81]

Mitch himself gave several end-of-year interviews with both local papers and a few Washington pundits. *The Hill* ran an article on December 21, 2010, that quoted him saying he would examine other potential 2012 presidential candidates' stances on the ever-expanding national debt when deciding whether or not to enter the field. He said he would decide in April whether or not to run.

---

[80]   Brent Budowsky, *Hill's Pundits Blog*, December 16, 2010.

[81]   Charles Krauthammer, *Fox News Special Report*, December 24, 2010.

Deanna Martin of the Associated Press quoted Mitch as saying, "Running for president would be much different than running for governor. That would involve leaving a state I lived in and planned to die in. It would involve dramatically greater sacrifice by my family."[82]

In a New Year's Eve interview with a local Fox television affiliate, Fox 59 News, Mitch reviewed the year in Indiana as a very successful one, particularly compared to that of the rest of the country. He said, "We were a leader in the growth of private sector jobs, but the problem is the national economy is still pathetically weak."

The news interviewer asked, "Is running for president the answer?"

Mitch replied, "We Presbyterians are inclined to think that what will be will be. There's a plan there somewhere, so we'll find out in due time."

---

[82] Deanna Martin, Associated Press, "Daniels: Presidential Hopefuls Must Address Debt," *Chicago Tribune*, December 26, 2010.

PART III
2011

The Year of Decision

Notwithstanding all the activity and new revelations coming out of December, Mitch started the new year, in the minds of most people, as one of the most serious potential candidates on the Republican side. If anything, the momentum continued to pick up speed.

One of the first stories of 2011 came from CNN, talking about Oval Office ambitions and interviewing Mitch about his current stance. CNN called him "a dark-horse favorite among many beltway insiders who believe his economic conservatism and no-nonsense personality might jibe perfectly with the broader mood of the electorate."

The story said Daniels stopped short of denying he is eyeing a presidential bid and said, "He's not happy with the national media's caricature of him as a 'cerebral and boring' politician. 'It's as if they think you couldn't be smart and funny at the same time,' Daniels said."

It went on to say, "In perhaps his biggest hint yet he is serious about a presidential bid, Daniels said his biggest concern when it comes to 2012 is how a campaign may impact his wife and four grown daughters. 'It scares them to death,' he said. 'And it should.'"[83]

In a GOP Insiders Poll, a new ranking was published that ranked the top five candidates, one through five, in terms of who was most likely to capture the 2012 Republican presidential nomination. The person with the greatest change in percentage points from 2010 was Mitch Daniels, nearly twice the increase of anyone else, and now second only to Mitt Romney.

You could also tell momentum was building for Mitch with the

---

[83] Alexander Mooney, "Daniels: Family Scared to Death about 2012 Run," CNN, January 3, 2011.

increasingly critical columns in the *New York Times* and other outlets trying to bring up negative stories.

Columnist David Leonhardt, in a *New York Times* column, attempted to make the case his record as a fiscal conservative had at least two blemishes. Both were old stories, his tenure at OMB and his criticism of Obama's stimulus bill and its impact on Indiana.[84]

We actually welcomed the fact the media were going after him on fiscal discipline issues because we knew that was never going to be a winner. However, it did raise some concerns over the timeliness of our response to such stories.

We also had the first communication on the very old story of Mitch's marijuana drug bust in college. In fact, notice of the impending story came from one of his classmates who was involved in the bust with him. He said someone named Ryan with *Talking Points Memo.com* wanted to ask some questions about the "incident" and contacted him. Apparently, the reporter acknowledged it was an old story, many times vetted and not a major story today. However, he said he was investigating a different angle and wanted to discuss it.

Mitch's classmate went to TPM's website; saw it was an outlet for, in his words, "the leftist liberal BS"; and ignored the call, but wanted to give us a heads-up. This was one story we truly didn't worry about. It was the oldest of news, in addition to the fact nobody really cared. Mitch had a great answer for it that he had given before, "It was a lesson; I was fined for an accurate offense, and I learned from it." End of story.

We also started noticing more and more commentary or remarks concerning Cheri and the divorce. In multiple articles, the subject was beginning to be mentioned. In some cases, the articles suggested that she and Mitch would have to answer some questions everyone still had about the episode. Mitch's comment was always, "If you like happy endings, you'll like our story," and that had apparently got them through two gubernatorial campaigns. We had concern about this story, even though it was old news. It wasn't the substance of the story that concerned us so much. As Mitch said, it had a happy ending. But we knew it wasn't something Cheri and the girls wanted to relive.

---

84   David Leonhardt, "Mitch Daniel's Fiscal Blemishes," *New York Times*, January 4, 2011.

Pundits continued to say Mitch was the odds-on favorite for the Republican presidential nomination in 2012. Jonathan Martin, writing in *Politico*, said, "The Indiana governor has been showered with favorable coverage from political thinkers and analysts in recent months, most of which heaped praise on his thoughtful and principled approach to governing while celebrating his serious yet down-to-earth mien. As David Broder, highly respected Washington political reporter wrote last fall—'his record of accomplishment is dazzling.'"

Martin also quoted *National Review* editor, Rich Lowry saying, "He's a Reaganite who is not trapped in 1980's nostalgia."[85]

* * *

One of the items coming out of the December strategy meeting was to think about who could be the chief communications person, someone to handle the national press both with strategy and tactics. We had discussed "famous names," such as Brit Hume, former high-level presidential staff like Dale Petrowsky (at the time with Major League Baseball), and a host of other lesser known but experienced people. As previously mentioned, Mitch had Trent Duffy, his press person at OMB in mind. Trent had also held a position in the White House press office of George W. Bush. After the December meeting, Mitch called him and asked whether he would be willing to help, to which he gave a strong affirmative answer.

Al Hubbard also knew Trent from his time in the White House and was a strong proponent. At the beginning of the year, Trent sent Al a memo with some initial thoughts on communication "to-dos" including ideas on how to announce the formation of the exploratory committee. He listed what he referred to as "strategic questions" for which Mitch needed to be prepared.

Mitch had great confidence in Trent, and he'd had a previous personal relationship with him at OMB, all very important in this particular position. Trent's initial comments and suggestions were quite valid and would become more so once he knew more about what had been done and what we planned to do.

---

[85] Jonathan Martin, "Mitch Daniels: Heartthrob of the Elites," *Politico*, January 22, 2011.

* * *

In early January 2011, I was still operating under the illusion that Mitch would now want to make a public decision based on all that had transpired in December. I called Charlie Black on January 5 to get his point of view on what type of announcement should be made and the strategy and logistics of such an announcement.

Charlie believed Mitch owed it to people who were supporting him, or agreeing to be neutral, to tell them he had made a decision and it was a no-go. He suggested doing an interview with *Politico* as the starting point, backed up with a formal statement released to the general press.

He suggested the message could include multiple points—his last TV commercial, when he'd said the governor's campaign would be his last; Indiana priorities must come first; too late to be competitive since he had raised no money; no campaign staff; no travel to any of the early primary states; had a message of tough medicine he wasn't certain people would accept. Therefore, he and his family had decided not to go.

Charlie believed he shouldn't blame anything on his wife or family. He also said he needed to be prepared to answer the question, who will you support? This was particularly relevant as it related to Haley Barbour (Haley had not yet announced his decision not to run). He said Mitch needed to decide whether or not he would go to Romney with the survival agenda and urge him to embrace it. In fact, Charlie believed a memo to all the candidates with that message should be considered.

And he said Mitch needed to have an answer to the question of whether or not he would accept the vice presidential nomination (Charlie advised he should indicate no).

The most pressing time issue was the CPAC speech. It was fast approaching, and we wondered if such an announcement as Charlie outlined should come before, after, or during that speech. Charlie asked whether or not Mitch wanted that speech to be about his message, his survival agenda, or about the fact he wasn't going to run if he announced it before the speech.

The decision was made not to announce anything before the speech, but perhaps right after might be the appropriate time.

January was also the beginning of people starting to pull away. Phil

Handy, a close friend of Al Hubbard and an attendee at a residence dinner, called to say he and a small group in which he was involved were being pushed hard by Pawlenty to make a decision and come aboard. He said they wanted to have important roles in the campaign and feared, if they did not get on board now with Pawlenty, the future opportunities for participation would be limited. Each of them preferred Mitch, but they didn't feel they could wait unless they knew Mitch was going to do it.

Al answered them by saying Mitch would be making a personal decision by late February and a public decision by late April. While wanting them to be a part of the campaign if Mitch ran, he certainly understood why they would have to go with Pawlenty if they had to make a decision now. He sent an e-mail to Mitch asking if this was the correct answer, and Mitch said yes.

January was also the State of the Union speech by Obama, and Mitch's State of the State speech in Indianapolis. Dennis Thomas watched both, Obama's live and a tape of Mitch. He sent a long e-mail message to Mitch the next day with some very personal, cogent remarks. Among other things, he said:

> I am not an Obama hater. But [after listening to his State of the Union] I believe he is leading the country in absolutely the wrong direction. And wrong not on the margin, but in a way that suggests the results of his approach and initiatives will be catastrophic.
>
> As to your remarks [in the State of the State] I feel and think it will be a real tragedy if you do not run for president. What I heard you describe is an approach that can begin to turn the country around. And shared in a way that people can believe and understand and embrace.

Mitch sent back a note thanking him for his thoughtful and touching message, saying, "If the family lights do not turn green, rely on my doing whatever I can to be of use in trying to help in other ways."

Dennis said to me later, "A nice response. I genuinely understand, but it breaks my heart. Someone who is willing to put his family first is precisely the person who should be president."

Two Major Events

Two major "events" in the first quarter of 2011 simply would not let this movement die.

The first we had already been working on, Mitch's speech before the annual CPAC conference in Washington that was to take place on February 11, 2011. Mitch had turned down this opportunity last year, but this year was the time to do it—to test out the survival agenda and to see what kind of response he would receive given his social truce idea that was an enigma with many in this audience. George Will was to introduce him in the prime speaking spot, the Friday night dinner known as the Reagan Address. Cleta Mitchell and David Keene, both friends and supporters, were on the dais with him as leaders of this conference. The conference was to be televised in its entirety.

The second event was unexpected. In January, we learned Mitch had been invited to be the Republican speaker at the annual Gridiron Dinner in Washington, DC, in March. This was the signature event of the nation's most prominent journalists. Each year, the dinner included three speakers—a Republican, a Democrat, and the president of the United States. For the first two years, Obama had stiffed them, but he was expected to be there in March.

Mitch sent out an e-mail to the group asking our opinion on whether or not to accept. As he said, Gridirons are much more downside than up. Speakers are expected to be funny. If they're not, which was often the case, they are pummeled by the press the next day. It's all about the quality of the material, inside DC baseball, and the comedic delivery of it. Mitch wondered if we knew the right people, various comedy writers for instance, who could help put this together and whether we thought he should do it.

Our response was, do it! We knew Mitch could actually be hilarious, but most of the press, therefore the world, knew him only as a serious, policy-oriented "wonky personality." We kicked around several names of people who had helped previous speakers prepare their remarks.

CPAC Speech, February 11, 2011

Perhaps more than any other singular event during the entire presidential decision making process, the CPAC event woke up a good portion of the nation that cared about presidential politics. It delayed the ultimate decision and thrust Mitch into the spotlight even more as a serious potential candidate for president.

In January, Mitch sent several of us his first draft of the speech he was preparing for CPAC. He had, of course, written every word himself, and it was comprehensive, and frankly, in the words of Al Hubbard, "fabulous in every respect."

Each of us had suggestions on some wording and a few ideas to ensure no misinterpretation of his meaning. I suggested using some references to Ronald Reagan (given the nature of the audience) and sent him several quotes from Craig Shirley's book that came from actual Reagan speeches to previous CPAC dinners. Al Hubbard had a few content related comments that brought greater clarity to what Mitch was trying to say.

All were well received by Mitch, and we thought he had a very strong message and were anxious to see how the audience would react.

On February 7, a week before the CPAC speech, I received a call from Mitch that I later reported to our group with an e-mail message. It said:

> Just got a call from Mitch, March 1 is the new deadline for decision. His rationale is simply that no one appears to be gaining any traction (true, I think), most everyone else is putting off their decision, and therefore, we have the luxury of waiting to make a final decision. He is seriously considering it, moving more and more towards saying yes,

but the family remains the issue. Will giving it more time enable him to turn them around? That's the question.

He has the major C-PAC speech this Friday and wants to judge the reaction to what he will say. I've seen the speech and think it is quite good, blunt and straightforward on what has to be done to save the country. It will be interesting to gauge the reactions. Additionally, a major profile piece is coming out in the *Wall Street Journal* by a writer who followed him around for a couple of days.

I believe he is correct that people (fundraisers, key volunteers in key states, other influencers) see no one is making any serious headway and therefore are more willing to wait and see. However, as I told him, don't think for a minute these other potential candidates aren't out there working hard doing things to get ready, which we aren't doing. We're going to talk again after the Friday speech and subsequent press coverage.

On Friday, February 11, George Will introduced Mitch, "the Harley-riding governor" as "the thinking man's Marlon Brando."

As chronicled by George Will in his column the next day in the *Washington Post* on February 17, 2011, "At first, the banquet audience at the 38th annual Conservative Political Action Conference (C-PAC) paid Mitch Daniels, Indiana's Republican Governor, the conventional compliment of frequently, almost reflexively, interrupting his address with applause. But as they realized they were hearing something unconventional—that they were being paid the rare compliment of being addressed as reflective adults—they reciprocated his respect with quiet attention to his elegant presentation of conservatism for grown-ups."[86]

The speech was a home run, perhaps a grand slam.

I immediately sent an e-mail. "Mitch, just watched the speech—congratulations—extraordinarily good in both content and delivery. No matter what develops you have made an enormous contribution and will continue to do so. Well done."

---

[86]   George Will, *Washington Post*, February 17, 2011.

His immediate response was: "Thanks. Didn't want to let down the team."

All of us were ecstatic. Lubbers said, "There isn't going to be another moment as portentous as this one."

Bob Perkins, who was in attendance, said, "Having seen Mitch 'in the environment,' it is hard to believe he won't run. I talked to the Yale group after Mitch talked with them and they were ebullient."

We were absolutely bombarded by e-mails and phone calls from across the country, both from friends and colleagues, but also from many people none of us knew.

Vince Harris, who Perkins was touting as the social media expert who could help us enormously, wrote, "Wow, fantastic speech. People ate it up on Twitter. A lot of what people re-tweeted and talked about his 'new red menace' line, so I went ahead and got the domain 'thenewredmenace. com' on private."

Dennis Thomas sent the following to Mitch: "Extremely well done in word and delivery. Take another look in the mirror, you may find someone looking very much like a President staring back!" To which Mitch replied, "I just ran and checked, same old mirror!" Dennis said to me later, "In addition to everything else, he's funny!"

Cleta Mitchell fired off a lengthy e-mail to Mitch that was both elegant and ecstatic. She said in part:

> I can't begin to tell you how inspiring your C-PAC speech was last night. It is all I've been hearing about, both last night and continuing today. So incredible. Everyone who heard it knew they were hearing something beyond ordinary and, actually, beyond special. It was transcendent.
>
> And not just because it was a great speech. It is special because of what it represents—a blueprint to save our nation. Nothing less. I know there are serious personal challenges to your deciding to make this race. And I am actually praying each day that God will help guide you and your wife as you make this decision. Of course, I'm also praying the decision you make is not just right for you, but also is the right one for America.

Later that day, Cleta sent me an e-mail:

> I sent Mitch a long email today about his speech and his decision. I've decided all I can do is pray—he is indeed the man for this time.
>
> And I believe God has been preparing him for this task his whole life. I hope his wife will be willing to make some sacrifice to save her country. Because that is, after all, what this is about—saving the nation.
>
> You have done wonderful service by helping to get him to this point. Now, I suppose, all we can do is hope and pray. What a speech! What a vision! It is utterly amazing. Keep me posted, I am standing by.

I responded that Mitch had forwarded her e-mail to me and was very moved by it, saying it was the most "incredible, thoughtful, direct from the heart message" he had received. I informed her that I'd then suggested he let Cheri and each of the girls read it; they needed to know the intensity of how people feel about this.

From Iowa, a friend e-mailed Eric Holcomb, saying he had watched the speech eight times. He said, "The excitement is building everywhere, you can't contain it! I hope Mitch runs; let me know when I can help."

From John McCain's former deputy political director in the 2008 campaign came this e-mail to Eric Holcomb: "Everywhere I've been this week, people are still abuzz about the Governor's C-PAC speech, in Washington and elsewhere. I came out to St. Louis today and it is still the talk of all the politicos I've been seeing. It is like no one else even spoke at the conference."

And Eric, himself, sent an e-mail to the group from an unknown person in New Jersey, which he said was one of many just like it that he was receiving from across the country, "Hello, Mr. Holcomb, my name is Jack Mozloom and I am writing to you from New Jersey. I'm a lifelong conservative and Republican, and like many of us I'm shopping for a presidential candidate. I was struck by Gov. Daniels' speech at C-PAC and I am convinced that he is the leader we need. I would be proud to help the Governor in my small way if he chooses to run, which I hope he will."

* * *

Then, the media itself began joining (and sometimes leading) the parade of enthusiastic reactions:

Garance Franke-Ruta, writing in the *Atlantic*, on February 12, 2011, said:

> There are candidates who are seeking to become the GOP's 2012 heartthrob. Indiana Gov. Mitch Daniels is the guy they never thought about dating who nonetheless may be able to talk them into it. One thing was clear at the Conservative Political Action Conference's Ronald Reagan Centennial Dinner Friday night, where the short, balding former George W. Bush budget director and possible 2012 presidential contender gave the keynote address: Daniels is a natural.[87]

On February 16, 2011, columnist John Ellis wrote an article for Business Insider.com saying:

> Last Friday night at the C-PAC conference in Washington D.C., Mitch Daniels gave the best speech of his political career and the most important speech of the 2012 campaign to date. He addressed the reckoning/restructuring head on. And he addressed it with refreshing candor, saying that the Party (and the country) must put aside all other matters and focus all of its attention on fixing our fiscal disaster.[88]

In *Commentary* magazine's blog, *Contentinos*, Peter Wehner wrote on February 16, 2011:

> As a statement on the major domestic threats we face—our fiscal crisis more narrowly and the efforts to undermine

---

[87]   Garance Franke-Ruta, "Mitch Daniels: The One to Watch," *Atlantic*, February 12, 2011.

[88]   John Ellis, "Daniels Goes for Broke," *Business Insider.com*, February 16, 2011.

self-government more broadly—the speech by Mitch Daniels at the recent C-PAC conference was superb.

Additionally, his point that Republicans need to appeal to their base and reach beyond it, which has been the formula for political victory pretty much since the beginning of time, while criticized by some, was right on point.

I have no idea whether Daniels will run; and if he does, whether he would be the best nominee. But his C-PAC speech, as a matter of substance and tone, was masterful.[89]

Noted conservative writer and columnist, Michael Gerson, writing in the *Washington Post* on February 17, 2011, said:

Another front-runner is Gov. Mitch Daniels of Indiana, who has come closest to providing an intellectual and political strategy for successful entitlement reform. His recent address to C-PAC, delivered with characteristic Coolidge-like coolness, was the most important Republican speech of recent years—the only one worth reading aloud to little conservatives around the hearth fire.[90]

Conservative talk radio, predictably, criticized Daniels. But he is one of the few politicians in America who are thinking like a president—a select group that, on the economy, doesn't include the president.

On March 4, 2011, in the *Tech*, MIT's oldest and largest newspaper and the first newspaper published on the web, staff columnist Keith Yost said:

Most of the speakers at the C-PAC conference in Washington followed the formula of pandering to the army of conservative organizers and activists that populate

---

89 Peter Wehner, *Commentary's* blog *Contentinos*, February 16, 2011.
90 Michael Gerson, *Washington Post*, February 17, 2011.

the conference. There was one man, however, who went beyond the cheerleader-ism and easy point scoring that so often characterizes C-PAC. Daniels is a rare politician, one who understands the scale of the problem that our nation faces, who has the courage to disown ideological purity in return for practical solutions, and who has the competence to not just cut government, but to make it better. He has displayed a level of leadership that the rest of the Republican field has not, and more importantly, has displayed a level of leadership that our own president has failed to provide.[91]

There were many other headlines and articles, both in electronic and print media, that Eric sent out to the group. As the onslaught of press and e-mails continued, a member of our group sent out a lengthy, highly charged e-mail to Eric, copying the group, saying we had to get some kind of deal done with Cheri. This had to happen; the country was at stake!

Eric's response was that Mitch had to want to run first, before any deal. He went on with a few other comments and then said, "We need a plan with a timeline we can take to him!"

I immediately replied to Eric:

> We had a plan, and a timetable! This is no longer our decision—it has to be his and he, alone, has to make it. The response to the speech has been everything we had hoped it would be, but we are kidding ourselves if we think this can go anywhere without a great deal of work in multiple areas where we are already behind. He has to make a decision—and he knows it.
>
> We just need to give him some room to do it and continue to try to get him to understand that even though we can put it off, we do so at our peril. But, most of all he has to come to grips with the answer—yes or no. "Maybe" isn't going to work much longer.

---

[91] Keith Yost, "Opinion-Mitch Daniels for President. Indiana's veteran leader is exactly what the country needs," *Tech*, March 4, 2011.

The Gridiron Dinner—March 12, 2011

One of Mitch's constant irritations was consistently being described as "serious and wonky," almost devoid of personality if you were to believe the press. Truth be known, he was a master at retail politics, not only because of his RV travels, home stays in regular citizens' houses, and Harley riding in parades, but also because he had a great sense of humor and was able to tell a story with great comedic timing.

I think that was one reason he relished the opportunity to do the Gridiron, to show the "eastern elites" and mainstream media he could not only hold his own, he could give as good as he gets.

This was a closed dinner with no live television coverage, so we had to wait on reports from people actually in attendance. The verdict, as communicated by Eric to the group the next morning, "The Governor hit another one out of the park."

Al Hubbard, who had breakfast with Karl Rove (who was in attendance) the next morning reported that Rove said Mitch was fabulous, and everything else he heard about the dinner speech was positive.

The *Washington Post*, in its Sunday editorial on March 13, 2011, said, "By all accounts, Mitch Daniels, the official Republican speaker of the night, slayed the room with a routine that was both self-deprecatory and snarky," and then proceeded to repeat many of his remarks.

Included in the story was Mitch turning to the President halfway through and saying, "Mr. President, you're not laughing. Who forgot to put ha-ha-ha on the teleprompter?"

Perhaps the biggest laugh, however, came when he said, "But I have to admit, all this favorable press I've been getting, it's hard not to let it go to your head. Just listen to a quick sample: 'Small, stiff, short, pale, unimposing, unassuming, uninspiring, understated, uncharismatic ... accountant-like, non-telegenic, boring, balding ... blunt, nerdy, wooden, wonky, puny, and pint-sized.' Really, it all points to one inescapable conclusion: It's destiny!"[92]

Margaret Carlson, liberal columnist writing in *Businessweek.com* on March 15, 2011, said, "When someone as staid as Indiana Governor Mitch

---

[92]   *Washington Post*, Sunday editorial, March 13, 2011.

Daniels turns out to have a sense of humor about himself, it may be time to take him seriously."[93]

In the days that followed, multiple articles, columns, and blogs all told the story of the Gridiron, and many published nearly all Mitch's remarks. They were delivered in his wry self-deprecating manner and, quite frankly, simply hysterical.

The last few minutes of his speech were devoted to the issue of running for president. He started out by saying, "Honestly, I never had any idea of running for president. After governor, my plan's been to go spend some time in a quiet place where no one can find me. First choice is Al Gore's cable network." He followed that with another dozen lines of equal hilarity.

He closed, however, with these thoughts:

> May I say in leaving how truly thrilled I was at this opportunity, and hope I did it justice. In the week the nation lost David Broder[94], might we hope that the spirit of this evening he loved could grow.
>
> To me, "singe, not burn" means to tease but not ridicule or demean those who must find answers that serve the interests of us all. It's the humor I encounter all the time among the regulars in Indiana coffee shops: the humor of common struggles, common purpose, and genuine, if carefully concealed affection. The humor of the needle, never the dagger.
>
> It is not for a visitor to say, but maybe this event should be shared more openly with our fellow Americans. Because it would be a fine thing for us all if the spirit of the Gridiron spread widely across this great but troubled land. Thanks for having me.

He was given a standing ovation—something rare, I'm told, in Gridiron history.

---

[93] Margaret Carlson, *Businessweek*, March 15, 2011.

[94] David Broder was considered the Dean of the Washington political press corps for many years, writing for the *Washington Post*. He died shortly before the Gridiron speech.

The Legislative Session

The other major event of 2011 was the Indiana legislative session. It had the potential for significant impact in multiple ways, both positive and negative.

The positive aspect was to give Mitch, with two houses now in firm control of the Republicans, a real opportunity to finish his agenda for the state. He had several major initiatives, including a major education reform program, a tax rebate proposal, and an effort to reform county government. Mitch had worked hard on these proposals for many months, and he believed passing them would be his crowning achievement as governor. Additionally, it could do nothing but help him nationally as a side benefit.

The only negative we saw was the timing issue. The session would go until the end of April, and while it gave us a solid excuse for not making a decision on the presidential question, it also limited the time he could spend on doing other things we needed to get done.

However, as often happens, there were more negatives than we anticipated. One came from the Democrats, and one came from our "friends," the Republicans.

The Democrats, knowing they were outnumbered and couldn't stop the reform initiatives proposed by the governor, took a page out of the Wisconsin playbook and left the state. Mitch labeled the move as a "complete contempt for the democratic process," but it put into question whether or not he could get anything voted on, in addition to the fact that the end of April deadline might come into question.

The other issue had to do with Right to Work[95] in Indiana. Several Republican legislators, including the leadership, wanted to include it as part of the reform agenda. Mitch balked, and a firestorm erupted among people both within the state and outside Indiana—many of them our key supporters. Mitch's position was that it was not included in the campaign for control of the legislature as a defining issue for this session; it would potentially derail his other reform initiatives; and it should wait until the next session when it could be a priority issue.

The end result was that the Right to Work proposal did get derailed with the legislators' walkout. Ultimately, they returned and Mitch's two most important reform initiatives, education and tax reform, were passed successfully. But, once again, unnecessary controversy was caused, in part, by his reaction in the press to some of these issues.

The fact is, Mitch had always been a supporter of Right to Work. By handling the issue as he did and getting hot under the collar with the Republican leadership, he riled up a group of people that were important to us. It was, as one of our group said, a repeat of the social truce/Mexico City fiasco. It didn't need to happen. If we had been consulted, we could have framed the issue differently and carefully communicated it with much less fallout.

The positive result was not only the reform initiatives being passed but, as blogger Alexis Levinson pointed out in an article entitled "Mitch Didn't Grandstand," "Mitch stayed focused on the job he was elected to do. He presented a broad and ambitious agenda with a single purpose—continuing Indiana's comeback. There is an implication here that Daniels would be equipped to facilitate the country's 'comeback' from its current economic troubles as well."[96]

From our standpoint, we were just happy to see the legislative deadline met and the session ended. We now had to proceed with the final step. What was the decision going to be and when were we going to announce it?

---

95   This statute (law in twenty-four states as of this writing) is about limiting labor unions' ability to require membership, among other things. It is not a law (despite the language) that guarantees employment.

96   Alexis Levinson, "Mitch Didn't Grandstand," *The Daily Caller*, April 29, 2011.

— Momentum Continues to Build

As 2011 unfolded, new polls and various analyses began to appear in the media. An interesting one (WSJ/NBC Poll) was sent to Mitch by Neil King at the *Wall Street Journal* on March 2, indicating pollsters had asked this specific question in "his honor:" Asked only of GOP Primary voters (N=282):

> Suppose a candidate running in the 2012 Republican primary for president says the party should focus MORE on issues such as the economy and the federal budget deficit and focus LESS on social issues such as gay marriage and abortion. Would you be more likely or less likely to vote for a Republican Presidential candidate who says this, or would this make no difference in how you might vote one way or the other?
> More Likely...............65
> Less Likely.................8
> No Difference............25
> Not Sure....................2

He indicated the cross tabs showed equally strong support for such a candidate even among social conservatives.

On March 4, 2011, Chris Cillizza, writing in the *Washington Post*, published what he called "Fixing the Line," a ranking of candidates most likely to wind up as the Republican presidential nominee in 2012. He would update this from time to time during the primary process. He listed

the top ten, with Rick Santorum being last and Mitt Romney being first.
At number six was Mitch Daniels with this commentary:

> He proved in his speech at C-PAC last month that if
> he runs, he would be a formidable voice in the race—
> sounding the alarm on the dangers of America's ever-
> mounting debt. While Daniels' speech won widespread
> plaudits in the pundit community, we still wonder
> whether someone who is almost exclusively animated by
> fiscal issues and has called for a truce on hot button social
> matters can win a Republican presidential nomination.
> Those close to Daniels—and there aren't many—insist
> he is genuinely undecided on the race. Whether Daniels
> ultimately runs or not may come down to his wife, Cheri,
> who is reportedly not keen on the idea.[97]

On March 6, 2011, it was reported by a friend of Eric Holcomb's that
Mitch won a straw poll at the forty-seventh annual Dorchester Conference
in Oregon. Romney was second, Sarah Palin third. Considering he had
virtually no name recognition and had never set foot in the state, this was
significant.

A new poll in New Hampshire was also released and sent to us by
Michael Sununu. It showed Donald Trump nearly closing in on Romney.
According to Sununu, the real message in this data was that there existed a
significant portion of the New Hampshire GOP primary subset that would
coalesce around a candidate that is the anti-Romney, not an opposite of
Mitt, but the person who takes on the role of being "not Mitt."

No one thought Trump would ultimately go anywhere, but he was the
current "placeholder" for the "anti-Mitt" sentiment. Following a decade
of political life in neighboring Massachusetts, in addition to owning a
home in New Hampshire, Romney had not moved the needle in any of
the surveys since the last primary. Many pundits believed this was a signal
of discontent.

We even heard from one of Romney's major fundraisers/bundlers. He

---

[97] Chris Cillizza, "Fixing the Line," *Washington Post*, March 4, 2011.

said although they were raising significant dollars, people were worried about Romneycare and his flip-flops, with a substantial number of people saying they wanted to wait for Mitch.

On March 10, 2011, the *National Journal* published the latest results of its Political Insiders Poll, saying the potential 2012 GOP White House hopefuls whose fortunes were most on the rise were Indiana Governor Mitch Daniels and former Minnesota Governor Tim Pawlenty. In the article, "Insiders: Buy Daniels, Pawlenty; Sell Palin," James Barnes asked which potential GOP presidential candidate's stock had risen the most in the past few months. A combination of Republican and Democrat responses said 47 percent for Daniels, ahead of all other potential candidates.

The article opened, "While no Republican could-be candidate towered above the field, GOP insiders focused on Daniels and Pawlenty as two whose stock has been rising in recent months but for very different reasons. Daniels, who has taken few overt steps towards mounting a national campaign, is seen as someone who could champion the Republican themes of shrinking government and cutting spending and also has the record in Indiana to back up that message in a campaign."[98]

Media Attention

The media, of course, continued its speculation and none among its voices ever felt reluctant to express opinions.

Jonathan Martin and Jim VandeHei did an interview with Mitch in *Politico* on February 10, 2011. The headline was a bit odd—"Daniels: I'd Have Cash, Support to Win," building off Mitch's answer to a question on whether or not he could win if he ran. The lengthy interview actually focused on his record in Indiana and his "survival agenda" of issues he thought important to the country. It also focused on his reluctance as a candidate. It said, "Daniels suggested three things that could keep him from plunging in: his wife's concerns, the calculation that his party or the country aren't ready for his tough-love message or the emergence of another capable candidate. 'What kind of life is it?' he asked. 'You take yourself

---

[98]   James Barnes, "Insiders: Buy Daniels, Pawlenty; Sell Palin," *National Journal,* March 10, 2011.

and your whole family for life into a very different sort of existence, and it's nothing I've ever thought about until last year or aspired to. But, I'm very concerned about seeing the country deal effectively with the problems we've got.'"

The article went on to say that the Daniels intrigue said much about the current state of the GOP establishment, noting many top Republicans were unenthused about the candidates who were clearly running. This group was increasingly worried that Obama was headed for a second term. It continued, "Such Republicans see Mitt Romney as stale and unable to get past his state healthcare law with the base; Newt Gingrich is seen as too erratic and baggage-laden; and others as lacking stature or even more deeply flawed than the big names."[99]

Peggy Noonan once again came through with an illuminating column in the February 19, 2011, edition of the *Wall Street Journal* with the headline "Where the Leaders Are." A large picture of Mitch accompanied the article. It was actually an article on governors showing the way in Washington, talking about both Chris Christie and Daniels and specifically discussing Mitch and his C-PAC speech.

Peggy took to task the conservative radio talk show hosts, saying, "If you really want to change your country, you cannot do it from a political base alone … And it starts with not alienating and proceeds to persuading, quoting the late Rep. Henry Hyde who said, 'Politics is a game of addition.'"[100]

Then, the column of all columns happened on February 25, 2011, when David Brooks, in his *New York Times* column, entitled his writing, "Run Mitch, Run." He said, "The man who would be the party's strongest candidate for the presidency is seriously thinking about not running. The country needs a substantive debate about the role of government. That's exactly what an Obama-Daniels contest would provide. Yet because Daniels is a normal person who doesn't have an insatiable desire for higher office, he's thinking about not running."[101]

Brooks then reiterated much of Mitch's record and accomplishments.

---

[99] Jonathan Martin and Jim VandeHei, "Daniels: I'd Have Cash, Support to Win," *Politico*, February 10, 2011.

[100] Peggy Noonan, "Where the Leaders Are," *Wall Street Journal*, February 19, 2011.

[101] David Brooks, "Run Mitch, Run," *New York Times*, February 25, 2011.

He pointed out, as had others, that Mitch couldn't match Obama on style but he certainly could on substance. He expressed the strong opinion in superbly written words that the country needed this debate and that he hoped we would have the opportunity to have it.

Veteran *Washington Post* columnist Dan Balz wrote a piece for the Sunday edition that compared Haley Barbour and Mitch in their decision-making processes. He said both were weighing whether or not to run in 2012 but approaching the decision in very different ways. He wrote, "Barbour is leaning in showing clear interest and taking steps to get ready. Daniels is engaged in a very public discussion about what to do but otherwise is holding back. Daniels is enjoying a surge of interest in the wake of his well-crafted and well-received speech at C-PAC this month. There he warned of a new 'red menace' of red ink and urged Republicans to reach beyond their base for support."[102]

David Shribman, a Pulitzer Prize-winning journalist, now executive editor of the *Pittsburgh Post-Gazette*, published an article on March 5, 2011, that said, "Politics has its moments, and right now Mitch Daniels is having his. Maybe Daniels, whose greatest asset is that he is normal, is what the Republicans need."[103]

Bill Glauber of the *Milwaukee Journal* did a lengthy piece on March 27, 2011, that Mitch himself praised for its accuracy—"This fellow did his homework and got it pretty much right." It was a thorough review of his tenure as governor, saying:

> It's a way of governing that America may hear about even more as Daniels publicly ponders joining the Republican field and making a run for the presidency in 2012. He's weighing it all, the toll on family, the punishing travel through the primary states and the prodigious fundraising that would be required for such an effort. "I do believe we could get table stakes together," he says, "I just believe a credible campaign on the side of freedom, on the side

[102] Dan Balz, "For Potential GOP Presidential Hopefuls Daniels and Barbour, the Decision Making Differs, *Washington Post*, February 27, 2011.

[103] David Shribman, "Indiana's Daniels Looking Very Much Like a GOP Star," *Pittsburgh Post-Gazette*, March 5, 2011.

of dealing with our debt before it destroys the American dream, will have lots of friends and will have its day in court."[104]

On April 19, 2011, Chris Cillizza posted an article quoting a new *Washington Post/ABC News* poll that said just 43 percent of the respondents proclaimed themselves satisfied with their options, a far cry from the 65 percent who said the same at this time in the 2008 race.

He then concluded by saying:

> Put simply: The opportunity is ripe for someone with the fiscally conservative focus of an Indiana Gov. Mitch Daniels or, less likely, New Jersey Gov. Chris Christie, to get into the race and immediately begin winning over Republicans dissatisfied with their current options.
>
> Daniels has agonized publicly about whether or not to run—making clear that he believes an opportunity exists for him but being unwilling (so far) to pull the trigger. An announcement is likely either by the end of the month or early May. He may look at these numbers and find it simply too hard to stay out.[105]

We all agreed it was humorous and, in fact, enjoyable to see the press floundering in what to think and what to say about Mitch and the final decision.

* * *

Speculation and suggestions on the best Republican ticket increased, with one person saying that a Daniels-Rubio ticket was the key to an Electoral College victory and another sending a message that his dream ticket was Daniels-Petraeus. In play too was constant speculation on what Haley

---

[104] Bill Glauber, *Milwaukee Journal*, March 27, 2011.

[105] Chris Cillizza, "Republicans Still Looking for Mr. Right," *Washington Post*, April 19, 2011.

Barbour was going to do, suggesting that he and Mitch had an agreed upon a mutual strategy.

On March 17, 2011, Sarah Lenti, wrote a commentary for NMpolitics. net entitled, "Haley Barbour and Mitch Daniels—It's One or the Other for 2012." She noted, "If I had to answer today, I'd say it's Governor Barbour."[106]

Then there were several media postings challenging Mitch to make the right decision and even suggesting he was shirking his duty if he declined. Mark Salter, in his March 18, 2011, column for *Real Clear Politics*, entitled "Will Daniels Step Up to Meet America's Challenges," wrote:

> Daniels has qualities that encourage the belief he might be indispensable to the country, a distinction that is accorded only to a few. A handsome indifference to power or his family's aversion to the sacrifices of public life are not sufficient reasons to excuse him from duty. Patriotism without sacrifice doesn't deserve acclaim.
>
> Thus if he doesn't consider the country's exigent circumstances, which he has described in the direst of terms, an unrefusable call to duty, then perhaps Daniels, for all his authentic and attractive qualities, will have revealed a serious character flaw and given solace— however unwanted—to Republican admirers who would reluctantly have to search for a second choice.[107]

"Wow" was all we were able to say to that one.

* * *

As the Indiana legislature finally came to a close (one of the many deadlines for decision making set earlier by Mitch), it was becoming more and more

---

[106] Sarah Lenti, "Haley Barbour and Mitch Daniels – It's One or the Other for 2012," *NMPolitics.net*, March 17, 2011. She was wrong on both accounts. There was no mutually agreed upon strategy, and Haley said no even before Mitch made his decision.

[107] Mark Salter, "Will Daniels Step Up to Meet America's Challenges," *Real Clear Politics*, March 18, 2011.

necessary to say something definitive. The press kept turning up the heat for a decision.

Dan Balz, the veteran *Washington Post* reporter, again came to Indiana for a personal interview. Balz pointed out that Mitch had been undecided about running for president for more than a year but, with the conclusion of the Indiana legislative session, was now in a position where he needed to make a decision. He wrote, "Asked where he was in his thinking, Daniels replied with a laugh, 'Oh, muddled.' Then he turned serious, 'I don't want to leave a misimpression. If we get in, we will go all out, and we know a little about how to do that. So reluctance or hesitation about running doesn't mean we would be a reluctant candidate if we got there.'"[108]

The article went on to discuss the importance of the family considerations. Mitch didn't offer any further comment except to agree that the family was a critical factor in the ultimate decision. It also suggested that Mitch was increasingly concerned that the issue of fiscal reform was not being adequately raised by any other candidate, a concern that made the decision even harder to make. Time was growing short, and everyone understood that a decision had to be made.

After an AEI speech on May 4, 2011, attended by many in the media who expected some kind of announcement, Jonathan Martin of *Politico*, wrote an article entitled "Mitch Daniels Campaign Only Lacks Candidate:"

> Mitch Daniels hasn't yet decided whether he'll run for President, but his Wednesday appearance at the American Enterprise Institute sure had all the makings of a campaign-in-waiting.
>
> Daniels in noting the rumors of some major announcement said that he literally was in town to speak at an evening event and was only trying to fill the day. He said, "As Calvin Coolidge once said, 'a man's got to eat somewhere.'" Daniels quipped that, 'Some pajama-clad blogger turned this speech into a major policy address.'[109]

---

[108] He was getting better and better at answering these questions.
[109] Jonathan Martin, "Mitch Daniels Campaign Only Lacks Candidate," *Politico*, May 4, 2011.

A final post prior to the decision by Chris Cillizza, *Washington Post*, came on May 8, 2011. He said:

> Indiana Governor Mitch Daniels continues to keep the political world waiting, saying recently that he will announce "within weeks" whether he will run for president in 2012. Daniels is regarded (and regards himself) as a candidate of considerable gravity, willing to focus on making tough choices about the nation's financial future even if that conversation is politically unpopular.
>
> "He will turn a race that is about less serious politics into a race about more serious policy," argued Alex Castellanos, a Republican media consultant who is not aligned with any candidate heading into 2012. "Daniels is the adult in the room saying the party is over, it's time to clean house."[110]

* * *

In addition to all the press speculation that occurred in this time period, individuals in the form of friends, colleagues, and total strangers also wanted to express an opinion. Many knew a decision was forthcoming at the end of the legislative session. Therefore, from February to May, hundreds of messages were transmitted. Many were communicated to various members of our group, but many also went directly to Mitch, all of which he personally answered.

Mercer Reynolds, the premier fundraiser from the Bush years, said, "The country needs you, and I hope that your family will lend you out for a few years."

Former colleagues from Mitch's Senate days began coming out of the woodwork to join longtime supporter and fellow former staffer, Dennis Thomas. These included Jann Olsten, former chief of staff to Senator Rudy Boschwitz, and Chris Koch, former chief of staff to Senator John McCain.

---

[110] Chris Cillizza, "Mitch Daniels: The Man Who Could Reshape the Republican Field," *Washington Post*, May 8, 2011.

Both were in new careers outside of Washington but urged him to run and offered support.

Positive comments were coming from South Carolina Governor Nikki Haley, who said that "it's not the time for social issues to be discussed" and that Romney's health care bill is "not right for South Carolina," while praising Mitch's record as governor.

Mitch was surprised at comments from Nikki Haley, saying he didn't know her well but had spent time talking with her recently at a National Governors meeting and liked her.

Charlie Black responded, "If you do this, you will be surprised how many people have the guts to support you … and disappointed in some friends who don't."

From a Democrat, former CIA Director James Woolsey, "Just in case you decide to go for it, you have an Okie Scoop Jackson Democrat supporter."

Former Congressman Dick Armey, one of the founders of the Tea Party movement, expressed support both privately and publicly, to which Mitch responded in a note, "Dick, just wanted to reiterate how good it was to see you yesterday and how much it meant to me that you expressed such confidence in me, both personally and in public. I don't know that I can make the national race, but if I do your advocacy will be a major reason that I did."

From veteran Washington insider and former president of Michigan State University, Peter McPherson, "Mitch, I have been watching events carefully and I do hope you can find a way to run. There is simply no one better to articulate how to deal with the deficit and how to make the necessary government work. Not easy to have such a burden on you but as a student of these matters over many decades, that is what I think."

Todd Stottlemyer, past President and CEO of the country's largest small business organization, NFIB, wrote, "I have come to believe that Governor Daniels may just be the right candidate at the right time for the party and the country. He recognizes that a country cannot be strong and a leader of the free world if it cannot put its own fiscal house in order and create an environment where innovation and entrepreneurship can flourish. If he does decide to do it, a hard decision and incredible personal commitment and sacrifice, I would like to do what I can to support him."

From former Intel CEO, Craig Barrett, who had attended a residence dinner with his wife, former Ambassador Barbara Barrett, "I am resisting active support of any presidential candidates pending my favorite throwing his hat into the ring. Any chance?"

* * *

Calls began coming in from other candidates, just to touch base and see if they could determine what Mitch was going to do. Tim Pawlenty called on April 28. It appeared that Pawlenty was trying to convince Mitch that he (Pawlenty) would be adopting the same strong positions as Mitch if the decision (by Mitch) was not to run. Private reports were that Pawlenty was more worried about a Daniels candidacy than anyone, including Romney.

Even former President Bill Clinton said to one of our key supporters that he watched Mitch's speech at CPAC from beginning to end and indicated it was the best policy speech he had heard in a decade.

In late April, Eric Holcomb sent the group a compilation of dozens of statements, letters, and e-mails he had received the past two weeks. All of them urged a positive decision while recognizing the difficult task ahead. Eric also was receiving dozens of letters and résumés from professionals who wanted to work on the campaign.

The last week of April, Haley Barbour announced he wasn't going to go. Many of us had been friends with Haley for decades, all the way back to when he was a Republican National Committee field man. Mitch and I had both expressed the opinion he was one of the smartest political minds in our party. That was the principal reason we both thought, in the end, he would say no. Haley knew that the politics were against him in a race against Obama.

Scott Reed, his principal political advisor, called Stan Anderson within days to say that all of their key people wanted to be involved with Mitch. On Tuesday, April 26, Haley called Mitch with a positive statement in regards to his potential candidacy.

As we moved into May, calls from people ranging from Congressman Paul Ryan to Governor Scott Walker to Governor Chris Christie came in with positive comments. Charlie Black reported that conservative Senator

Jim DeMint (R-SC) was a likely supporter, thus providing a grassroots network in South Carolina.

A similar call came to one of our group from a representative of House Speaker John Boehner, who said all our candidates so far were second tier, but if Mitch entered the race he would be a first-tier candidate.

Finally, from the true grassroots of America, came this report from Mark Lubbers to the group on May 13, as he was getting ready to board a flight from Washington Reagan Airport to Indianapolis:

> The agent-in-charge was a very bright, black, 30-something with an east African accent. As he was taking boarding passes, he was loudly reminding people that this is the flight to Indianapolis and he was doing a little comedic stand-up as he goes, saying:
> "This is the flight to Indianapolis, home of the Hoosiers, home of Mitch Daniels, our next President, although Cheri hasn't said yes yet ..."
> As Lubbers said, you can't make this stuff up.

Mark asked the agent how he knew Mitch, and he said he's just read about him in the newspaper, saying, "He balances the budget."

Mark asked him if he had read about him in the *Washington Post*.

"No," he said. "I'm a conservative; I read about him in the *Wall Street Journal!*"

Mark said the agent, a Kenyan by birth, wrote down his name and e-mail address. If there was to be a campaign, this immigrant from East Africa wanted to work on it.

* * *

The Final Two Months

As we entered the final few weeks of the legislative session, approaching mid-April, I had a concern that Mitch was still not ready or prepared to make a decision. As we often remarked within our group, he really doesn't want to say no. I didn't want him to say no. I completely understood why *he* didn't want to say no. However, the fact was we needed a decision, yes or no.

We were starting to lose significant people, key staff in particular. Travis Thomas told us he had been promoted into a new demanding role in his company as the number two person for global development. He said he would not be able to do the job of finance director full time but would be willing to make a few calls and give advice to whomever we did recruit. He suggested a few names for Al Hubbard to contact. This was a key loss if we were to go ahead.

Our first choice for campaign manager had been Nick Ayres, executive director of the Republican Governors Association and a highly regarded organizational pro with good experience. I always thought Nick would go with Haley (who was chairman of RGA), but Nick said he was very interested. However, after a lengthy discussion with Mitch, he determined Mitch wasn't going to do it. He certainly wouldn't be making a decision in time for Nick's own timetable. He ended up going with Pawlenty.

More of our key volunteer fundraisers were also bailing out. These individuals wanted to play at a high level, and that meant getting involved early with a candidate.

About this time, a longtime Washington lobbyist and political operative sent Mitch an e-mail suggesting a new strategy. Basically, he was saying, because of all the noise and fights between Congress and Obama, the terrible economy, and other candidates out there making noise, we should just stand down. We should do nothing publicly. There was no need to make a decision yet. We should just wait until after the Iowa, New Hampshire, and South Carolina primaries were over and then announce as the white knight to come in and save the day.

Mitch sent his e-mail to me, saying, "Read this as a different perspective than most."

I did and was flabbergasted. The only thing that flabbergasted me more was an e-mail from one of our own group to Mitch saying, "I think he's right!" Double flabbergast!

After conferring with Charlie, Al, and others, all of whom were in agreement, I sent a message to Mitch on April 19, 2011, that said:

Where to start? This is not about Washington and insider pundits. You are already a part of the debate and will have to answer all these questions regardless, questions in fact you want to answer since you, more than anyone, started this adult conversation.

The fact is no one is "moving quickly," everyone is holding back with public announcements of actual candidacy which is all to the good. However, as we've always said, this doesn't mean they aren't doing hundreds of things to get ready. Fundraising is only one aspect, although a critical one.

Congress is historically out of control and having the luxury of not being there (i.e., you) is still a great asset that enables you to have some control over how you enter the debate. This is true whether you are an "announced" interested potential candidate or not.

The bottom line is you can't wait to be anointed. Ultimately people expect you to earn it. There are hundreds of people out there right now who are still waiting and thousands more we don't even know about. These people want, need and deserve some indication that in the end, you're going. How we do that is still open to discussion. However, waiting until the fall or later to at least make the personal decision that can be communicated to the potential group of key supporters is a mistake.

I like the idea of going directly to the announcement and bypassing an exploratory committee except for one reason: the exploratory committee buys you time. It allows you more control over when and how you enter the debate, and provides a period of time to get organized. It just gives you more flexibility in how you proceed.

Mitch's response was, "Agree. I wasn't endorsing sitting around much longer, just playing mailman. If it ever turns to 'go' we might as well just be direct about it."

I was getting concerned, not just because of the inane idea but because

I knew Mitch in his heart of hearts didn't want to say no. So I arranged a call with Hubbard and Bell to talk about what we ought to do with Mitch to get him to understand we had to make a decision, even if it was no.

In the meantime, Eric had prepared a large "reading" book of clips and letters and e-mails from people. He sent it to Cheri with a request for her and the girls to just read it over the weekend when they were all going to be together at the Greenbrier house.

We agreed that Bell would call Mitch and go see him for dinner on Monday, April 18. I told them I would fly to Indianapolis also, but it wasn't particularly convenient for just a two-hour meeting. Additionally, I thought Tom with a one-on-one session might be better. We arranged for me to call Al's house (where Tom was staying) following the meeting with Mitch to get a report. I told Tom I would send him some thoughts regarding the conversation that needed to take place.

That memo on April 17 said:

> I have two additional points to consider in the conversation with Mitch:
>
> 1. Somehow we need an answer that is more than: "I'm still seriously considering it. I'll ask people to wait until the end of April when I'll make my decision. There is still a good chance I might do it if I can move the family." That's the answer we have now. That's what I repeat daily to people. It has obviously kept some on the sidelines and will continue to do so, but it has also lost some major players. That erosion will also continue.
> 2. What we need is: "I now want to do it. I think there is an excellent chance I can get the family to neutral, which will allow me to do it. I don't want to announce anything until the end of April when the legislative session concludes." That enables us to begin to say to people: "I think he's going to go—if he does, can we count on you to do … whatever." That is a different conversation. One I could have with all these people that keep calling, most of who have given up.

If he can't answer that Monday night when you meet because he hasn't talked to Cheri yet then try to get a day next week when he can give you an answer. If, in fact, he could answer it in that manner, there are multiple things that need to be done. Just to give you some idea of the scope, I will go through all my notes this weekend and come up with the top 10 or 20 "things to do right now." You could even discuss this list with him if appropriate.

* * *

I had a telephone conversation late in the evening on Monday, April 18, with Tom and Al Hubbard following Tom's dinner with Mitch. Tom said Mitch understood the necessity of making a decision soon. He clearly understood that we needed a core group on board, and we were at risk of losing people. He was concerned about leaks on the decision. It was clear to Tom he didn't want to say no.

Other questions regarding what the Aiming Higher PAC and the state party could do legally in terms of setting up an initial office during transition were discussed. We needed some type of repository for inquiries while we put our own infrastructure together. We required a clear understanding of the type of expenditures that could be made and the process of paying them back. Questions regarding record keeping, contribution limits, and numerous other subjects needed to be clarified.

I told Tom that Cleta Mitchell[111], Eric, and I would have a telephone conference call the next day to iron out all of these details.

However, the most important summary points of the dinner were:

- The family was going to be together at the Greenbrier for the week, and he'd hopefully return with an answer by next Sunday.[112]
- If the signal was green or even yellow, we would move forward.
- He didn't want to do an exploratory committee—just go. He needed to know exactly what was involved with starting, and I indicated I would get that from Cleta also.

---

[111] Advising us now as our FEC attorney
[112] It didn't happen.

Tom asked him six questions (Mitch's responses follow in *italics*):

1. Are you willing to do it?
   Yes
2. Do you think you should do it?
   Yes
3. Do you think you can win?
   Yes
4. Will you do this without the support of the family?
   No
5. Can you get their support?
   Don't Know
6. Have you told the family that you now want to do this?
   No, but will this weekend

* * *

The next day, Eric and I had a lengthy call with Cleta Mitchell trying to answer all the questions of what it would take to go, how the process of filing worked, what could be spent when, and various record-keeping requirements. It was all straightforward. We would file a Form 1 setting up the campaign committee with a treasurer and open a bank account, and Mitch would personally sign and file a "statement of candidacy." We then reviewed the other questions Mitch had asked during his talk with Tom.

On Wednesday April 20, I sent Mitch an e-mail telling him Haley Barbour would be announcing on Friday that he would not be running. I said:

> Apparently he has put together quite an excellent group of people, particularly in Iowa, New Hampshire and South Carolina. He determined he could possibly win the nomination, but in his mind a southerner can't beat Obama. Additionally, he was concerned about the stress this effort would put on both his wife and son. Just another element of the on-going saga. I assume he will call you if he hasn't already. The primary reason I was called was to

say there are a substantial group of people now that will be looking for another place to go.

Mitch responded early the next morning, "I had not heard. Surprised. Thanks for passing it on."

* * *

On Monday, April 25, Mitch was quoted in an interview with Jonathan Martin of *Politico*, as saying, "I would have backed Haley if he had decided to run," he said. "Haley Barbour is a great citizen; he'd have made a great president. I'd have been proud to try to help him had he chosen to run."[113]

Charlie Black reported some reporters thought Haley got out because Mitch was going to get in.

At the same time, word got back to Eric Holcomb that Pawlenty was struggling both organizationally and in raising the necessary dollars. The assumption was that the hiring of Nick Ayres would produce ample funding through Republican Governors Association donors, but it wasn't happening. Everyone believed that Pawlenty would be a good second choice. Even his supporters from Minnesota told us he didn't have the policy depth, political instincts, or gubernatorial record to equal Mitch.

On Tuesday April 26, Tom Bell sent Mitch a message asking if there was any news from the Easter weekend at the Greenbrier. He made the point that, with Haley out, we should be making some calls if the light was green or yellow.

Mitch replied later that day, "She did her homework[114], but no real news. I'm digesting the Haley decision now. Marsha's comments[115] are more likely to reinforce than convert her, but we'll see. Haley called … if we go, I think he'll be right there with us."

Tom responded, "Encouraging. Hang in there and let me know when we can go to work."

---

[113]   Jonathan Martin, *Politico*, April 25, 2011.
[114]   A reference to the packet of clippings and messages Eric had compiled for Cheri to read
[115]   Marsha Barbour, Haley's wife

* * *

Also on Tuesday April 26, Trent Duffy sent a memo to Mitch entitled "Cutting Bait." He listed the basic points that needed to be covered in announcing an exploratory committee. Trent was still not privy to many of our internal deliberations, but his thoughts were basically on target. He then said, "Whatever your decision, it's been an honor serving you and your stealth campaign."

The Final Twenty Days
to a Decision

On late Sunday evening, May 1, I sent an e-mail to Mitch: "Congrats on a great legislative session and huge accomplishments across the board. If you want to discuss 'plans' any further, call me. I know you're probably tired of talking about it and perhaps don't want any further review/discussion. I know you understand what's at stake and all the issues with which to deal. However, if you want to talk about it one more time, just let me know."

Early the next morning, he responded: "I'll try to call. Incredible how the game has come to us … don't we wish we were really all that smart. Next two weeks will decide things."

May would continue as a month of great speculation, both among friends and the media. A previously planned trip to Washington to address the American Enterprise Institute (AEI) conference and the upcoming Indiana State Party dinner (featuring Cheri as the keynote speaker) helped stoke the fires.

One of the AEI hosts said of Mitch's appearance, "He did a good job for us today. A luncheon with our donors, an education speech, and an interview with our magazine editor. He sounded to me like a guy who is planning to run."

Later that week, Al Hubbard sent a note to Mitch with a report on calls made to him by some of our key financial supporters. Those types of calls were coming into all of us from many people across the country, saying, "You've had enough time; we need a decision."

Mitch's response, "Understood, understandable."

On Friday May 7, I sent Al an update after talking to Eric Holcomb at length that morning. He called to give a report on the Washington/New York trip and discuss the May 12 state party dinner. I said:

> Apparently C-SPAN is covering the dinner live. This morning CNN called and is also seriously considering live coverage. A video will be shown at the dinner, followed by Mitch's introduction of Cheri. A "spontaneous" appearance of hundreds of *Run Mitch Run* signs for all to see will then appear. They expect a thousand people, the largest state party dinner ever.
>
> Eric is seeing Mitch at 5:30 today and is going to give him a list of people he is suggesting for leadership positions in the campaign. He will also review with him a list of people on the finance side who need to be called immediately. Eric and I will review that list later this morning and compare notes. He said Mitch was besieged by many significant people in Washington and New York to run. He came away as in the past buoyed by all the potential support, still believing it isn't too late but also indicating nothing has changed at home. So, there you go—same old same old—we'll see!

Tom Bell, just returning from an overseas trip, asked Al Hubbard if he was going to attend the GOP dinner on May 12 to hear Cheri. Al said:

> I wouldn't miss it for the world. I met with Eric yesterday and it sounds like he has organized quite an event. A great introduction of Cheri by Mitch and a "spontaneous" *Run Mitch Run* chant with posters is planned. I have no clue as to what will happen. I suppose Cheri will not change her position of opposition. Eric says he thinks Mitch's hope/assumption is that all this support will convince her to at least be neutral. But I can't believe she would say that at the event. It will be interesting. It is amazing the number

of folks who continue to wait on him. My odds today are 75-25 he runs.

Of course the media was continuing to get worked up. Rick Powell sent a message saying he had received e-mails ten minutes apart from Christiane Amanpour (ABC News) and Mike Allen (*Politico*) asking if he would talk to them about Mitch. He wondered if they were hearing something. He said, "They both know I am acquainted with Mitch but don't know about our group or my involvement."

On May 11, 2011, I received an e-mail from Dan Balz, *Washington Post* national political correspondent[116], saying: "Dear Don, like other reporters, I've been following the decision-making process of Mitch Daniels as he weighs a presidential run. Could we have a brief conversation tomorrow about that?"

I responded that I was traveling across the country with my wife and attending a couple of graduations. I then said, "I'm always happy to talk with you, but I will have nothing to say about Mitch's situation. The decision is now in his hands, and I'm hopeful we'll all know his decision soon."

Balz replied to me, "Thanks for your reply. Depending on the decision, I would like to talk to you about the meeting at your home in early 2010 that kind of kicked off the deliberation process. No rush."

My initial reaction was, *How did he know that?*

I sent it to Mitch, saying, "Just got this tonight and sent back my response. I don't know him, never met him or talked to him, and don't know where he got my name or his information."

Mitch responded, "He's straight and a good reporter. But your instincts are right, as usual."

Then on May 14, Mitch sent a message to several members of our group. He was receiving multiple calls from people such as Governor Scott Walker and Congressman Paul Ryan (who said he was getting calls from people panicked that he [Mitch] wasn't going to run).

Mark Lubbers responded by saying, "You have put in all the air this balloon will hold. Time to pop it or launch it. You have undoubtedly

---

[116]   Whom I had never actually met

thought through how you want to launch, which from all appearances is what you are doing. Do you want any thoughts from us on this?"

Mitch replied, "Yes, stand by for a requested conference call fairly soon."

The next day, the call was scheduled with Eric and the seven members of our group for noon eastern time, Saturday May 21, 2011.

* * *

As we waited for that day, an article in an online publication that was published several months earlier reminded us of the difficult decision Mitch was now going to make. It was entitled "2012 Run Not an Effortless Decision for Daniels." It was posted on www.jconline.com on March 21, 2011.[117]

We never could locate the author of this particular piece, but we all agreed it hit the mark. It asked us to try to imagine the difficulty of the decision Mitch and his family were preparing to make. This was arguably the most important, prestigious job in the world, yet at what cost to the individual and his family?

Simple things we take for granted—walking the dog, going to a movie, spontaneously taking your spouse to dinner. None of that was possible without a heavily armed security detail wherever you traveled. Notwithstanding the little inconveniences, what if running for president and then assuming the presidency meant suffering the slings and arrows of the opposition, the media, and anyone else with a different point of view? Your integrity, past actions both personal and political were all subject to withering attacks and many times twisted meaning.

Then there was the job itself. The world is your office and every single American your responsibility in terms of safety and security. What does that do to an individual's health and the sanity of his or her family? The article reminded us that this was a decision that was hard, and it was fast approaching the deadline in which it had to be made.

---

[117] "2012 Run Not an Effortless Decision for Daniels," *JConline*, March 21, 2011, www.jconline.com/article/20110321/opinion/103210312/0/NEWS09/2012-run-not-an-effortless-decision-Daniels?odyssey=nav/head.

Cheri and the Family

A s we progressed through 2011, there was some indication in the press that Cheri had perhaps softened in her opposition to the idea of Mitch running for president. That was fueled entirely by press speculation, as the media saw her sitting for more interviews than perhaps normal.

A *RealClearPolitics* article written by Erin McPike said, in part:

> To hear the average wise-guy political strategist in Washington tell it, Indiana first lady Cheri Daniels ultimately may be what stands between Republican Gov. Mitch Daniels and a 2012 presidential bid. Story after story about Daniels' national plan reads that an impediment to the Hoosier State governor's success in a GOP presidential primary is a spouse with no stomach for a national campaign. That may prove to be a myth, one that overlooks a steady rise in Mrs. Daniels' profile over the past year—and evidence that she appears to be steeling herself for the rigors and scrutiny of a presidential campaign.[118]

The odd thing about the article was that Cheri had actually passed on an interview for this very story, so most of what the author said and quoted was mere speculation. The author did use the article, however, to

---

[118] Erin McPike, "Cheri Daniels Raises Her Profile," *RealClearPolitics*, March 11, 2011.

again raise the specter of the divorce and remarriage. She pointed out that the 1994 divorce and 1997 remarriage could be an obstacle, and certainly was something that ultimately had to be addressed.

Alexis Levinson, writing for *The Daily Caller*, also brought up the divorce issue. Levinson said, "Another potential issue that has been raised regards Daniels' marriage, a subject the Governor is exceptionally reluctant to speak on and into which he has never allowed much scrutiny. Despite the Daniels' reluctance to talk about that period, it is something that other candidates would certainly bring up in a presidential primary—if not directly then perhaps through intermediaries."[119]

Additionally, at this time other people tried to talk to Cheri with some successful, some not. Laura Bush did call her, and when Cheri returned the call to the house, the former president himself actually answered so she ended up talking to them both at some length. The response later communicated to us was no commitment.

A close friend of the family met with two of the Daniels daughters, and their response when asked about a potential race was, "No way." They said it would change their lives forever.

* * *

Probably the single event behind much of the speculation was the state party's announcement that Indiana First Lady Cheri Daniels would be the keynote speaker at the annual Spring Dinner to be held May 12, 2011. This caught us all, including the new state party chairman, Eric Holcomb, by surprise.

The press reaction was immediate. Was this to be the official announcement? Had Cheri changed her mind? Her chief of staff said to the press the speech wasn't a signal of her feelings one way or the other regarding the presidential race but simply the first time she had been invited.

Later that week, I called Mitch and asked him how this had happened. He said he was literally sitting at the dining room table having breakfast with her, and it just popped into his mind. Eric had been after him to nail down a keynote speaker. He asked her, she said yes, and that was it. He

---

[119] Alexis Levinson, "As Daniels Considers White House Run, Supporters Venerate, Critics Unload," *The Daily Caller*, March 18, 2011.

said the point was to sell the maximum number of tickets, and who better to do it at this particular time than Cheri!

Several of us considered that, perhaps, in the back of his mind was the thought that she would be so well received by an enthusiastic crowd (as stated previously, *Run Mitch Run* signs had already been printed and were to be handed out), it might just turn her around.

Anthony Dalke, writing in *Politico*, picked up on the story weeks later, saying, "We could be seeing a signal that suggests Mitch Daniels now leans toward a presidential bid. Daniels' wife, Cheri, did a recent appearance at the Indianapolis Indians home opener and plans to appear as the headliner at the Indiana State GOP dinner next month. GOP County Chairman Steve Shine says that means Daniels is likely to enter the race."[120]

It also prompted a lengthier article in *Politico* by Molly Ball that focused on all the spouses of the potential GOP candidates. It started out by noting the "frenzy of interest" generated by the announcement that Cheri was going to keynote the GOP dinner.

In the article, Myra Gutin, a historian at Rider University in New Jersey whose research focuses on First Ladies, was quoted as saying, "As a people, we want to see the spouse, whoever it is, and hear from the spouse. At the very least we certainly like to see that the partner has given tacit approval to the candidate."[121]

This unusual role for Cheri, in addressing the dinner, also brought out even more distasteful articles and questions. In many ways, these were examples right at the heart of the family's reluctance for a national campaign. Even though they had been through two successful gubernatorial campaigns, this stage was different. The onslaught of press articles just reinforced that reality.

Jason Horowitz, in a *Washington Post* article, said, "If the first lady is the deciding vote, she is not an easy sell. She has expressed her own reservations about the consequences a presidential bid might have on her family."

Horowitz went on to say (revealing a sobering example of what we could expect) that in exchange for anonymity, an official for another GOP prospect provided him with contact information for the ex-wife of

---

[120]   Anthony Dalke, "A Tasty Tidbit about Daniels," *Politico*, April 13, 2011.
[121]   Molly Ball, "In Spotlight for 2012, Spouses Glare Back," *Politico*, April 23, 2011.

the man Cheri married in the years between her divorce and remarriage to Daniels.[122]

On May 12, 2011, the *New York Times* jumped into the fray with a front page story. Author Jeff Zeleny, in a lengthy article complete with pictures and sidebars, recapped the entire divorce story, comparing it to other personal narratives of well-known personalities. He said:

> [Daniels] has been married twice—to the same wife. Should he run that chapter in his life would no doubt be picked over in public and become a part of the personal narrative that springs up around any serious candidate: in this case a three-year gap in their marriage in the 1990s, when she filed for divorce, moved to California with a new husband and left Mr. Daniels to raise their four daughters, then ages 8 to 14. She later returned and remarried him. He has discussed it only once publicly, telling the *Indianapolis Star* in 2004: "If you like happy endings, you'll love our story."[123]

Following the *New York Times* article, one of our group received a message from a veteran senior Democrat campaign consultant who said, "I thought that story on Daniels' wife was outrageous. Why would they write a piece focusing on his remarriage? I know Zeleny—he is 100% for Obama."

But the crowning blow was an article by Janice D'Arcy in the *Washington Post* following the Indiana dinner that brought up the idea of Cheri "abandoning her children."[124]

Mitch, when confronted with this article, said, "Nothing could be

---

[122] Jason Horowitz, "Whether Mitch Daniels Runs for President May Come Down to his Wife's Vote," *Washington Post*, May 11, 2011. Speculation in *Double Down* by Halperin and Heilemann suggested it was Huntsman campaign officials who obtained her cell phone number.

[123] Jeff Zeleny, "Weighing a White House Bid as Opening a Door to Past Pain," *New York Times*, May 12, 2011.

[124] Janice D'Arcy, *Washington Post*, May 18, 2011.

further from the truth and everyone that knows the situation understands that. She is and has always been a fabulous mother to our children."

It was also reported around this time that the ex-wife of the doctor (with whom Cheri went to California and married) approached *RealClearPolitics*. That story was also beginning to make the rounds with some unflattering comments.

* * *

The dinner speech was a huge success. There were no announcements, no revelations, just a strong, funny, well-received speech to a completely sold-out audience who kept chanting, "Run, Mitch, Run!" with a huge contingent of national press waiting for something significant to report.

It did remind all of us that opponents and the press weren't going to ignore Mitch and Cheri's marriage history. South Carolina Governor Nikki Haley, appearing the next day, May 13, on ABC's *This Week*, called the focus on Indiana Governor Mitch Daniels's wife as a reluctant political spouse, "ridiculous." She continued, "What you need to be looking at—and what I'm certainly looking at—is what type of governor he was. He was an amazing reformer in his state. He needs to give his stance on where he stands with family values and what he'll do to make sure those stay strong in this country. But I think to go into a candidate's personal life and try to attack them and distract the country—people are smarter than that."[125]

All of us believed that, but it didn't erase the fact that attacks would be painful at times.

---

[125] ABC's *This Week*, May 13, 2011.

The Final Decision

P rior to the scheduled call with Mitch on Saturday May 21, 2011, Tom Bell called to talk about the upcoming call and discuss what the decision might be. I had shared nearly everything with Tom over the past two years, and either he or I were the ones always tasked with talking to Mitch at critical periods. However, he had not experienced a conversation with Cheri as I had done.

He asked me what I thought the decision would be. He said in his opinion (and the opinion of every other member of our group, with the possible exception of one), Mitch was going to say yes. "What do you think he will do?" he asked.

I said, "I think he will say no."

Tom then replied, "That's why we were such good partners [in business], we complement each other."

The call took place from Mitch's home, and the rest of us—Tom Bell, Al Hubbard, Rick Powell, Bob Perkins, Mark Lubbers, Eric Holcomb, and myself—were on the telephone. Charlie Black was in Ireland and couldn't be on the call, but I had arranged to call him shortly thereafter. That was our group, the same group that met nearly two years previously in my living room in Scottsdale, Arizona, that started this journey.

Mitch started by thanking everyone on the call for all the support and encouragement in his consideration for a run at the presidency. He then wasted no time and quickly said, "But, I will not be a candidate for president in 2012."

He said he believed it was doable, and he had reconciled all the objections and barriers in his own mind. He simply couldn't convince the family to let him do it.

Mitch said he believed the Obama campaign was most concerned about his candidacy and the issue focus he would bring, the debt and the size of government. He said, "I believe the American people are ready for someone with a business background who would tell the truth about real issues."

He said he was all right with all of it. He could live without doing it, but his greatest concern was he was "letting people down who expected me to ultimately say yes."

He requested if we talked to reporters—and he thanked us again for never leaking anything in nearly two years—that we try to counter the argument he was "boring" as a candidate. That description really bugged him. He said we would have shown them something about how to do "Indiana retail politics."

Someone also suggested we characterize this as a person who didn't just talk family values but actually lived them.[126]

The call lasted about twenty minutes; everyone praised Mitch for his willingness to do it and expressed regret we were unable to continue.

As I indicated previously, I believe most of the group had felt as if he was going to say yes. I never did. Ever since my meeting with Cheri, I believed, in the end, she would never say yes, and therefore, he wouldn't do it. The press, particularly the Indiana press, was stunned. But so was the national press; they all thought he was going to say yes.

* * *

An official statement was released to the press, embargoed until after midnight for the Sunday papers and to allow us time to call select people, and then an e-mail was sent that evening, May 21, 2011, to our in-house list of supporters from Mitch saying:

> I hope this reaches you before the public news does. If so, please respect my confidence for the short time until I can make it known to all.

---

[126] An obvious shot at Tony Perkins and the Family Research Council

The counsel and encouragement I received from important citizens like you caused me to think very deeply about becoming a national candidate. In the end, I was able to resolve every competing consideration but one. But that one, the interests and wishes of my family, is the most important consideration of all. If I have disappointed you, I will always be sorry. If you feel this was a non-courageous or unpatriotic decision, I understand and will not attempt to persuade you otherwise. I only hope you will accept my sincerity in the judgment I reached.

Many thanks for your help and input during this period of reflection. Please stay in touch if you see ways in which an obscure Midwestern Governor might make a constructive contribution to the rebuilding of our economy and our Republic.

* * *

In retrospect, reading his statement, it is evident that he felt people would be upset with his decision, and he sounded almost defensive about it. Both things were true and understandable. It had taken him two years to accept the idea he could actually do this—be a serious candidate for president of the United States. Then to not do it because he couldn't get his family to even be neutral was a staggering blow. Mitch was good at moving on with things, and he would successfully move on after this decision, but initially it was a difficult time.

After the call, I sent Mitch the following e-mail:

What to say? Ever since December 12 when I had my meeting with Cheri, I have felt this would be the outcome, but ever optimistic, I was still hopeful. I'd be less than honest if I didn't admit I am in a bit of depression right now. But, I can only imagine what you are going through so I will simply say it was a privilege to be involved and I thank you for the opportunity of the exploration. You have made significant contributions to the entire debate, framing it really in the terms it needs to be discussed. I believe you have many more contributions to make. I hope we can somehow continue the journey, just in a different way.

He responded, "Many thanks for everything … we'll figure out a way to chip in."

* * *

The next day, early Sunday morning May 22, 2011, I sent the following to our list of key supporters:

> A difficult decision was made today in Indianapolis and I wanted to make certain you received the notice as soon as possible. Mitch delivered a statement to the *IndyStar* late Saturday night that will be in Sunday's paper and is embargoed until 1:00 a.m. Sunday morning online. He is announcing he will not be a candidate for President of the United States.
>
> You will no doubt see his explanation in any number of publications tomorrow and throughout the next few days so I will not repeat his statement. Suffice it to say there is only one thing that surpassed his love of country and that was his love of family. I think it is significant that you have in Mitch Daniels a person who not only talks family values but who also lives them.
>
> He believes, as do I, that this was a doable challenge. The people that were waiting on him and were prepared to support him comprise a list that would have been unmatched by any current candidate in the field. From multiple Governors to major finance players to key professional and volunteer staff—it would have been a powerful group of individuals. They believed in him as a person and equally important, in his message—that we

are a country at the crossroads that needs to decide what kind of future we will leave for the next generation.

I believe it is true his candidacy was the one of most concern to the present Administration. Mitch has vowed to continue his participation in raising the difficult issues and insisting on an adult conversation with the American people. I know his greatest concern is feeling he has let people down by his decision, but I for one, believe he made it for the right reasons. While disappointed that we will not have our best candidate running, I understand it and support it.

As to the media's characterization of him as boring and wonky—we haven't had a candidate since Ronald Reagan that could connect with the common person like Mitch Daniels. Just ask the people of Indiana who elected him twice and specifically the hundreds of ordinary citizens in whose homes he stayed the past six years. He would have shown America something about retail politics!

So, a sincere thank you for all the support, encouragement and willingness to wait on him. There is still a contribution to be made by Mitch and all of us who believe in preserving our country for our children. Feel free to drop him a note at his personal email.[127]

Then I received an onslaught of personal messages, and the media unleashed a barrage of stories.

My first e-mail was from Tom Bell. "You did all you could," he said, "and we came a long way but as you always said, 'She ain't going to change her mind'! Now what?"

My second was from Rick Powell: "Even though I knew it was coming, that was a profoundly disappointing call. I respect his decision, but you can tell he wanted to do it. Thanks for including me in this amazing trip."

From Al Hubbard, "It is such a bummer. You did see it coming. I just couldn't believe he would be doing all he was doing and getting such a

---

[127] I included Mitch's personal e-mail address here.

positive reception without figuring out a way to run. It would have been so much fun working with you."

From Eric Holcomb, "I felt like I was standing at the casket all day today, shaking everyone's hand and saying, 'he is in a better place.' One of the best outcomes of this adventure was meeting the 'Arizona Gang' when it all started. I understand why Mitch looks to you as much as he does. I hope we can find another project and this time punch it across the goal line!"

Other messages included:

Roger Helms, Scottsdale businessman—"I thought he was THE choice for us … Thank you for allowing me to get involved with him."

Former Congressman George Nethercutt—"That lets a lot of air out of the political tire for me. I was hoping, yearning for a yes, and really ready to go to work, but understand and respect family decisions."

Cleta Mitchell, FEC attorney who would have been our general counsel—"I feel as though someone died. Just hope it isn't the country. Thanks for your yeoman work in getting him to move from 'no way' to 'yes, if' … So odd to me that Cheri is so adamant, but I guess only she can know her own heart. Thanks for letting me be part of it."

Tim Clayton, NFIB Chairman—"Sorry to hear about Mitch's decision but understand it completely. The media craziness is driving away our best possible leaders. I'm sure the team in the west wing will be breathing easier today."

Joe Allbaugh, President George W. Bush's campaign manager—"Do not like it, but totally understand. It is so brutal on families. Hard for most to see that from the outside. You are a trooper for steering all of this. I know that role is not easy."

Jann Olsten, former chief of staff to Senator Rudy Boschwitz (R-MN)—"An understandable decision, but no less disappointing. A sad day for America."

Harold Burson, Chairman Emeritus, Burson-Marsteller—"Too bad about Mitch's decision not to make the run, but even not knowing much of the background, I can empathize with and respect his decision."

Chip Andreae, former chief of staff to Senator Richard Lugar (R-In.),

"I am sad about the decision. I believe he would have made a great President and I believe that we need him now more than never."

There were many additional messages sent directly to Mitch, including one from Dina Powell, Bush Administration senior official and Goldman Sachs partner. "They say that at the end of the day there are no perfect ways to make really tough decisions," Dina wrote. "I disagree. There is always one guidepost that stands out—what is the right thing for my family and me. You are picking the right legacy. The other part of life, of course, is when God shuts one door, he opens another we couldn't even see, so hang on because you are too talented to not serve our country and continue to make an impact."

Mitch sent me his response to Dina: "Getting a lot of these messages, but this is a very special one that I intend to keep. Thank you, good friend. Sun came up this morning, as I thought it might."

(The late) Jim Cannon, former advisor to President Gerald Ford, wrote, "Kudos for your stout decision and your valid reasoning. Like millions of others, I am disappointed that you will not be our next President; but I compliment you on your demonstration of courage and conviction. 'Fondly do we hope, fervently do we pray,' as Lincoln said, that you will continue to be the voice of candor and reality about the state of our nation. Continue to talk sense to the American people. Tell us where we are, where we need to go, and what we need to do to get there."

Karen Keller, my assistant for ten years and then Mitch's at OMB and finally President George W. Bush's as his executive assistant in the White House, wrote, "Mitch, you are a brave and courageous man. I admire and respect you more than ever. Thank you and your amazing family for what you have been through and what you have done for this country. Rest assured knowing that you have given more than anyone should ever ask."

And then, we did receive a few that expressed the great frustration we all felt but didn't express so graphically. A Mitch supporter forwarded one such message from New York. Our supporter, while not the author of the message, thought Mitch needed to see these opinions also. It read:

How terribly disappointing. Thank heavens the founding Fathers on down to Ronald Reagan were willing to make untold sacrifices in accepting the burden of leadership. As Ike told Mamie, "Duty will always come first."

What is the message to those making greater sacrifices, including those with families who have volunteered to serve in harm's way to defend our country on the front lines? A single term for Mitch, equal to one contract for a Marine officer, could perhaps have changed the country's course for the better in an hour of great peril and need.

Merely campaigning at the top of the ticket could have helped improve the prospects for Republican dominance in Congress and a certain end to the Obama agenda. At the end of the day, this exploration feels like a giant tease at the nation's expense. A shame he ever announced publicly his interest. This is a man I respected a lot more yesterday.

I responded myself to our supporter who'd sent it by saying, "Thanks for sending, but completely unfair and wrong in my view. Duty is not only to country. We tried everything possible to change the five family minds but the inappropriate ugliness of the media-led process was just too much."

Obviously, strong feelings were held by many people.

* * *

The media explosion was also expected, and it didn't disappoint. Among the many stories, columns, blog posts, and articles were these: *Politico*'s Mike Allen on May 23, 2011, said:

> Why we kept saying Daniels wouldn't run (and stuck to it, even when some of the top Republicans in the land claimed otherwise): If you're not sure, you're not running. It's too hard. D.C. buzz about Daniels was largely wishful thinking. The Halperin-Heilemann book[128] will say that

---

[128] 2013's *Double Down*

if Daniels could have gotten Cheri to neutral, he would
have gone.[129]

Politico's Alexander Burns and Jonathan Martin followed with a
lengthy article entitled "Team Daniels Plots Next Moves." It quoted me,
Tom Bell, and several other former colleagues trying to ascertain what, if
anything, we would now do in the presidential race. It said, "A group of
top Daniels supporters predicted Sunday—as they were still reeling from
their candidates announcement—that there would be no mass migration
to another 2012 contender. Instead, many will keep their political and
financial might in reserve, waiting for one of the current candidates to gain
momentum—or for a new champion to show up and transform the race."

Politico had received my e-mail from someone and quoted me saying
our support would have been unique and powerful. I then said for
attribution, "I don't plan to pick another candidate. For me, it was very
personal with Mitch. I believe the major issue we face as a country was his
issue, the debt and size of government."

Burns and Martin also quoted Tom Bell as saying, "Most of the people
I know that were strongly encouraging Mitch to run not only felt like he'd
be a strong retail candidate, but were embracing his message. I don't see
another candidate out there right now on the Republican side that really
has the same message. Unless someone adopts it or is more articulate or
forceful in focusing on the debt and deficit issues, I don't know that we'll
get very excited about anyone."[130]

Peter Wehner, writing in *Commentary Magazine*, said:

> The decision by Governor Mitch Daniels to forego a
> presidential run because of family considerations is an
> example of something exceedingly rare in the political
> arena—selflessness and grace. I say that because Daniels
> wanted to run for president, and if he had chosen to do
> so, he would have been a front-runner. But because of

[129] Mike Allen, *Politico*, May 23, 2011.
[130] Alexander Burns and Jonathan Martin, "Team Daniels Plots Next Moves," *Politico*, May 23, 2011.

concerns expressed by his wife and four daughters, he decided to take a pass.

I'm not cynical about politicians. They're capable of acts of courage and perseverance. It isn't easy being in the arena; those who endure the slings and arrows deserve ample credit. And there are genuine sacrifices that accompany public service. But there's also enormous ego gratification that occurs, even though public officials rarely acknowledge it (they stress the sacrificial nature of serving in public life, not the inflated pride and public adoration that usually accompany it). And for a public official genuinely to put the desire of others ahead of his own—to step back from the stage when you have a realistic chance to become the next president of the United States—happens about as often as does a solstice lunar eclipse.

I wish Daniels had decided to run. But in an age when the order of our lives is easily corrupted, even in ways we don't see, it's hard to criticize a man for not forcing his wife and daughters to relive a terribly painful episode not of his own making.[131]

In the online version of the *Evansville Courier Press*, a staff editorial said:

> Some television talking heads were making light of Daniels on Sunday and Monday for allowing his family to ultimately decide for him whether or not to seek the most powerful political office on the planet. Shame on them. Daniels demonstrated with his decision that he is someone with solid core values, someone you could trust as a man of his word. How many major political players would merit that same trust?[132]

---

[131] Peter Wehner, "You Can't Criticize a Man for Sparing his Wife and Daughters," *Commentary Magazine*, May 23, 2011.

[132] *Evansville Courier Press*, May 24, 2011.

Ross Douthat, writing in the *New York Times*, said:

> The world may not have ended on Sunday, May 22, but
> for conservatives pinning their hopes for 2012 on a Mitch
> Daniels presidential campaign, the weekend felt a little bit
> like the opening of the sixth seal in the Book of revelation.
> As with any apocalyptic development, commentary is a
> bit superfluous: 48 hours later, there's not much to say
> about his family-driven bow-out except that it's a big
> disappointment to anyone who cares about American
> conservatism.[133]

A Gary Varvel cartoon in the *IndyStar* had Mitch in a Superman
costume, greeting a downcast elephant at his front door with a Mitch 2012
sign. The caption read, "My family won't let me come out and play."[134]

Perhaps the most compelling article in those closing days came from
Mark Salter, writing in *RealClearPolitics* on May 24, 2011, in a piece
entitled "Mitch Daniels, and Why We'll Miss What Might Have Been."
He said:

> I am disappointed by his decision, and I'm sorry for the
> country, too. No other prospective candidate had a record
> of accomplishment as impressive as his. More importantly,
> Daniels has personal qualities that Americans yearn for in
> public leaders even as our political culture impedes them.
>
> Had he run, I would have wagered on his nomination.
> I also believe he would have been our best candidate in
> the general election.
>
> His decision, he tells us, was a choice between his
> family's needs and his country's, and I have no doubt
> this was true. Repeated in every press account of his
> announcement was an assurance that his marriage, once
> broken and now repaired, would have been subjected to

[133] Ross Douthat, "Exit Daniels," *New York Times*, May 24, 2011.
[134] Gary Varvel, *Indy Star*, May 24, 2011.

painful scrutiny. It would be foolish to believe it would not have been. It's right to believe it shouldn't have been.

It really was none of our business. No one believes the matter reflected poorly on Daniels' character of leadership qualities. And the fact we believe such intimate truths are our business will probably dissuade other talented Americans from subjecting their families to vivisection by a gossip-hungry press and public.

I wrote on this site a couple of months ago that patriotism obliged Daniels to run for President—"A handsome indifference to power or his family's aversion to the sacrifices of public life are not sufficient reasons to excuse him from duty," I chided him.

In the email to his supporters Daniels gave an honest acknowledgment of that point of view—"I love my country; I love my family more." I felt ashamed of myself when I read it. But I expect to benefit in the future from that lesson in humility.[135]

After the decision was made by Mitch not to run, one of the more lengthy media articles was one by Maggie Haberman and Jonathan Martin in *Politico*. They reported:

> Daniels message to his supporters said that his wife and four grown daughters had veto power on a campaign and they had exercised it. If anyone wondered about the depth of Cheri Daniels concerns about the prying eyes of the public, these questions were more than answered in a string of stories and columns focused on her and her husband around the time of her May 12 speech to the GOP dinner. Those family concerns weighed heavily on the Daniels' clan, and ultimately won the day.[136]

---

135   Mark Salter, "Mitch Daniels, and Why We'll Miss What Might Have Been," *RealClearPolitics*, May 24, 2011.

136   Maggie Haberman and Jonathan Martin, "Behind the Daniels Family Veto," *Politico*, May 22, 2011.

* * *

Also coming after the announced decision was a feature article in *Indianapolis Woman* with an extensive interview with Cheri. Written by Anne Ryder, the article revealed much about Cheri's feelings and attitude about being in the national spotlight. She wrote, "Cheri is a public person who straddles the line of privacy. Her vision of the next chapter of life was not in sync with the grind of a national campaign. Incognito photo shoots with her grandkids go out the window on a presidential bus tour. 'When you take the world stage, your anonymity is gone,' Cheri said. 'You lose your life as you know it forever.'"[137]

The interview went on to cover many of the personal considerations that had been expressed by Cheri and the family in private conversations. The media scrutiny remained a constant concern with all of them. Cheri articulated the subject of obligation to country and family and the inherent conflict between the two. She claimed that the ultimate decision was not up to her alone, although admittedly she had a major voice in the discussion. She recognized that people were disappointed, but indicated most were very kind about the decision once made.

There are some people who will never forgive Cheri and the family for preventing Mitch from making the run for the presidency, people who were convinced it was his time, his "obligation" to his country.

But most people said the same thing: "We would have liked to see him run, but he turned it down for all the right reasons."

Cheri, flooded with relief once the decision was announced, certainly agreed.

---

[137] Anne Ryder, "Family First: Down to Earth and True to Her Roots, Cheri Daniels is Right Where She Wants to be—in Indiana," *Indianapolis Woman*, July 1, 2011.

The Remaining Months

O ne would think that with the fury of activity and response to the announcement on May 21, the spectacle of a Mitch Daniels candidacy would slowly fade away. We often discussed the fact that, once he had taken himself out of the race, that would be it—no more calls from the morning talk shows or reporters wanting time for feature articles.

The attention clearly subsided for a while, but various things kept cropping up that kept him in the mix.

Paul Bedard, writing in *Washington Whispers*, asked, "Is Mitch Daniels Looking to be *Drafted* for President in 2012?" The article was centered on the anticipated release of his book, *Keeping the Republic: Saving America by Trusting Americans*, which was due out September 20.

Bedard said, "He's rejected running for president, but an upcoming book from Indiana Gov. Mitch Daniels that lays out a comprehensive 'reconstruction' plan for the United States is sure to revive the 'Draft Mitch' effort, especially if the economy continues to sputter and no GOP candidate catches fire."[138]

In the book's forward, Columnist George Will, wrote, "This book is a conservative blueprint to restoring American faith in the nation. It is the Daniels Doctrine, or conservatism for grown-ups."[139]

---

[138] Paul Bedard, "Is Mitch Daniels Looking to be Drafted for President in 2012?" *Washington Whispers*, August 10, 2011.

[139] George Will, foreword to *Keeping the Republic: Saving America by Trusting Americans*, by Mitch Daniels, (New York: The Penguin Group, 2011), xiii.

Mitch himself, in a letter to friends and supporters regarding the book, said:

> Why do people write books? For some it's to seek fame and fortune. For others it's an exercise in narcissism. For politicians it's often part of a quest for higher office. In my case none of those applied. I was just deeply concerned about the country's direction and hoped I might have something useful to say about it.
>
> The book title comes from Benjamin Franklin. As he was leaving the Constitutional Convention in 1787, someone in the crowd asked what sort of government the delegates had created. He called back: "A republic, if you can keep it." I do believe that despite the seriousness of our problems, and the bitterness of our politics, we can still pull together a broad coalition to do what is necessary to preserve the American dream, do right by our kids and theirs, and keep the republic.

Mike McCarville, veteran Oklahoma journalist, upon reading Bedard's column, said, "If a draft would work, put me down! I had not known about the book and must get a copy. Mitch has always been a solution ... not a problem."

The Chairman of a Fortune 500 company in New York, after seeing Mitch on a television broadcast in mid-September, sent him a message saying he was fabulous and hoped he was changing his mind.

Mitch responded, "Terrific to hear from you. If you are sitting around watching me on TV, you need to find a hobby or strengthen your social skills. I don't expect to reverse field, unless my five women suddenly do, but it means a ton that you would suggest it. Many, many thanks."

And, then of course, talk about the vice presidential choice inevitably began to surface.

Politico, in an article by Jonathan Martin, said:

> Some Daniels enthusiasts are eyeing him for vice-president, but the ever-modest Indiana governor, while

not ruling out the prospect, doubts he'll be asked. Some Republicans saw the joint interview Daniels and his publicity-shy wife, Cheri, did on *CBS Sunday Morning* as a signal that the family may be up for the Naval Observatory if not the White House. By addressing their divorce and reconciliation in the interview, the thinking went, the Daniels' could point to the sit-down next year as a sign of having sufficiently addressed the matter. The Hoosier Governor wearily dismisses the notion as "Beltway over-analysis."[140]

* * *

On the final day of 2011, December 31, Mitch sat for an interview with the local media and answered the question, "I know you are tired of being asked about this, but do you have any second thoughts about not running for President, and would you accept a draft at the Republican National Convention if no one has the requisite number of delegates?"

Mitch answered: "Well, that isn't going to happen. As intriguing as it would be for everybody in your business and for all of us, nominations get settled before conventions. No, I don't really sit around thinking about [the decision]. People bring it up so when they do, that's when it comes back to mind. I opted for a different way to try to contribute and I'm happy with that course."

140   Jonathan Martin, *Politico*, September 30, 2011.

PART IV
2012

Election Year

J anuary started out politically with the annual State of the Union address by the president. The Republican response was given by someone chosen by the Republican leadership in Congress (Speaker John Boehner and Senator Mitch McConnell). They wanted someone not running for the nomination and not aligned with any one candidate. They chose Mitch Daniels.

The problem was he was fabulous, and all the rumors started up again, even in January of the election year!

On January 25, 2012, Ron Radosh posted an article on pjmedia.com. He wrote:

> Any viewer who stayed tuned after our campaigner-in-chief's State of the Union speech last night had the opportunity to watch the GOP response by Gov. Mitch Daniels of Indiana. The feeling of many Republicans and conservatives, including myself, is an instant one: why isn't this man a candidate for the presidency?
>
> So, I support those who hope for a brokered convention, at which time neither Mitt nor Newt will have enough votes to win on a first ballot, and the Republican Party can turn to someone else with real chance against Obama. At this point, I think, that candidate is Mitch Daniels.[141]

---

[141] Ron Radosh, "Why Mitch Daniels Should Enter the Race: The Real Conservative Alternative," *pjmedia.com*, January 25, 2012.

It was a nice theory, but Charlie Black had told us months before that it was just mathematically impossible, given the way delegates are now selected, for someone to go into the convention without the nomination secured.

Peter Wehner wrote a piece for *Commentary Magazine* on January 27, 2012, called "Read It and Weep." He said:

> I had some critical things to say about President Obama's State of the Union address. But the evening was not a total waste, thanks to the response by Indiana Governor Mitch Daniels. Needless to say, those of us who wanted him to run for president this year were reminded why. In that sense, listening to Daniels's speech left some of us more depressed than listening to Obama's speech.[142]

In *RealClearPolitics*, Mark Salter wrote:

> We had an excellent example of the statesmanship missing in our public affairs a few minutes after the president high-fived his way out of the House chamber when Indiana Gov. Mitch Daniels offered the Republican response.
>
> In the long ago, pre-Trump, Bachmann, Cain, Gingrich, Santorum, Romney and Gingrich yet-again days, I used this space to plead with Daniels to run for president. He declined for personal reasons. But, really, after Obama's feckless performance and the histrionics and other silliness of the Republican nomination race, is it any wonder why I still find myself chanting this week, "Run, Mitch, Run!"?[143]

* * *

[142] Peter Wehner, "Read It and Weep," *Commentary Magazine*, January 27, 2012.
[143] Mark Slater, "After Obama's Empty Words, Daniels Said it All," *RealClearPolitics*, January 26, 2012.

In addition to the media articles and numerous messages from friends and colleagues, the governor's office in Indianapolis began receiving dozens of handwritten letters from people all across the country following the State of the Union response. His personal assistant, Maggie Ban, picked out a dozen or so and sent them to me. She said, "I'm not trying to stir anything up, but thought you should know that there are people out there still encouraging him to ride into the convention on a white horse to save the party."

A sampling of these letters include:

Dear Governor Daniels,

To introduce myself, I am a 77-year-old retired RN, mother of 10, grandmother of 24, great grandmother of 4 and wife of a retired army man. I have paid close attention to politics over the years.

I've been following your career. I've read your book and heard your amazing response to the President's State of the Union message.

My wish is for you and your family to reconsider your decision to run for president. I sincerely believe you are exactly the man to lead our country. Your country needs you.

And, as a Catholic mother, I'm pretty good at assigning guilt.

(Bonner Springs, Kansas)

We are not from the state of Indiana, we are from Texas. With tears on our faces last night we stood up and took notice we want you as President of our United States. No one has spoken to us like this in all our years.

(A couple in their late sixties)

I do not want to live to see the end of America, but I fear I will. It is not too late for you to enter the race.

(An eighty-six-year-old widow)

Respectfully, and with deep appreciation for genuine sacrifice I am asking you to make, I implore you to take on a historic responsibility: to lead the way back to our uniquely American destiny as a candidate for the presidency. Your country needs you. Our history needs you. It is a pivotal moment, after which things will never be the same, one way or another.

(A chief executive officer in Virginia)

I rarely write handwritten letters, but I felt compelled to send a personal appeal to you after hearing your response to the State of the Union address. I am asking you to reconsider a run for the presidency. Our party and country needs you. You are the only person that can combine a solid conservative record and impressive executive experience with pragmatic ideas and passionate rhetoric. Please rethink your decision and lead America out of the mess we are in.

(A doctoral candidate in the field
of Plasma Physics at Princeton University)

There were dozens and dozens of similar letters, and according to Maggie, Mitch answered them all.

* * *

As we approached convention time and continued the journey through multiple primaries and debates, Mitch took himself out of all of it by accepting a future appointment (once his term ended in January) as president of Purdue University. He and I had talked about this possibility earlier in the year, and I knew he was interested. He had asked my opinion, and I was positive, although I had hoped he would wait until after the convention in the slight chance he would be considered for the vice president slot.

We had talked about the VP slot on several occasions, and there is no doubt in my mind he would have accepted it, if asked. It made a great deal of sense in multiple ways. He came from a midwestern state we needed to carry (Obama carried it in 2008); he had a record of achievement as a governor and a business executive; he could talk about the principal issue we faced, the debt and fiscal matters; he had appeal to young people; and, unlike Romney (through no fault of his own), he was fabulous at retail politics, he could relate to the common man.

By accepting the Purdue appointment, even though he wouldn't assume the office until January 2013, he had to agree to refrain from any active political involvement from that day forward. We not only missed out on the best running mate, but we also gave up a great campaigner who could have contributed significantly on the campaign trail if used wisely. It effectively took him off the grid politically for the rest of his term.

The choice of Paul Ryan, in many ways, was a salute to Mitch. He was a clone without the gubernatorial or business experience. He was a serious thinker, understood the fiscal issues as well as anyone in the country, and could be counted on to talk about big solutions to big problems. He could be relied on to tell the truth to the American people in an adult conversation. The *Wall Street Journal*, in an editorial following his selection, used all that language that Mitch actually brought to the conversation.

Cleta Mitchell, following the convention, sent this message to Mitch: "As I listened to the GOP convention I couldn't help but think that your influence was reflected everywhere. "Have an adult conversation with the American people," "tell the voters the truth" … the very words you've used these past several years. So, while we didn't get a Mitch Daniels presidency, maybe we are going to get a Mitch Daniels presidential campaign. Thanks for your inspired leadership—it was evident in Tampa."

Mitch replied with thanks and said he did feel we gave things a little shove in the right direction, and that he and Paul Ryan thought a great deal alike on key issues. He also said, "Yesterday my second grandchild was born. The first came on the night before the New Hampshire primary. One doesn't have to be a Presbyterian to sense a little meaning in that, because had I been a candidate I'd have missed both events. I think I was where I was supposed to be."

There are those who would always disagree with that observation. Skype and fast airplanes are wonderful inventions—but it was what it was. Mitch was at peace with the decision and at peace with himself and his family.

* * *

The election, of course, was a disaster. There were lots of reasons, not the least of which was that Romney's voter projection model was completely wrong. The ground game the Romney campaign kept saying was ready to execute was a failure. Obama outsmarted them at every turn in every aspect of the campaign. And, Romney just could never "relate" to the common voter.

Henry Payne, writing in the *Detroit News* a couple of weeks after the election, asked the predictable question—"Would Mitch Daniels have Defeated Obama?" He wrote, "Romney was simply a weak candidate. How weak? Rick Santorum almost beat him in Michigan. In Michigan! So weak that a dozen challengers entered the primary to try and defeat the man who should have been formidable after his runner-up primary finish in 2008. So weak that the GOP pleaded with conservative governors like Mitch Daniels (is there anyone today who doesn't think the folksy, successful, businessman-turned governor from Indiana would have beaten Obama?) to enter the primary"[144]

It is a question that is impossible to answer and probably even unfair to ask.

* * *

As 2012 came to a close, Mitch ended his eight years in the governor's office and prepared to begin a new life as president of Purdue University. It was his goal to create the model public university. He believed he still had a great deal to contribute.

In one of his closing interviews as governor, he was asked if he was sad to leave and whether he'd have run again if there weren't term limits. He said:

---

[144] Henry Payne, *Detroit News*, November 20, 2012.

I want this state to be a state of innovation and leadership. I think it's a good idea to have new people come in ever so often. We might not run out of good ideas, but they might have more than we did.

My own conception of public service is a citizen, if he or she gets the chance, should go do it. Whatever you can find to do. And then go back into the society and live under the laws that you were a part of making.

For those reasons, I think that, even without term limits, I would have felt it was time to try something different.

President Reagan said in the wings after a talk one time when I was with him, and the crowd was cheering and wanting him, "Always leave 'em wanting a little more."

In his final letter to state employees as he was preparing to leave, Mitch said, "For eight years, we have asked state government to operate on the basis of continuous improvement, on the principle that 'good enough never is.' I leave your ranks with heartfelt thanks for what you have done to prove that government can shoot straight, and can treat taxpayer dollars with the care and respect they deserve. And I go in the hope that you will never rest but will keep on delivering results that are better every single year. Thank you for everything."

Epilogue

Politics at the national level is hard. The advent of social media and the new communications environment in which we now live, where anyone can say anything without any accountability for truth or accuracy, makes it even harder.

We came to Mitch Daniels initially because we knew him. We knew his capabilities, his values, and his persona. He was a friend, but he was also a person who had a gift, an extraordinary mind with keen political instincts, and an ability to relate to people of all walks of life. He knew how to manage and how to lead. He could put words on paper like a seasoned author and could deliver a speech or a story with the timing and clarity of a performer.

Could Mitch Daniels have been elected president of the United States in 2012? No one knows. The subtitle of this book is *The Hard Decisions One Man Faced for the 2012 Presidential Election.* That's what the process demands, and who knows where it would have ended?

Mitch stopped before the real scrutiny began, prior to all the opposition hammering that would have occurred, short of all the unanticipated crises that come with any national campaign. So, I am not naive enough to think he would have been able to just play offense. The Obama campaign was a master at political attacks. There would have been multiple challenges as the campaign progressed.

Yet, one has to wonder, *What might have been?* Here was a candidate who believed an adult conversation with the people of America was due and could be had. A candidate who had proven, as governor of a state heavily in debt, now in surplus, that through creativity, good management, and the right philosophical approach, you could succeed. A candidate who believed you could tell the American people the truth, thereby not just winning but also winning with a chance to actually govern. A candidate who could ride his Harley up to a complete stranger's modest home and stay the night, listening to his or her concerns and dreams.

In one of our very first conversations about this journey, Mitch said, "The real issue is what kind of country do we believe in?"

All of us involved believed a battle was raging in our country. It was not a traditional battle between Republicans and Democrats, conservatives and liberals, the young and the old. It was a battle for the soul of the country, a battle to answer the question posed by Mitch: "What kind of country do we want to be?"

He meant simply that one belief is based on the idea that America should be the land of equality and fairness and the right to happiness and success for every individual regardless of his or her status in life. This view believes that government is the engine that can provide that guarantee and is a safety net to ensure every person is covered with the cloak of equality.

The other view, our view, believes in an America that provides every individual the *opportunity* to succeed, the opportunity to find happiness, and the personal freedom to succeed or fail depending on his or her own hard work and merit. Government's role is to be a facilitator of that opportunity, not a guarantor, and to foster programs to ensure that those unable to help themselves receive special attention to help them succeed.

As Arthur Brooks once said, "The America our founders envisioned was a country that believed in equality of opportunity, not equality of outcome."

And, as Mitch himself said in an address at Yale University following the 2012 election, "We overlooked and omitted the most powerful appeal (to voters) available. We believe in *you* and your ability to decide for yourself; the other side doesn't."

* * *

In the end, Mitch determined that love of family trumped love of country. Even though he has moved on, the decision not to run was a wrenching one because he also thought of "what might have been." Many messages were sent (as described earlier) that summarized most people's feelings—he made his decision for the right reasons; that is the type of person we would have wanted to be our president.

On January 16, 2013, in the *Miami Herald*, former presidential speechwriter and now columnist Michael Gerson posted a column entitled: "Mitch Daniels, The One Who Got Away."

It was a superbly written conclusion to the Mitch Daniels story and raised once again the spectrum of "what might have been," which was on the minds of so many people as the Obama years continued.

The article talked about Mitch's new role in academia, a prestigious one for certain, and interviewed Mitch about his entering a new phase of his life. Michael, a colleague of Mitch in the Bush White House, talked about the necessity of having leaders like Mitch who were willing to talk truth to the American people.

His appeal to the youth, his willingness to prioritize on "survival" issues, his tolerance and sensitivity to the disenfranchised, his positive attitude about the necessity of a limited but active government that would bring real solutions to real problems—all of it wrapped up into a Harley riding, retail politician who had the courage of his convictions not just to win but also to govern.

Gerson concluded his article on January 16, 2013, by saying:

> Returning quietly to private life after public service is honorable and admirable. But this doesn't change one fact. The best Democratic politician in America is about to take his oath as president of the United States.
>
> The best Republican politician will soon be president of Purdue.[145]

145 Michael Gerson, "Mitch Daniels, The One Who Got Away," *Miami Herald*, January 16, 2013.

—— Afterword by Mitch Daniels

There are people in public service who grew up imagining a life in elected office and have spent decades plotting and working for it. I'm not one of them. I had not expected to hold office at any level, let alone the top office of them all—the one that every US senator, for instance, is supposed to believe is his destiny. As I told one reporter during the events covered in this book, "I have never once looked in the mirror and seen a President of the United States looking back."

Similarly, it's often observed that the crushing demands of modern presidential campaigns require candidates whose fixation on winning the prize verges on obsession. I'm not one of those, either. As a friend said, "As a presidential candidate, you'd have a fatal flaw. You can live without it." There's probably some validity in that.

From my youth, I was interested in politics and spent years either full-time or as a volunteer helping candidates I admired pursue election, but I never was at all driven to pursue office myself. That changed only in my fifties, when circumstances—me between jobs after a stint in the cabinet of President W. Bush, a home state in bad shape, and an Indiana Republican Party casting about for a candidate who could end a sixteen-year losing streak—combined to bring about my first and only elective bid.

Arriving in office so late in life, and with no ambition beyond the very big job of governor, I told myself daily to concentrate on making big positive change for the citizens of our state, to aim high and act boldly, and let the chips fall. Of course there were times when we pulled a punch or ducked a dispute, but in the main, our administration tackled the toughest issues and problems head on, and tried a constant stream of new ideas in a state never known for governmental innovation. Even our strongest detractors agreed with that assessment; for much of the first term, the conventional wisdom was that reelection would be extremely difficult not because we had done too little but because we had brought too much change, too soon.

We never took a poll to decide what ideas to advance. We barely took them at all, outside of the two campaign years when we measured our status and learned where to concentrate our campaigning. Ronald Reagan used to say that many people seek public office to be something, but the best seek it to do something. I aspired to the latter category. Countless times someone would warn of the ire we would generate from this group or that with one of our policy initiatives, to which I usually responded, "What are they threatening to do, give me my life back?"

I made the point over and over, in the first campaign (2004) and again in 2008, that I was not a careerist and had no interest in running for any other office. In the closing advertisement of the 2008 reelection, which I had written a year before, I said, "Regardless of your outlook on politics, I have some very good news. This is the last time you'll have to watch me in an ad like this!" I went on to reiterate that governor was the only office I had ever sought or intended to seek, that if rehired by the people of Indiana, we would deliver four more years of activist government aimed at lifting our state in areas we had not already attacked.

It's easy to understand the cynicism with which people dismiss a statement like that, but I always meant it and was determined to live up scrupulously to that assertion and to every other pledge I made. I believe in limited government but have always argued against letting skepticism about Big Government turn into a corrosive contempt for *all* government. I wanted to show that now and then people can come and go from public life without being on the make for higher office or personal gain, people whose words can actually be relied on.

All that made the idea of running for president utterly farfetched and unthinkable, when it began to surface and intensify after the Republican defeat by President Obama in 2008. And, after a deep concern about the future of our stagnating, indebted nation and the appeals of an astonishing number and variety of people I respected, moved me to think very seriously about running, I wound up returning to the position I had adopted at the outset—to compete for one public office, the one with by far the most potential to improve life for my fellow Hoosiers, to do that job as well as I could, and then return to private life.

When I finally made the choice not to run, the decisive factor was the unified and strong opposition of my wife and children. That alone would have settled the matter. But it was not the only thing on my mind. The issue above weighed heavily. First, I would be going back on a compact I felt I had made with the citizens of Indiana, to put in two full terms with no agenda other than building a better state.

Second, with two years left to serve, there was work yet to do; our team never accepted the inevitability of lame duck status, and we went on to prove it can be successfully avoided. Finally, I did not relish the prospect of watching our administration's record, seen by many as one of the strongest in Indiana history, trashed for two years by adversaries, probably in both political parties, with no scruples, respect for the facts, or stake in the success of our state.

On that score, the decision sits very well with me now. No one else thinks about this, but a host of important accomplishments would never have happened if I had run for president. In 2011, we delivered another balanced budget that solidified Indiana's first-ever AAA credit rating, and handed our successors the strongest fiscal foundation in the country, with more than $2 billion in reserves *after* refunding $ 720 million in "surplus reserves" to our taxpayers. We achieved the long-sought extension of full-day kindergarten to every Indiana school district. We fixed the state's unemployment insurance system and put it on a path to repay its recession-driven borrowings (at this writing, the repayment is four years ahead of schedule).

We codified Indiana's civil service reforms, previously in place through executive action, preventing the public sector union abuses that have paralyzed and bankrupted state governments in many other places. And we ran the table on the education reforms that are necessary if our unacceptable K–12 results are ever to improve—returning management to superintendents and school boards by narrowing collective bargaining to wages and benefits; performance evaluation of teachers; and the nation's first and still largest school choice program, to ensure that low- and moderate-income parents have the same range of options in educating their children that rich people do.

In 2012, we repealed the state's inheritance tax, and Indiana made more history by becoming the first Right to Work state in the industrial heartland since the early days of the Taft-Hartley Act. Along with the seven previous years' enhancements of the state's business climate, this breakthrough cemented Indiana's top-tier ranking as a good place to invest. In 2012, Indiana's per capita net income growth rose to second in the country, behind only oil-rich North Dakota. In short, we got more accomplished in years seven and eight than most of our predecessors did during their entire terms of service.

If I had been off running for president, it is likely that none of this would have occurred. A national political juggernaut would have encamped in Indiana, dissecting, distorting, and attacking every proposal we made. Each of these initiatives, even those I had espoused for many years, would have been viewed through a lens of political calculation, not the public interest that was our real motivation. National labor unions in particular would have invaded Indiana, as much to damage our presidential bid as to defeat civil service and Right to Work reforms.

No one, of course, can know how the campaign that wasn't would have turned out. Several of those who encouraged the idea remain utterly convinced that we would have won. While they could be right, my own best guess is that we would have captured the nomination but lost to an Obama campaign that had several powerful advantages—a monolithic, unpersuadable base of black and strongly liberal voters; an electoral college head start through its ownership of a few big coastal states; a clear superiority in its grasp of the political uses of social media; and its track record of success in personally demonizing its opponents.

Still, the thing had a shot. Viewing it as dispassionately and clinically as I can, I had never seen so open a door to a party's nomination as that which beckoned our little group in 2010–11. As the parade of visits and entreaties rolled on, it was clear that we had the unique potential to assemble a coalition spanning virtually the entire Republican Party.

Our fundamental positioning was pretty near ideal. Geographically, a midwestern candidate would have been preferable, and there wasn't another viable one around. Governors benefit from having held executive office, and the Indiana record through the first six years was a strongly positive one that would have held up even through the inevitable slanders and misrepresentations of a national campaign. Most of my thirty-plus fellow GOP governors, notably my old amigo Haley Barbour, would have been on board from the outset. And I believe we had enough credibility and avid supporters among the social issues leadership to have conducted an economically focused campaign under the flag of "truce" I had suggested the party adopt in order to appeal to moderates and less ideological voters.

Organizationally, we would have started with several entire networks—my fellow Reagan alumni, from whom I heard daily; the Bush 43 and Bush 41 networks, overlapping but not identical; Freedom Works, the largest and best organized of the so-called "Tea Party" structures (its leader Dick Armey made two trips to see me urging the run); the McCain organization (befitting our previous nominee, Senator McCain stayed neutral, but I got a strongly encouraging phone call from him and a slew of others from his top supporters); and the largely East Coast network of intellectual and financial leadership, the folks who fund and support publications like the *Weekly Standard*, *National Review*, and the *Spectator*, each of which ran cover stories promoting a run.

And in terms of the field, well, I think it's fair to say it wasn't the strongest. That part was largely luck; the Republican Party was in between generations, with a cohort led by John McCain having left center stage and a lot of promising younger officeholders just getting their careers airborne but not yet ready for the big show.

But no need to take it from me. Confirming accounts we had heard many times before and after my negative decision, the president's friend and strategist David Axelrod, in front of a large audience in Chicago at which we made a joint appearance in the spring of this year, said, "We were very relieved when Governor Daniels took himself out. He was the one we were most worried about."

Still, when the questions come, as they do almost every day, the answers come quickly. "Don't you wish you had run?" ("Thank you, but no.") "Won't you please run in 2016?" (Same reply, with emphasis.) On this question, the answer is both personal and practical; timing is truly everything in politics, and timing as fortuitous as that circumstance spread before us in 2012 never comes twice.

A thousand things could have gone awry, and many would have. I often told the gang of friends to be careful what they wished for, that "This might be the most interesting campaign anyone has seen for a while, for the six weeks before it blows up." Aside from the many mistakes I would surely have made, the fundamental purpose of the run, to call Americans to our duty as citizens not to bankrupt our nation and plunder our youth, would probably have been too easy to distort and demonize.

The whole endeavor might have ended on the stage in Des Moines, during the most interesting of the generally dreary "debates" into which the field was enticed. When Fox News's Bret Baier asked the year's single best question ("If you knew you could get a debt reduction deal that was 90 percent spending cuts and 10 percent tax increases, would you take it?"), not one hand went up. Mine would have.

I would have said, "Yes, probably, but first tell me a little more. What's the enforcement mechanism to make sure the spending cuts really happen? And what kind of tax increases? If, for example, they involve the elimination or capping of exemptions and special preferences, sign me up. If they leave a wreck of a tax code as is and just raise rates, hurting the economic growth we must have for greater revenues, let's negotiate a little more."

So that's one moment when things could have unraveled. Surely the other candidates would have piled on vigorously. But, just as the "truce" idea had far, far broader agreement among primary voters than many understood, the reaction to the CPAC speech in early 2011 told me that Republicans were ready for an honest addressing of the mortal threat that our runaway, autopilot spending and escalating debt poses to the American experiment.

In a wretched economy, with deficits and debts exploding to levels beyond comprehension, maybe a campaign pitched relentlessly to young people, to the unemployed, to the "yet to haves" of our society, a campaign that studiously declined off-putting negativism and divisive "wedge" issues and tried to unite Americans, might have had a chance.

At least in my case, the decision not to run was an intensely personal one, and that was reflected in the process of making it. Some will find fault with the fact that I conferred closely with only a small circle of longtime friends, all men and most of similar background. But such a group, chosen for their candor, willingness to tell me the plain truth as they saw it, and ability to keep a confidence, was for me exactly right for the threshold choice of whether or not to run. Had there been a campaign, then of course it would have immediately involved a very wide and diverse circle; in fact, its distinguishing characteristic would probably have been the breadth of the coalition I believe we would have assembled.

One dimension in which the decision should be personal, but sometimes isn't, has to do with its essence, the reasons for which the candidate is offering himself up at all. If a person needs guidance to decide what a candidacy stands for and what its program in office would be, then he shouldn't be running in the first place.

Any campaign we would have mounted would have minimized the use of paid political consultants, at least in the dominant and highly visible roles now prevalent in our politics. I already knew the themes and issues on which our effort would center, and we'd have seen no need to spend precious campaign dollars to be told what to talk about. Our two statewide races worked out well without hiring a single such consultant, and each was highly specific as to the initiatives and policies that we would pursue if selected. Especially at the presidential level, a person, his views, and values, either match the moment or they don't.

The other respect in which the counsel of others is of limited value has to do with the brutally public and intrusive nature of today's presidential campaigns. A candidate now exposes not only himself but his family to criticism, ridicule, and often hurtful falsehoods, which are never fully refuted. And winning the presidency means an end to private life, and an artificial existence of ongoing public scrutiny, limited mobility and friendships, and constant Secret Service presence. My wife and daughters were largely unaffected by my gubernatorial service, taking part in those aspects that interested them and absenting themselves from the rest. That can't work at the presidential level; when you decide to run, you take your loved ones into the hurricane with you.

As it happens, I am writing this in the cottage Cheri and I own in the beautiful mountains of West Virginia. Daughters, sons-in-law, and four beautiful grandchildren two years old and under are asleep in the rooms around me. At this moment, I feel as fortunate and blessed as a person can be in this world. Ben Johnson wrote, "To be happy at home is the end of all human endeavor." By that standard, I am among the luckiest of all God's creatures.

People in a position to know argued that our family would experience a net positive from presidential service. We'll never know. But it's hard to believe that family life could be much better than it is, at least for now.

One of the most memorable instances chronicled in Don's narrative occurred in Scottsdale when the ever-insightful Tom Bell leaned forward and said, "Listen, here's what matters. Have you settled in your own mind what thousands of people believe, that you can be a good president of the United States?"

Anyone who can say yes to that question without any hesitation probably shouldn't be president. The hubris it takes to make that claim with certainty about the world's most difficult job is exactly the trait that has gotten presidents, and our nation, into trouble before. I never got further than "I think so" or "at least as well as any of these other guys."

Charles DeGaulle is credited with the aphorism, "The cemeteries are full of indispensable men." Clint Eastwood's Dirty Harry Callahan said it even better, "A man's got to know his limitations." I still feel amazed and grateful that circumstances conspired to make the decision described in this book a serious one and to have been forced to think it through in the company of trusted old friends.

Appendix A

Governor Mitch Daniels's Speech to Conservative Political Action Conference Washington, DC, February 11, 2011

D avid Keene, George Will, good friends, thank you for the enormous privilege of this podium. Even a casual observer of American public life knows how many great ideas have been born here, how many important debates joined here, how many giants of our democracy appeared on this platform. When David broached the invitation, my first reaction was one I often have: "Who cancelled?" But first choice or fifteenth, the honor, and the responsibility to do the occasion justice, is the same. I am seized with the sentiment best expressed by Hizzoner, the original Mayor Richard Daley, who once proclaimed a similar honor the "pinochle of success."

We are all grateful to our cosponsors, the Reagan Foundation and the Reagan Ranch. How fitting that we convene under their auspices, as we close this first week of the centennial. Those of us who served President Reagan were taught to show constant respect for the presidency and whoever occupies it. But, among us alums, the term "the president" tends to connote just one of those forty-four men, that great man with whom God blessed America one hundred years ago this week.

The prefix in *cosponsor* is meaningful tonight. It is no state secret that the two foundations have not always been *co*operative, or *co*llaborative, or *co*llegial. So it is a tribute to the stature and diplomacy of David Keene that they have come together to produce so warm a moment as this. I am now converted to the view that yes, the Israeli-Palestinian conflict will be solved. Well done, David; Nobel Peace Prizes have been awarded for far less.

I bring greetings from a place called Indiana. The coastal types present may think of it as a "flyover" state or one of those "I" states. Perhaps a quick anthropological summary would help.

We Hoosiers hold to some quaint notions. Some might say we "cling" to them, though not out of fear or ignorance. We believe in paying our bills. We have kept our state in the black throughout the recent unpleasantness, while cutting rather than raising taxes, by practicing an old tribal ritual—we spend less money than we take in.

We believe it wrong ever to take a dollar from a free citizen without a very necessary public purpose, because each such taking diminishes the freedom to spend that dollar as its owner would prefer. When we do find it necessary, we feel a profound duty to use that dollar as carefully and effectively as possible, else we should never have taken it at all.

Before our General Assembly now is my proposal for an automatic refund of tax dollars beyond a specified level of state reserves. We say that anytime budgets are balanced and an ample savings account has been set aside, government should just stop collecting taxes. Better to leave that money in the pockets of those who earned it than to let it burn a hole, as it always does, in the pockets of government.

We believe that government works for the benefit of private life and not the other way around. We see government's mission as fostering and enabling the important realms—our businesses, service clubs, Little Leagues, churches—to flourish. Our first thought is always for those on life's first rung, and how we might increase their chances of climbing.

Every day, we work to lower the costs and barriers to free men and women creating wealth for each other. We build roads and bridges and new sources of homegrown energy at record rates, in order to have the strongest possible backbone to which people of enterprise can attach their investments and build their dreams. When business leaders ask me what they can do for Indiana, I always reply, "Make money. Go make money.

That's the first act of 'corporate citizenship'. If you do that, you'll have to hire someone else, and you'll have enough profit to help one of those nonprofits we're so proud of."

We place our trust in average people. We are confident in their ability to decide wisely for themselves, on the important matters of their lives. So when we cut property taxes, to the lowest level in America, we left flexibility for localities to raise them, but only by securing the permission of their taxpayers, voting in referendum. We designed both our state employee health plans and the one we created for low-income Hoosiers as Health Savings Accounts, and now in the tens of thousands, these citizens are proving that they are fully capable of making smart, consumerist choices about their own health care.

We have broadened the right of parents to select the best place for their children's education to include every public school, traditional or charter, regardless of geography, tuition-free. And before our current legislature adjourns, we intend to become the first state of full and true choice by saying to every low and middle-income Hoosier family, if you think a nongovernment school is the right one for your child, you're as entitled to that option as any wealthy family; here's a voucher, go sign up.

Lastly, speaking now for my administration colleagues, we believe in government that is limited but active. Within that narrow sphere of legitimate collective action, we choose to be the initiators of new ideas or, as we have labeled ourselves, the Party of Purpose. In President Reagan's phrase, "We *are* the change." On election nights, we remind each other that victory is not a vindication; it is an instruction, not an endorsement, but an assignment.

The national elections of 2010 carried an instruction. In our nation, in our time, the friends of freedom have an assignment, as great as those of the 1860s or the 1940s or the long twilight of the Cold War. As in those days, the American project is menaced by a survival-level threat. We face an enemy, lethal to liberty, and even more implacable than those America has defeated before. We cannot deter it; there is no countervailing danger we can pose. We cannot negotiate with it, any more than with an iceberg or a Great White.

I refer, of course, to the debts our nation has amassed for itself over decades of indulgence. It is the new Red Menace, this time consisting of ink. We can debate its origins endlessly and search for villains on ideological grounds, but the reality is pure arithmetic. No enterprise, small or large, public or private, can remain self-governing, let alone successful, so deeply in hock to others as we are about to be.

Need I illustrate? Surely the consequences, to prosperity, world influence, and personal freedom itself are as clear to this audience as to any group that I could appear before.

Do I exaggerate? I'd love to be shown that I do. Any who think so please see me in the hallway afterward, and bring your third grade math books.

If a foreign power advanced an army to the border of our land, everyone in this room would drop everything and look for a way to help. We would set aside all other agendas and disputes as secondary and go to the ramparts until the threat was repelled. That is what those of us here, and every possible ally we can persuade to join us, are now called to do. It is our generational assignment. It is the mission of our era. Forgive the pun when I call it our "raison debt."

Every conflict has its draft dodgers. There are those who will not enlist with us. Some who can accept, or even welcome, the ballooning of the state, regardless of the cost in dollars, opportunity, or liberty, and the slippage of the United States into a gray parity with the other nations of this earth. Some who sincerely believe that history has devised a leftward ratchet, moving in fits and starts but always in the direction of a more powerful state. The people who coined the smug and infuriating term— have you heard it?—"the Reagan Interruption."

The task of such people is now a simple one. They need only play good defense. The federal spending commitments now in place will bring about the leviathan state they have always sought. The health care travesty now on the books will engulf private markets and produce a single-payer system or its equivalent, and it won't take long to happen. Our fiscal ruin and resulting loss of world leadership will, in their eyes, be not a tragic event but a desirable one, delivering the multilateral world of which they've dreamed so long.

Fortunately, these folks remain few. They are vastly outnumbered by Americans who sense the presence of the enemy but are awaiting the call for volunteers and a credible battle plan for saving our Republic. That call must come from this room and rooms like it.

But we, too, are relatively few in number, in a nation of 300 million. If freedom's best friends cannot unify around a realistic, actionable program of fundamental change, one that attracts and persuades a broad majority of our fellow citizens, big change will not come. Or rather, big change will come, of the kind that the skeptics of all centuries have predicted for those naive societies that believed that government of and by the people could long endure.

We know what the basic elements must be. An affectionate thank you to the major social welfare programs of the last century, but their sunsetting when those currently or soon to be enrolled have passed off the scene. The creation of new Social Security and Medicare compacts with the young people who will pay for their elders and who deserve to have a backstop available to them in their own retirement.

These programs should reserve their funds for those most in need of them. They should be updated to catch up to Americans' increasing longevity and good health. They should protect benefits against inflation but not overprotect them. Medicare 2.0 should restore to the next generation the dignity of making their own decisions, by delivering its dollars directly to the individual, based on financial and medical need, entrusting and empowering citizens to choose their own insurance and, inevitably, pay for more of their routine care like the discerning, autonomous consumers we know them to be.

Our morbidly obese federal government needs not just behavior modification but bariatric surgery. The perverse presumption that places the burden of proof on the challenger of spending must be inverted, back to the rule that applies elsewhere in life: "Prove to me why we *should*."

Lost to history is the fact that, in my OMB assignment, I was the first loud critic of congressional earmarks. I was also the first to get absolutely nowhere in reducing them—first to rail and first to fail. They are a pernicious practice and should be stopped. But, in the cause of national solvency, they are a trifle. Talking much more about them, or "waste, fraud, and abuse," trivializes what needs to be done and misleads our fellow citizens to believe that easy answers are available to us. In this room, we all know how hard the answers are, how much change is required.

And that means nothing, not even the first and most important mission of government, our national defense, can get a free pass. I served in two administrations that practiced and validated the policy of peace through strength. It has served America and the world with irrefutable success. But if our nation goes over a financial Niagara, we won't have much strength and, eventually, we won't have peace. We are currently borrowing the entire defense budget from foreign investors. Within a few years, we will be spending more on interest payments than on national security. That is not, as our military friends say, a "robust strategy."

I personally favor restoring impoundment power to the presidency, at least on an emergency basis. Having had this authority the last six years and used it, shall we say, with vigor, I can testify to its effectiveness and to this finding: You'd be amazed how much government you'll never miss.

The nation must be summoned to General Quarters in the cause of economic growth. The friends of freedom always favor a growing economy as the wellspring of individual opportunity and a bulwark against a domineering state. But here, doctrinal debates are unnecessary; the arithmetic tells it all. We don't have a prayer of defeating the Red Threat of our generation without a long boom of almost unprecedented duration. Every other goal, however worthy, must be tested against and often subordinated to actions that spur the faster expansion of the private sector on which all else depends.

A friend of mine attended a recent meeting of the NBA leadership, at which a small-market owner, whom I won't name but will mention is also a member of the US Senate, made an impassioned plea for more sharing of revenue by the more successful teams. At a coffee break, Mr. Prokhorov, the new Russian owner of the New Jersey Nets, murmured to my friend, "We tried that, you know. It doesn't work."

Americans have seen these last two years what doesn't work. The failure of national economic policy is costing us more than jobs; it has begun to weaken that uniquely American spirit of risk-taking, large ambition, and optimism about the future. We must rally them now to bold departures that rebuild our national morale as well as our material prosperity.

Here, too, the room abounds with experts and good ideas, and the nation will need every one. Just to name three: It's time we had, in Bill Simon's words "a tax system that looks like someone designed it on purpose." And the purpose should be private growth. So lower and flatter, and completely flat is best. Tax compensation but not the savings and investment without which the economy cannot boom.

Second, untie Gulliver. The regulatory rainforest through which our enterprises must hack their way is blighting the future of millions of Americans. Today's EPA should be renamed the "Employment Prevention Agency." After a two-year orgy of new regulation, President Obama's recent executive order was a wonderment, as though the number one producer of rap music had suddenly expressed alarm about obscenity.

In Indiana, where our privatization of a toll road generated billions for reinvestment in infrastructure, we can build in half the time at two-thirds the cost when we use our own money only and are free from the federal rulebook. A moratorium on new regulation is a minimal suggestion; better yet, move at least temporarily to a self-certification regime that lets America build and expand and explore now and settle up later in those few instances where someone colors outside the lines.

Finally, treat domestic energy production as the economic necessity it is and the job creator it can be. Drill and frack and lease and license; unleash in every way the jobs potential in the enormous energy resources we have been denying ourselves. And help our fellow citizens to understand that a poorer country will not be a greener country but its opposite. It is freedom and its fruits that enable the steady progress we have made in preserving and protecting God's kingdom.

If this strikes you as a project of unusual ambition, given the state of modern politics, you are right. If it strikes you as too bold for our fellow Americans to embrace, I believe you are wrong. Seven years as a practitioner in elective politics tells me that history's skeptics are wrong. That Americans, in a vast majority, are still a people born for self-governance. They are ready to summon the discipline to pay down our collective debts as they are now paying down their own; to put the future before the present, their children's interest before their own.

Our proposals will be labeled radical, but this is easy to rebut. Starting a new retirement plan for those below a certain age is something tens of millions of Americans have already been through at work.

Opponents will expect us to be defensive, but they have it backward. When they call the slightest spending reductions "painful," we will say, "If government spending prevents pain, why are we suffering so much of it?" And "If you want to experience real pain, just stay on the track we are on." When they attack us for our social welfare reforms, we will say that the true enemies of Social Security and Medicare are those who defend an imploding status quo, and the arithmetic backs us up.

They will attack our program as the way of despair, but we will say no, America's way forward is brilliant with hope, as soon as we have dealt decisively with the manageable problems before us.

2010 showed that the spirit of liberty and independence is stirring anew, that a growing number of Americans still hear Lincoln's mystic chords of memory. But their number will have to grow, and do so swiftly. Change of the dimension we need requires a coalition of a dimension no one has recently assembled. And unless you disbelieve what the arithmetic of disaster is telling us, time is very short.

Here I wish to be very plainspoken: It is up to us to show, specifically, the best way back to greatness and to argue for it with all the passion of our patriotism. But should the best way be blocked, while the enemy draws nearer, than someone will need to find the second best way—or the third—because the nation's survival requires it.

Purity in martyrdom is for suicide bombers. King Pyrrhus is remembered, but his nation disappeared. Winston Churchill set aside his lifetime loathing of Communism in order to fight World War II. Challenged as a hypocrite, he said that, when the safety of Britain was at stake, his "conscience became a good girl." We are at such a moment. I for one have no interest in standing in the wreckage of our Republic saying, "I told you so," or, "You should've done it my way."

We must be the vanguard of recovery, but we cannot do it alone. We have learned in Indiana, big change requires big majorities. We will need people who never tune in to Rush or Glenn or Laura or Sean. Who surf past CSPAN to get to *SportsCenter*. Who, if they'd ever heard of CPAC, would assume it was a cruise ship accessory.

The second worst outcome I can imagine for next year would be to lose to the current president and subject the nation to what might be a fatal last dose of statism. The worst would be to win the election and then prove ourselves incapable of turning the ship of state before it went on the rocks, with us at the helm.

So we must unify America, or enough of it, to demand and sustain the big change we propose. Here are a few suggestions:

We must display a heart for every American and a special passion for those still on the first rung of life's ladder. Upward mobility from the bottom is the crux of the American promise, and the stagnation of the middle class *is* in fact becoming a problem, on any fair reading of the facts. Our main task is not to see that people of great wealth add to it but that those without much money have a greater chance to earn some.

We should address ourselves to young America at every opportunity. It is their futures that today's policies endanger and in their direct interest that we propose a new direction.

We should distinguish carefully skepticism about Big Government from contempt for all government. After all, it is a new government we hope to form, a government we will ask our fellow citizens to trust to make huge changes.

I urge a similar thoughtfulness about the rhetoric we deploy in the great debate ahead. I suspect everyone here regrets and laments the sad, crude coarsening of our popular culture. It has a counterpart in the venomous, petty, often ad hominem political discourse of the day.

When one of us—I confess sometimes it was yours truly—got a little hotheaded, President Reagan would admonish us, "Remember, we have no enemies, only opponents." Good advice, then and now.

And besides, our opponents are better at nastiness than we will ever be. It comes naturally. Power to them is everything, so there's nothing they won't say to get it. The public is increasingly disgusted with a steady diet of defamation and prepared to reward those who refrain from it. Am I alone in observing that one of conservatism's best moments this past year was a massive rally that came and went from Washington without leaving any trash, physical or rhetorical, behind?

A more affirmative, "better angels" approach to voters is really less an aesthetic than a practical one—with apologies for the banality, I submit that, as we ask Americans to join us on such a boldly different course, it would help if they *liked* us, just a bit.

Lastly, critically, I urge great care not to drift into a loss of faith in the American people. In speech after speech, article upon article, we remind each other how many are dependent on government or how few pay taxes or how much essential virtues like family formation or civic education have withered. All true. All worrisome. But we must never yield to the self-fulfilling despair that these problems are immutable or insurmountable.

All great enterprises have a pearl of faith at their core, and this must be ours—that Americans are still a people born to liberty. That they retain the capacity for self-government. That, addressed as free-born, autonomous men and women of God-given dignity, they will rise yet again to drive back a mortal enemy.

History's assignment to this generation of freedom fighters is in one way even more profound than the tests of our proud past. We are tasked to rebuild not just a damaged economy and a debt-ridden balance sheet, but to do so by drawing forth the best that is in our fellow citizens. If we would summon the best from Americans, we must assume the best about them. If we don't believe in Americans, who will?

I do believe. I've seen it in the people of our very typical corner of the nation. I've seen it in the hundred Indiana homes in which I have stayed overnight. I've seen it in Hoosiers' resolute support of limited government, their willingness, even insistence, that government keep within the boundaries our constitutional surveyors mapped out for it.

I've always loved John Adams' diary entry of 1774, written en route to Philadelphia, there to put his life, liberty, and sacred honor all at risk. He wrote that it was all well worth it because, he said, "Great things are wanted to be done."

When he and his colleagues arrived, and over the years ahead, they practiced the art of the possible. They made compacts and concessions and, yes, compromises. They made deep sectional and other differences secondary in pursuit of the grand prize of freedom. They each argued passionately for the best answers as they saw them, but they never permitted the perfect to be the enemy of the historic good they did for us, and all mankind. They gave us a Republic, citizen Franklin said, if we can keep it.

Keeping the republic is the great thing that is wanted to be done, now, in our time, by us. In this room are convened freedom's best friends but, to keep our republic, freedom needs every friend it can get. Let's go find them and befriend them and welcome them to the great thing that is wanted to be done in our day.

God bless this meeting and the liberty which makes it possible.

Appendix B

Governor Mitch Daniels's Speech to Gridiron Club of Washington, DC March 12, 2011

I bring greetings from my beloved Indiana, a land of surprises where, as we say, South Bend is in the north, North Vernon's in the south, and French Lick is not what you hoped it was.

Thanks to the organizers and the staff. It's been a perfect evening so far—well, almost perfect. I asked for cream in my coffee, and the waiter said "Sorry, you'll need a waiver from Secretary Sebelius."

Again, the Gridiron brings us together in all our diversity, united only by our patriotism and our passionate love of America. We all express that passion in different ways: I in mine, Secretary Sebelius in hers, Newt Gingrich in his. But that's what's special about tonight.

I never expected to be here making this speech, but then, life's so accidental. I wouldn't ever have been governor to start with, but a group back home decided the state needed to elect a small businessman, and I was the smallest one they could think of. I guess the Gridiron Committee was equally hard up.

I overheard someone at the reception saying, "Daniels? Sebelius? Who did the vetting, John McCain?" But they'll think differently after tonight. Daniels versus Sebelius—it's a classic matchup. Will be remembered always, like Lincoln versus Douglas on slavery, Nixon versus Kennedy on the missile gap, Romney versus Romney on health care. (That was a damn good line until Judy Woodruff stepped all over it.)

In the end, it was Vice President Biden who talked me into it: He told me it was a momentous, monumental matter. I'm paraphrasing slightly.

Still, it's scary. Me, in front of all these celebrities, and in white tie, for Pete's sake! No way I was paying top-dollar for something I'll never wear again. I went to see the bearded guy at Men's Wearhouse. Has anyone else noticed, you never see him and Wolf Blitzer in the same place at the same time?

Nancy Pelosi is here, still so intimidating, even back in the minority. I just knew that Speaker role was never going to work out. A high-pressure, high-stress job like Speaker of the House, it's just no place for a woman. They're so fragile, emotional, prone to break down crying …

But the scariest part is, no matter how well I do, there'll be no way to top the president. You watch, he's gonna steal the show. I know this because I read his speech last Tuesday on Wikileaks.

I suppose I'm the first Gridiron presenter ever to show up in a sling, and I need to start by coming clean about it. Rotator cuff surgery was really a cover story. The truth is I broke a rib traveling to last month's governors' conference. I drew a middle seat between Haley Barbour and Chris Christie.

But that wasn't the really embarrassing part. I couldn't get up to go to the bathroom. Their tummies were stuck in the full upright and locked position.

I can't wait to heal up, because this is frightening, too. Until this thing comes off, I can cling to my gun or my Bible but not both.

Mr. President, we often disagree, but sometimes I think you get a bum rap. For instance, after watching our Indiana House Democrats hide out in your home state the last three weeks, people who vote "Present" are starting to look like real statesmen to me.

Actually, it's a little hard to feel humorous with the economy still so tough. As if our state budget wasn't tight enough, now after the Chicago mayor's race, we have to build a missile defense system against F-bombs.

But again, let me stick up for the president. His policies *are* starting to create a lot of high-paying job openings—senator from Virginia, senator from New Mexico, senator from Hawaii … I see the secretary got together that death panel she was trying to start.

And I know the president agrees that our top priority has to be to get every American back to work. Except Larry King. That was a Charlie Sheen joke, but Judy stomped on that one too.

I love this event; I'm a traditionalist. But it's a new media world, and you've got to change with the times. When you think about it, today's bloggers are walking in the shoes of the giants of journalism. They're today's Edward R. Murrows. That is, if Edward R. Murrow had gone to work in his pajamas and hadn't talked to a woman in thirty years.

And all right, I confess; I miss Keith Olbermann. We Hoosiers have a tolerance for people who curse, throw things, and generally trash anyone who disagrees with them. Remember, we had Coach Bobby Knight. The analogy's not perfect; Coach Knight actually beat his competition most of the time.

But I'm glad Mr. Olbermann landed on his feet. If you hadn't heard, he debuts next week as the perky weekend weatherman on Al Jazeera.

Mr. President, you're not laughing. [*Turning to chairman*] Come on, Susan, we went over this. Who forgot to put "Ha, ha, ha" on his teleprompter?

Okay, I know I have to confront it. All this presidential speculation. It's always best to face things head-on—unless you're Michelle Bachmann; then you're better off facing them sideways.

Honestly, I never had any idea of running for president. After governor, my plan's been to go spend some time in a quiet place where no one can find me. First choice is Al Gore's cable channel.

But I have to admit, all this favorable press I've been getting, it's hard not to let it go to your head. Just listen to a quick sample—"small, stiff, short, pale, unimposing, unassuming, uninspiring, understated, uncharismatic … accountant-like, non-telegenic, boring, balding … blunt, nerdy, wooden, wonky, puny, and pint-sized." Really, it all points to one inescapable conclusion: It's destiny!

So, I'm thinking about it. This is the point in the presidential process where candidates are hinting and exploring and jockeying for position, and seriously, I like my chances. If anyone is built for jockeying, it's me.

But it's awkward watching people you admire bicker. Mike Huckabee mistakenly says the president is from Kenya, and right away Sarah Palin pounces: "Wrong, Mike, he's never even been to Europe!"

It hasn't been completely smooth so far. I caused some stir saying that maybe we should have a truce on those controversial, divisive, secondary issues, which might get in the way of solving the nation's biggest problems. I still think it's a good idea. So if my potential primary opponents promise not to talk about either height or hair, I promise I won't either. Unless Donald Trump is serious, and then all bets are off.

The field is starting to thin out. Within the last month, my friends Mike Pence and John Thune have both declared they are not running for president. In the same spirit of realism, I choose tonight to announce that I will not … be entering the NBA draft.

But I probably won't run for president, either. So much of life is timing, and I think I missed my best chance already. I really thought my shot at national office was 2008. I got all excited when I heard that Senator McCain's criteria in a running mate were a first-term governor from a moderate-sized state, smart, and good-looking. Damn, John, if three out of four was good enough, why not me?

May I say in leaving how truly thrilled I was at this opportunity and hope I did it justice. In the week the nation lost David Broder, might we hope that the spirit of this evening he loved could grow.

To me, "singe, not burn" means to tease but not ridicule or demean those who must find answers that serve the interests of us all. It's the humor I encounter all the time among the regulars in Indiana coffee shops—the humor of common struggles; common purpose; and genuine, if carefully concealed, affection. The humor of the needle, never the dagger.

It is not for a visitor to say, but maybe this event should be shared more openly with our fellow Americans. Because it would be a fine thing for us all if the spirit of the Gridiron spread widely across our great but troubled land. Thanks for having me.

Notes

Books

Daniels, Mitch. *Keeping the Republic: Saving America by Trusting Americans.* New York: The Penguin Group, 2011.

———. *Notes from the Road: 16 Months of Towns, Tales and Tenderloins.* Indianapolis: Print Communications Inc., 2004.

Halperin, Mark and John Heilemann. *Double Down: Game Change 2012.* New York: The Penguin Group, 2013.

Kahn, Herman. *The Coming Boom: Economic, Social and Political.* Horizon Book Promotions, 1982.

Special thanks to Eric Holcomb, Al Hubbard, and Marc Cogman for editorial help. Particular thanks and acknowledgment to outstanding photographers R.P. Gentry, Kim Alfano, Ben Ledo, Adam Horst, and Nathaniel Edmunds Photography.